EVERYDAY LIFE

Also by Agnes Heller

Renaissance Man
A Theory of History

EVERYDAY LIFE

Agnes Heller

translated from the Hungarian by
G.L. Campbell

ROUTLEDGE & KEGAN PAUL
LONDON, BOSTON, MELBOURNE AND HENLEY

First published as A mindennapi élet
© Akadémai Kiadó, Budapest 1970

This translation first published in 1984
by Routledge & Kegan Paul plc

14 Leicester Square, London WC2H 7PH, England

9 Park Street, Boston, Mass. 02108, USA

464 St Kilda Road, Melbourne,
Victoria 3004, Australia and

Broadway House, Newtown Road,
Henley-on-Thames, Oxon RG9 1EN, England

Photoset by Thomson Press (India) Ltd., New Delhi
and printed in Great Britain
by Unwin Brothers Ltd, Old Woking

Library of Congress Cataloging in Publication Data

Heller, Agnes.

Everyday life.
Translation of: A mindennapi élet.
Includes index.
1. Life. 2. Man. I. Title.
BD431.H39713 1984   128   83–24619
British Library CIP data available

ISBN 0–7100–9701–8

CONTENTS

Preface to the English edition

This book was written in 1967–68 and first published in Hungarian in 1970. Italian and Spanish editions followed suit. I soon became aware of certain redundancies in the original version, somewhat aggravated by the overabundance of examples. This is why I consented to an abbreviated version in German, published in 1978 (second edition 1981) by Suhrkamp. In spite of my respect for the work of the editor, my ideas about a properly abridged version were different from his. As a result, when the idea of an English publication presented itself, I decided to abbreviate the Hungarian original myself.

To prepare a shorter version of a book written almost twenty years ago is almost always an unwholesome enterprise; there are several pitfalls involved in it. First and foremost, one must resist the temptation of rewriting certain parts, of bringing certain analyses into harmony with one's present views and works. To give in to such temptations would have been tantamount to the destruction of the coherence of the book which had to be avoided at all costs. I have therefore not changed any ideas or any solutions. Even the categorical vocabulary of the original has been left intact. I have not added any knowledge to it gained from books written on the same or similar topics which I have appropriated since. The work presented in English is not only true to the message of the original, it is indeed the translated shorter version of the original work itself.

Everyday Life was written in the midst of a period when the slogan of the 'renaissance of Marxism' was coined. The first objective of the book was exactly what the title suggested:

outlining a theory of everyday life. However, the enterprise was even more ambitious. I decided to embark on new paths by working out a philosophical method, on the one hand, and the outlines of a new philosophical framework, on the other hand, while remaining faithful to the spirit of Marx and, at the same time, breaking with certain dominant traditions of 'historical materialism'. It is in this book that I established the very framework of my philosophy which I have never changed since, short of elaboration or occasional modification.

The method of the book can be described as a combination of a phenomenological approach and an analytical procedure. By the latter I mean the Aristotelian procedure. Since I had written a book on Aristotle (1958–9), I was intimately familiar with, and sympathetic to, his analytical procedure. But I was also aware of the fact that in modern times, where norms and rules are no longer taken for granted, where traditional values have been dismantled, the analytical method of Aristotle cannot be implemented, unless the 'phenomena' themselves are constructed. Husserl, and a critically modified Heidegger, had to provide the method with which to construe the phenomena themselves.

The philosophical framework of the book cannot be summarized with similar brevity, and I shall therefore confine these prefatory remarks to basics. It was in this book that I worked out a specific version of the paradigm of objectivation: the paradigm of the sphere of objectivation 'in itself'. Since this sphere of objectivation is an empirical universal, all social categories can be understood by having recourse to this objectivation, and thus the procedure of transcendental deduction could be avoided. Since it is this sphere of objectivation which in the main – even if not exclusively – regulates everyday life in our age as well, the centrality of the theory of everyday life has been theoretically established. The anti-historicist character of such a conception is obvious. However, it is equally obvious that 'anti-historicist' is here not synonymous with 'anti-historical'. I have sought rather, to emphasize the historical variability of social structures and, simultaneously, the historical variability of the *content* of the norms and rules presented by the sphere of objectivation 'in itself'. Moreover, I then shared the *evolutionism* of Marxism in full, and subscribed to a philosophy of history, characteristics which I have since abandoned. All the same, I have insisted that the sphere of objectivation 'in itself' and, as a result, the patterns of everyday life, include historical constants, and these historical constants have to be reflected upon in conjunction with the historical variables. I argued that everyday life can be changed, humanized and democratized, in spite of the constancy of some of its patterns. The emphasis put on the possibility of such a change was intended as a challenge to the Heideggerian position. As far as the practical intent of the theory is concerned, the anti-Heideggerian message cannot possibly be mistaken.

How everyday life can be changed in a humanistic, democratic, socialist direction is the practical issue the book addresses. The answers provided in it express the conviction that social change cannot be implemented on the macro-scale alone, and further-more, that the change in human attitudes is co-constitutive of every change, be it for the worse or for the better. I have argued for the possibility of a change in attitudes on the grounds that the attitude essential for the change for the better does exist, and that it only needs to be generalized. I coined the term 'individual personality' (in contrast to 'particularistic person') when referring to this attitude. True to the phenomenological approach, I commence my discussion with the distinction of these two kinds of attitude. I never had 'perfectibility' in mind; the 'individual personality' is anything but perfect, yet it is good enough to be the subjective bearer of a humane everyday life (which I called non-alienated, using a then voguish but fairly vague term.) Despite dismissing perfectibility, I did raise the most ancient problem of philosophical speculation, the problem no one can solve, but which no philosophy envisaging a change for the better can fail to address, namely 'Is suffering injustice better than committing it?' If this is 'moralizing', then so be it.

The British reader, educated in a quite different philosophical tradition, will perhaps find the continental categorial system of the book puzzling, sometimes even artificially over-complicated. The Hegelian distinction between 'in itself', 'for itself', 'in and for itself' and 'for us' is applied to the three spheres of objectivation and, respectively, to their appropriation. But given that these categories are properly defined (or redefined) in the book, their use should not cause undue difficulties for the reader. Another central category of the book, 'species-essence' or 'species-essentiality', was borrowed from Marx, in particular from the *Paris Manuscripts*. All spheres of objectivation are termed 'species-essential'. They are divided into objectivations which are 'species-essential in itself', 'species-essential for itself' and, finally, 'species-essential in and for itself'. 'Species-essential in itself' stands for the empirical human universal which is appropriated as 'taken for granted', whereas 'species-essential for itself' stands for a sphere of objectivation which is appropriated of free volition, and reflection for it embodies the crystallization of previously willed and reflected acts. It would have been sufficient to define these spheres as 'species-essential' on introducing the categories. The repetition of the qualification at every point where the term is used, seems to me now to be entirely superfluous and redundant. But I did not want to delete it, for the notion of 'species-essentiality' indicates my indebtedness to the Marxian legacy in general, and to that of Lukács in particular. It was Lukács, in the first chapter of his *Aesthetics* (on everyday thinking), a work to which I make frequent references, who placed the category of species essentiality at the forefront of discussion. Even though I have modified the Lukácsian interpretation of 'species-essentiality' in the present work, the continuity is to be taken into consideration as much as the discontinuity.

After the first, rough, German translation of *Everyday Life*, I sent the manuscript to several friends abroad, among others to Professor Kurt Wolff. In his most complimentary reply, Professor Wolff pointed out the similarities of my conception with that of Schütz. It was for the first time then that I heard the name of this famous author, for which I have no excuse other than the insularity of East-European cultural life in that period. After having read *The Phenomenology of the Social World*, I too was struck by the coincidental similarities, even if, on second thoughts, it was not particularly astonishing. Since Husserl, and to a lesser extent Weber, inspired me to an extent no less than they influenced Schütz, the similarities are easy to explain. At any rate, certain ideas are always 'in the air', more precisely, in the historical consciousness of a given age, and coincidence must occur whenever the same problems are addressed. Certain similarities notwithstanding, my conception was, in the main, basically different from that of Schütz. First and foremost, in my book 'everyday life' is not identical with the 'life world'. The notion of 'life world' refers to an attitude (the natural attitude) in action and thinking, which is to be contrasted with institutionalized (rationalized) action and scientific thinking. Everyday life, however, is not an attitude, rather it encompasses (or at least it can encompass) *different* attitudes, including reflective-theoretical attitudes. It is the objective fundament of every social action, institution, of human social life in general. Although the sphere of objectivation 'in itself', as the backbone of everyday life is to be contrasted with all objectivations 'for itself' (not only with science, but also with art, religion, abstract moral norms and ideas), everyday life itself

xi

is not necessarily conducted under the guidance of the sphere of objectivation 'in itself' alone. In our everyday lives, we can have recourse to higher objectivations, and as well we can test and query norms and rules which are 'taken for granted'. The practical intent of my book on everyday life then, is at cross-purposes with Schütz's solution which ended up in the vicinity of a positivistic systems-theory. In spite of its phenomenological approach, the present work is far closer to the so-called 'critical theory' than to Schütz. And the impetus to argue for the possibility of changing everyday life (and thereby social life altogether) has undoubtedly come from the legacy of Marx and Lukács.

Agnes Heller

PART I

Particularity, individuality, society,
species-essentiality

CHAPTER 1

The abstract concept of 'everyday life'

If individuals are to reproduce society, they must reproduce themselves as individuals. We may define 'everyday life' as the aggregate of those individual reproduction factors which, *pari passu,* make social reproduction possible.

No society can exist without individual reproduction, and no individual can exist without self-reproduction. Everyday life exists, then, in every society; indeed, every human being, whatever his place in the social division of labour, has his own everyday life. But this is not to say that the content and structure of everyday life are the same for all individuals in all societies. Reproduction of the person is always of the concrete person: the concrete person occupying a given place in a given society. The activities required to reproduce a slave or a shepherd are quite different from those required to reproduce the inhabitant of a *polis* or a city worker.

Very few types of activity are invariant, and even these are invariant only as abstractions in the lives of all persons. We must all sleep (if not in identical circumstances, and not in the same way) and we must all eat (though not the same things and again not in the same way); and, if we take a social cross-section of populations, we must all reproduce our own kind, that is to say, engender offspring. Such common activities are, then, those we share with the animals: they are, in so far as we can abstract them from their concrete content, the activities which serve to sustain man as a natural being.

From the foregoing examples we can see to what extent the primary or natural sustenance of the person is socially determined.

3

But even in the most 'primitive' societies, the sustenance of the human person demands far more, and far more manifold types of activity. Why should this be so?

As I said above, persons can reproduce society only by reproducing themselves as persons. But the reproduction of society does not follow automatically from the self-reproduction of persons, in the same way as a breed of cattle is spontaneously reproduced by the reproduction of its individual members. Man can reproduce himself only by discharging his social functions, and self-reproduction becomes the impetus to social reproduction.

On the plane of the person, our everyday life depicts the reproduction of a current society in general; it depicts the socialization of nature on the one hand, and on the other hand, the degree and manner of its humanization.

Man is born into a world which exists independently of him. This world presents itself to him as a ready-made datum; but it is in this world that he must support himself, and put his viability to the test. He is born into concrete social conditions, concrete sets of postulates and demands, concrete things and concrete institutions. First and foremost, he must learn to 'use' things, to acquire the customs and meet the demands of his society, so that he may bear himself in a way that is both expected and possible in the given circumstances of that society. Thus, reproduction of the person is always of a historical person existing in a concrete world. In general, we can say that – within certain degrees of tolerance – man must learn to 'use' the concrete things and custom patterns of the world into which he is born, however great their variety and their complexity.

The stipulation 'within certain degrees of tolerance' is important. Not every person learns how to use things and institutions, how to find his way in the nexus of customs, in uniform fashion. But we have to acquire an average competence *vis-à-vis* the system of objects, habits and institutions of our surroundings; in the development of such skills we have to reach a certain minimum degree of competence below which the person is not 'viable'.

The process of acquisition proceeds 'naturally': it may not always be easy, and persons vary in aptitude, but every normal human being can and does see the process through.

Appropriation of the system of objects, habits and institutions is never simultaneous, nor is it something that is concluded when the child becomes an adult. To be precise – the more highly developed, the more intricate the patterns, the less speedy and efficient the acquisition process. In static societies, or static circles

4

within these societies, the stage of minimum capability in everyday life is reached on becoming adult. What remains for the person thus equipped is to accumulate experience of life, at first and second hand: but that he can now successfully reproduce himself as a person, upon attaining maturity, is no longer in doubt. But even in static societies this must be modified if the person is detached from his native environment – if he is called up for military service, for example. In the army he must learn many new things if he is to 'stand his ground' and reproduce himself as a person.

The more dynamic the society, the more fortuitous the relationship between the person and the society into which he is born (and this is particularly true of capitalist society from the eighteenth century onwards), the more sustained is the effort which the person is required to make throughout his life to substantiate his claim to viability, and the less true is it that appropriation of the given world is completed on attaining maturity. For modern man, every new situation, every change of job, even admission to a new social set presents him with new problems of acculturation: he must learn to 'utilize' new customs and new proprieties. What is more, since he lives in a fluid setting of continually varying social demands, he must develop an ability to 'change gear' where necessary, to any one of a number of social stereotypes. His daily existence throughout his life is a battle with the world's sharp 'edges'.

But if the more dynamic type of society engages man in a perpetual struggle with the world's edges, it offers him at the same time a wider choice of alternatives. Since the emergence of dynamic society, i.e. non-communal society, the ready-made world into which man is born is not identical with his narrower local world. In so far as his minimum appropriation (upon attaining maturity) of this narrower world's skills is successful, the more chance he has of choosing for himself a variant, a relatively new 'local world'.

But whenever and however the process of exploring and manipulating the available skills of his milieu is completed for the person, the practice of these skills is constant and unremitting. This is not to say that they are of daily occurrence. At certain times and in certain societies, women have to learn how to sew, otherwise they will not be able to play their part as women in a given social setting at a given time. Sewing belongs to their 'coming of age', to their reproduction as persons, and thus it is constant and continuous – which is not to say that they spend every day sewing! Constants, i.e. activities which are constantly and continuously practised, may of course include some which are, in the narrower sense of the word, 'everyday', but they also cover activities which may relate to certain periods only in a person's life.

In a given period of life, unconditional continuity, in the sense of 'happening every day' is a characteristic of a cluster of everyday activities. This is the ongoing basis of our way of life. The proviso 'in a given period of life' is very important. Age plays a very big part in deciding what role a person can take in the share-out of work and activities in a tribe or even in a family. In modern social conditions – given the development in productivity – the connection between the position actually occupied in the work share-out and the position into which one is born has become contingent, and is susceptible to change within a given 'natural' age period (youth, maturity, etc.), which involves a redistribution of the cluster of 'everyday' activities as well.

In everyday life the person objectivizes himself in many forms. He shapes his world (his immediate environment) and in this way he shapes himself. At first sight, 'shape' may seem too strong a term; after all, we have done no more than define everyday activity as the process of growing into a 'ready-made' world, the internal process of accommodation to the world's requirements. Of course, 'growing into' includes a causative component as well – 'making to grow'. The 'everyday' includes not only what I learned about life's fundamental rules from my father, but what I teach my son as well. I myself am the representative of a world into which others are born. My own personal experience of life is bound to play a part in the way I 'make to grow', that is, rear others by representing the 'ready-made' world to them: when I relay my world to others, I am expressing my experience of it; when I 'convey' my world, I am at the same time objectivizing myself who once appropriated this world. And this happens not only in education but in all transmission of experience (work experience) in all forms of counsel – in fact, every time one consciously sets an example. In my relationship with the everyday datum, in the affects connected with this relationship, in my reactions to it, in the possible 'breakdown' of everyday activity – in all of this we are dealing with objectivized processes. (Here, I am not speaking of material objectivation in the narrow sense – a piece of sewing, a fire laid in the grate, a pot of soup.)

Everyday life always takes place in and relates to the immediate environment of a person. The terrain of a king's everyday life is not his country but his court. All objectivations which do not

6

relate to the person or to his immediate environment, go beyond the threshold of the everyday. This is not to say that the effective radius of the objectivation of everyday life stops short at the person and his immediate environment: on the contrary, as we shall see in some detail later, it extends to the highest reaches of objectivation, if only because all the basic skills, the fundamental affects and attitudes by means of which I transcend my environment and which I correlate with the total world accessible to me, and with the aid of which I objectivize myself, are appropriated by me in my everyday life. Here I only mention some of these fundamental affects and attitudes – courage (if, as a child, I pluck up the courage to enter a dark room); self-control (if I don't heap my own plate without considering others); coping with problems; feeling pleasure in success; loyalty; gratitude; etc. So, what matters is not merely that the influence which I exert on my environment should continue tacitly and covertly: what matters is that, without the skills I am to appropriate in this environment, without objectivizing myself in everyday life, I would not be able to objectivize my abilities in higher forms.

In human history up to date, spontaneous and, at the same time, conscious 'generic' activity – as we shall see in what follows – has been only exceptionally possible as far as the average run of humanity is concerned. As regards the average human being we can say with some confidence that the unity of personality has always been constituted in and by everyday life. It is in everyday life that human beings are tested as to whether they are – in Goethe's words – 'grain or husk'.

CHAPTER 2

The 'person': a breakdown of the concept

When we say that in everyday life the 'person' directly reproduces himself and his world (his local world) and, indirectly, the social aggregate, the 'wide world', we are using concepts in a very loose and figurative fashion. So far, we have established the historicity of the concepts 'person' and 'world' (people, society) without trying to distinguish between the separate categories of this historicity. This is what we shall now try to do.

(a) The category of the 'person': (i) particularity

Every human being is a particular person who comes into the world equipped with a given set of qualities, capabilities and aptitudes. From the person's point of view, the qualities and dispositions with which he is born are natural gifts. They accompany him throughout his life; he must reckon with them whenever he takes stock of himself.

From the moment of birth onwards, the person is increasingly aware of his environment, its objects and its social postulates: which is to say that from the moment of his birth he begins to cultivate his inborn qualities. The fluctuating requirements of a variable everyday existence demand the cultivation of more and more of these qualities. In a world where brute force was indispensable, man cultivated his bodily strength to a far greater degree than is called for in the arena of modern civilization. And when we say that the individual is above all concerned with survival in his immediate local community, his local instance, this is tantamount to saying that he begins to cultivate those qualities

8

and dispositions which are likely to promote his survival in the given circumstances. The *cultivation of these particular qualities* is, then, the minimum without which the appropriation of the requisite everyday life would not be possible.

So much for particular propensities; we turn now to the particular viewpoint. Man always perceives the world into which he is born in a certain perspective which has himself as origin; and in terms of this same perspective he seeks to manipulate it. The process whereby he discovers the world centres round his *self*.

Man's uniqueness, his non-repeatability, is an ontological fact. But this is not to say that real communication between men is impossible, nor that man is closed off in his uniqueness; nor does it mean that this uniqueness, in and for itself, constitutes the essence of man.

In the first place, man's uniqueness and non-repeatability are only realized in his objectivized world. Without self-expression there can be no self-determination or self-preservation for the human being; and self-awareness as the synthesis of consciousness takes shape as the world becomes objectivized – primarily in work and in language. Only he who generalizes can have self-awareness, awareness of his particularity. Work is such a generalization, and so is even the most primitive form of linguistic exchange. Where there is no generalization, where there is no promulgation of human species-essentiality, there is no human particularity.

Let us repeat: there is no self-awareness without generalization. But does this generalization not act as a brake or a fetter on self-expression? Does not the essence of the self tend to be lost, as it were, in the generalization of the self?

One man cannot know another – so runs the argument – because he cannot perceive things in exactly the same way. No two men will perceive exactly the same shade of red (not that this could be verified) just as no two men will feel joy or sorrow in exactly the same way. Thus are we shut up in our individual natures: we cannot get to know others, we cannot communicate ourselves to others.

It is, of course, true that we cannot know whether persons do or do not perceive and feel in precisely the same way: but this has nothing to do with inscrutability and incommunicability. It is only in practice that things acquire significance for man. The question whether we are perceiving exactly the same shade of red never arises; what does matter is whether I can react to what I perceive as red in the manner agreed through consensus with others with regard to 'red', and this goes for every situation, from the everyday humdrum to the loftiest reaches of aesthetics. If I can – then, by expressing my awareness of 'red', I express my own individual observation and I communicate in overt and comprehensible manner with others. The situation with regard to feelings and emotions may be more complicated, but it is essentially the same. If I feel love, what is significant for me is not whether someone else should feel exactly the same love – my love, as I feel it – but that he/she should, by reading off from my objectivation, take cognizance of my love, recognize it as such and react with love – his/her own love – to it. We may not feel the pain or grief of others, but we can comprehend it. Only a psychopath could insist that others should feel *his* pain or *his* sorrow; what matters for normal people is that the same things should awaken joy or sorrow in others as in them. Implicit in the summons to 'feel with me in my suffering' is the postulate that the cause of my suffering can be the cause of yours.

It is not because singularity as such cannot be expressed in its own 'thus-am-I-ness' that communication between men is difficult; on the contrary, rather, the problem only arises where (and because) communication as expressed in objectivation becomes alienated. Mystification of individual singularity is mystification of one aspect of alienated particularity.

So far, we have discussed two aspects of particularity: its basic nature as a datum, and, secondly, its generation of a particular viewpoint. Mention of alienation raises a third aspect for analysis: particularistic motivation.

From the ontological and anthropological fact of the particular viewpoint, it follows that no human being can exist without some degree, greater or less, of particularistic motivation. As we shall see in more detail later, the hierarchy of values that links human beings never takes shape on the basis of whether or not we have particularistic motivations, but rather in relation to what precisely these motivations are, what is their concrete content, at what intensity they operate, and, finally, what relation subsists between us and our own particularities – to what extent we can relate to our own *subjectum* as to an *objectum*.

The functioning of the particularistic viewpoint as motive is the most primary and most spontaneous form of particularistic motivation. I am hungry, and therefore I take bread from my neighbour; *I* have a low opinion of someone because he does not like *me* (or at least I suspect that he does not like me); if I can't make something of *myself*, I begin to ask myself – why am *I* in the world: on whatever plane of existence this takes place, the way in which the particularistic viewpoint acts as motive is unmistakable.

All my affects are in some way related to my particularistic viewpoint, but this is certainly not to say that all my affects are based on this particularistic viewpoint, or can be derived from it. There are very few purely particularistic affects and emotions, the primary ones being envy, vanity and cowardice; jealousy and selfishness take second place to these. Other affects and emotions are not purely particularistic in character. They may relate to (a) particularity or individuality or (b) to species-essentiality (*Gattungsmässigkeit*): as we shall see, these two, (a) and (b), necessarily condition each other. In essence, this has been known for a very long time, even if these categories were not specifically recognized. For example, when analysing self-love, Aristotle says that by identifying 'who loves what' in oneself, we can assess the value or lack of value of the affect. Self-love may point to a simple undifferentiated affective relationship with one's own self, an affectionate relationship with everything that 'I am'; but it can also indicate, for example, that when pressed I hold my own ground – that is, in myself I love the generic-individual values and their outward manifestation. In general the affects are neither particularistic nor generic-individual *per se,* but can take on these specific identities depending on referent and concrete content.

We have made a distinction between the particularistic affects (few in number as we have seen) and those which are not purely particularistic. It must now be stressed that the former have no ontological or anthropological priority *vis-à-vis* the latter. In plain words: growing up into the everyday world is not a process whereby one is born selfish (jealous, cowardly, etc.) and only gradually thereafter adapts oneself to the world's demands. Man is born equipped with particular properties and with a particular viewpoint, but not with particularistic motivations. Certain particularistic motivations unfold and develop from the matrix of inborn qualities and viewpoint. But since man is born into the world, into systems of regulations and habits, into affective relationships of which he is aware in his experience though they are independent of his self, these are, as far as he is concerned, fundamental data just as much as is the fact of his particularity, and motivations arise from these as necessarily as from the inborn matrix. The two sets work upon each other in a reciprocal relationship, in correlation, but neither is the cause of the other. The extent to which a man will relate the world he discovers around him to his own self, the extent to which particularity will predominate in his appropriated world of affects – these things depend on many factors. Primarily, they depend on the kind of world into which the person is born, and thereafter on his particular fundamental qualities (not on his motivations): on their specific nature, and on the extent to which they can be 'cultivated' in the given milieu.

When we speak of the affects which are related to particularity, we cannot stop short at the undifferentiated self. In its simplest forms, particularity is still more complicated than the self. In the first place, it extends to all that emanates from the self, all that the self cognizes and recognizes as belonging to it. One of the particularistic affects – vanity – has itself such a force field: my vanity extends not only to that which I am or do, but also to whatever is even adventitiously mine or connected with me – my wife's appearance, my child's intelligence, etc. Thus, affects linked to 'we-awareness' can be just as much particular affects as those linked to self-awareness. I shall go into the relationship between person and community in more detail in a later chapter, but some anticipatory remarks may be in order here.

When the person appropriates his environment, his 'world', he recognizes it as *his own*. He perceives his own individual nature as one subject to integration (or in more complex cases to a series of integrations). Integration appertains to him, as he does to integration: the effective field appropriated by integration is his effective field, its requirements are his. The person identifies himself with his own integration. This identification proceeds spontaneously and in tandem with the formation and development of self-awareness. The opposition set up between *our* family, *our* town, *our* people, on the one hand, and 'others' on the other hand – *their* family, town, etc. – is as real and natural for the person as self-motivation itself.

The 'we' is that *via* which 'I' am. And if my we-awareness amounts to a spontaneous identification with a given integration, then all the affects relating to that integration can be just as genuinely particularistic affects as if I were relating them to myself.

I say 'can be': it is not necessarily so. As I have already said, affects related to the self do not necessarily become particularistic: let us recall Aristotle's analysis of what we like or love in ourselves – that is to say, what is it within me that I identify myself with? Complications arise when we-awareness replaces self-awareness. If I identify myself with nothing more than the satisfaction of my particularistic desires, my affect is necessarily particularistic; but if I identify myself with the particularistic requirement of my integration from the viewpoint of my self, I can

12

then surmount particularity. If I throw my weight into furthering my own selfish interests, this is undifferentiated particularity; but I can throw my weight into what can be construed as the purely selfish interests of my nation, *to the detriment of* my own personal and selfish interests. The transition to we-awareness, identification with we-interests and activity towards the realization of these interests can lead to the suspension of particularistic motivation, even when the specific aims of the integration are particularistic. In the defence of we-consciousness, in the defence of integration, particularistic and non-particularistic motives are usually inextricably intertwined.

So far in my discussion of particularity I have spoken only of the affects, making a distinction between the purely particularistic affects and those which can relate to particularity as well. I have now to say something about the objectivation of particularity in linguistic usage – particularity, that is, as expressed in judgments, deductions, etc.

Linguistic-cognitive formulation of affects is related to particularistic affects, or to the particularistic relations between affects in a specific way – it tends to conceal them. This concealment varies in type and in intensity: the scale of possibilities runs all the way from impromptu dissembling to hypocritical and deliberate cover-up. Impromptu dissembling occurs when the person is simply not clear in his own mind as to his motives; his relationship with himself is so vague, he has failed so completely to make himself a *cognoscendum,* that he simply does not know what he feels or why; and he expresses his sympathies and his antipathies in ready-made formulae borrowed from his environment. Deliberate deception arises in the case of those who know and acknowledge the system of norms confronting them (including the moral norms) but who are aware that these are not the norms by which they themselves are motivated: that is to say, they are fully aware of the particularity of their own motivation, but studiously translate this motivation into the moral language of their consuetudinal environment. In this case, the defence of particularity is duplicated. On the one hand, the particularistic motivation, or the motivation brought to bear on particularity takes up a defensive posture; and this is reinforced by the concealment of this motivation which turns the person into a *'comme il faut'* member of another world of morally demanding beings. In the extreme form of this attitude, the linguistic expression, the generalization is also reduplicated. The person articulates the defence of his particularity and turns it into a way of life – while at the same time, for the benefit of others, he is careful to adopt the postures of a rationalized morality.

The weapons of concealment which particularity chooses for its own lingual-conceptual defence are usually drawn from the defensive arsenal of integration, of we-awareness. This is a simple stratagem, the more so since, as we saw, defence of we-awareness can also be defence of particular motivation, and, at least as far as these related to the given integration are concerned, unreservedly acceptable and plausible. The more intellectually complicated the person, however, the more complicated are the forms taken in the lingual-conceptual defence of particular motivations.

It was only in the development stage of bourgeois society that particularity put its cards openly on the table (we are, of course, talking of an average social cross-section, not of individuals); there and then egoism became a principle. But even there, there was one rationalization of a general ideological nature: the persuasion that, on the general social plane, looking after one's own interests was, in the long run, conducive to the 'benefit of all'.

General lingual-conceptual cover-up of our motivations is only one manifestation of particularity. Inseparable from it, and of central importance in everyday life, is assessment of others. The extent to which one's own particular motivations play a part in passing verdicts on others, whether individuals or groups, is too well-known to need elaboration. Heroism is idiotic – because I am incapable of it; I run down somebody's wife – because I envy her; I denounce a custom as 'immoral' – because I've got used to doing something else; examples can be found ad lib.

In defending my particularity I am, of course, not merely defending my particular motivations and other motivations bearing on my particularity, but the whole system which is founded on these as its basis. To this system belong my actions in the past, my views, my thoughts, the various attitudes I have adopted. I have to defend everything that I have done – or everything the group has done with which I identify myself: otherwise I cannot successfully defend my particularity. I rationalize my past. My mistakes were due to *other* factors – heredity (which I can't help! – another rationalization), the intrigues of others, tricks of fate, or, just 'bad luck'.

Rationalization is, of course, not just rationalization of the past; it applies to the future as well and to what I shall do in it. Before the wolf devours the lamb, it must first motivate its action – why it

14

must devour it; even before the deed is done, the aureole of 'justice done' surrounds it.

As long as an immediate identification with the self and an equally immediate identification with we-awareness characterizes man – average man, civilization will nourish and foster particularity. According to Marx, the human essence develops via an 'emptying-out' of individual existence, the efflorescence of human wealth proceeds *pari passu* with the impoverishment of persons. It is this process of alienation which has nourished particularity. Particularity is the subject of alienated everyday life.

It is a tough world into which we are born and in which we have to make our way. In this tough world, people work, eat, drink (usually less than they need) and make love (usually by the rules); people rear their children to play a part in this tough world and timorously guard the nook they have managed to corner for themselves; the order of priorities, the scale of values in our everyday life is largely taken over ready-made, it is calibrated in accordance with position in society, and little in it is movable. There is little opportunity to 'cultivate' our abilities beyond, at best, very narrow confines. Where life is comparatively full, it is obtuse or 'narrow-minded' (Marx). Where it is not narrow-minded, it is no longer protected by a solicitous community. What is surprising is not that the alienated development of human essence creates persons with particular motivations, that it fosters particularity, but that free individuality can – as it does – develop at all.

(b) The category of the 'person': (ii) individuality

No person is without particularistic motivation, nor is there any person who never in any way whatever, transcends, in some degree, his own particularity. No hard and fast line can be drawn between the particularistic person, on the one hand, and the individuality on the other. Individuality is a development; it is the coming-to-be of an individual. This coming-to-be takes different forms in different ages. But whatever form concrete individuality, or its ideal, takes in a given age, individuality is never complete but is always in a state of flux. This flux is the process of transcending particularity, the process of 'synthesization' into individuality.

A random sample from persons belonging to two different societies tells us little or nothing as to how and to what extent these societies promote development and efflorescence of the human essence. From comparison of two random samples we could assess neither the value-content nor the stage of development. As we saw, persons are particularistic units as regards their social average status and propensities; as they have no conscious relationship with their species-essence, they neither incorporate nor express its values *in toto*. Of course, some information can be gleaned from them which is of importance in the assessment of a society – e.g. the possibilities afforded by a given class of a given society for the self-development and efflorescence of its average persons. But it is not from such information but rather from its individualities that we can assess the value-substance of a society. It is the individualities – particularly those most developed individualities who have most successfully absorbed the value-substances, to whom we shall refer as 'representative individuals' – who individually incorporate the evolutionary generic maxima of a given society.

This is not to say that the gallery of representative individuals gives a complete picture of the way in which a given society sponsors or impedes the development of species-essential values. Such a complete picture becomes available only when the object of our scrutiny is not the individual but the structure of society as a whole. The individuality represents the potentialities of the person, albeit at maximum pitch, absorbing the potentialities of the species-essence, and is therefore representative.

This means that, in so far as there is an increment in value-substance from one society to another – that is to say, in so far as a society sponsors more values, or does so in more effective fashion than its predecessors – this increment in value-substance will be discernible in the representative individuals of that society. It is not only that the representative individual of one age is different from that of another age: there is also qualitative development. The evolution may indeed be contradictory, but this will then express the contradictions of the society's general attitude to the development of value-substance.

So far we have no more than hinted that individuality represents generic development. To understand how and why this should be so, we have to go rather more deeply into the concept of 'individuality'.

✱ According to Marx, man, like animal, is a specimen of its species. But, depending on the extent to which a given society, a given structure of society, contributes to the development of the

16

species essence, the person can – as species-being 'in itself' – *become* the representative of the human essence.

'The practical creation of an objective world, the fashioning of inorganic nature, is proof that man is a conscious species-being, i.e. a being which treats the species as its own essential being, or itself as a species-being . . .' (Marx, *Economic and Philosophical Manuscripts*, Penguin, 1975 (hereafter *EPM*), pp. 328 – 9). Man differs from the animals in that his vital activity is conscious; this is why man is a species-being. Or we can say that he is a conscious being, i.e. his life is an object for him, *because* he is a species-being. Because of this, his activity is free activity. 'Estranged labour therefore turns man's species-being . . . into a being alien to him and a means of his individual existence. It estranges man from his own body, from nature as it exists outside him, from his human essence.'

So, as a result of alienation, as far as the average person living in society is concerned, man's consciousness, i.e. his species charac-teristics, becomes a means of discrediting his own species-essence by making that essence a means of his existence. This is the particular, the alienated person. But every man need not necessarily without exception carry out this transposition of ends and means. There can be, and indeed always are, those who win through to seeing the species in the person, and who relate to themselves as to species-beings: who see themselves – from the point of view of species-being, from the point of the actual stage reached in the development of the species at a given time – as objects, who see that they should not be identified with the needs of their own existence, and that they should not make their being, the forces of their being, nothing more than a means of satisfying the needs of their existence. So, we give the name of 'individual' to the person for whom his own life is consciously an object, since he is a conscious species-being.

Of course, the conscious apprehension of his own life as object can happen for man at different stages and on different levels; and a species being can emerge at differing levels of consciousness. The upper content level of this consciousness is always that level to which the human generic essence has objectively developed in the given society. The lower level is always the particularity of the person which – as we shall see – is never annulled, even in individuality.

Thus does Marx differentiate between the particular relation (man as simple existence) and the individual relation (man

17

developing his essential powers) from the standpoint of work and consciousness. Elsewhere – in the third part of *EPM* – he substantiates this differentiation in the light of a third relation of the human being – totality:

> Man appropriates in integral fashion his own integral essence: that is, as total man. All his human relations with the world – seeing, hearing, smelling, tasting, feeling, thinking, contemplating, sensing, wanting, acting, loving – in short, all the organs of his individuality, like the organs which are directly communal in form, are in their objective approach or in their approach to the object, the appropriation of that object. This appropriation of human reality, their approach to the object, is the confirmation of human reality. (It is therefore just as varied as the determinations of the human essence and activities. [Marx's note].) It is human effectiveness and human suffering, since suffering, humanly conceived, is an enjoyment of the self for man.
>
> Private property has made us so stupid and one-sided that an object is ours only when we have it, when it exists for us as capital, when we directly possess, eat, drink, wear, inhabit it, in short, when we use it ... therefore all the physical and intellectual senses have been replaced by the simple estrangement of all these senses –the sense of having. So that it might give birth to its inner wealth, human nature had to be reduced to this absolute poverty. (Marx, *EPM,* p. 351.)

In communism, according to Marx, with the positive abolition of private property, the unity of being and existence is realized: every man has the possibility of developing his species potentialities, and everyday life itself can provide the terrain for the conscious deployment of this process. Thus (as Lefèbvre rightly points out) when analysing alienation Marx speaks of the alienation of everyday life as it affects the individual. If work, if deployment of the species capabilities becomes a means to serve man's existence, if the sense of ownership takes the place of all man's natural senses – this can only mean that it is maintenance of existence and ownership and nothing else, round which man's whole life, average man's life, everyday life centres. This can only mean that everyday life gravitates round particularity, round the sustenance of existence – an existence orientated on property ownership. Hence (and this is not a trivial corollary) the Marxist theory of alienation is a critique of class society, of private property, of daily life as lived out in the division of labour. For, from the viewpoint of society as a whole, alienation in the Marxist sense is by no means a negative category: in the aggregate, on the species plane, it involves the efflorescence of production and its economics, of science and the arts. The trouble is that man develops his species-essence in such a way that it is embodied in powers that are external to him – from the standpoint of individuals belonging to different classes, in differing degree, of course, and in different manner; and that, as a result of the economic and social structure into which he is born, man is, at least in the average, unable to cultivate his potentialities in the manner necessary if he is consciously to appropriate species-essential development.

Marx, however, never fails to remind us that it was class society itself that provided not only the material means for the development of communism but also those human qualities and attributes – the human relationship with the species – without which the aims of communism could not have been formulated. When he speaks of the 'human dignity' embodied in individual workers, or of 'great theoretical acumen' it is always this he has in mind. For Marx, a certain stage of development to be attained by the individual was as much a pre-condition of communism as the pushing back of natural barriers.

As we have seen, according to Marx, man has so far deployed his human essence in such a way that it is de-essentialized and now gravitates round the particularity of his life. But – and this is where the deployment of individuality comes in – not every historical period, social class or human group exhibits alienation in equal measure: emptying-out of the species essence does not take place to the same degree in all persons. Second, society itself and its needs have brought about certain attitudes and ideological forms which have made the human essence explicit for individuals, and which have created an individual 'movement' between particularity and a conscious relationship with the species: morals and politics, the arts, science and philosophy. And this remains true even though these objectivations can be and have, up to a certain point, been alienated. The existence of these species objectivations 'for itself' (i.e. for the species) – an existence which, as we have seen, arises from the needs of society – provides the opportunity for the person to transcend his particularity, to formulate his conscious relationship with the species, to become an individuality. Man is born into a concrete world which has been more or less alienated. But it is not obligatory for every person to receive the world in its concretely given existence; it is not necessary for every person to identify himself with the alienated attitudes.

As we have seen, particularity tends towards self-preservation, and subordinates everything else to this self-preservation. But if the person becomes an individual, this is no longer a law to which he is subject: the individual does not necessarily wish to preserve himself 'in all circumstances' and 'in any way possible'. His everyday life is also motivated by certain values (among other things) which can be more important for him than self-preservation. The individual – simply because of his conscious relationship with the species-essential values – can choose his own destruction or his own suffering. To quote Marx again: thus can suffering become an 'enjoyment of the self'. We may add that the choice of one's own destruction is a 'borderline situation' with the individuality as well, but one which is included in the category of individuality. But what is true of every individuality is that he will seize upon his particular potentialities and gifts as a situation which is not only to be sustained but also developed.

The individuality, then, is the person who has a conscious relationship with the generic, and who 'orders' (naturally within the given conditions and possibilities) his everyday life on the basis of this conscious relationship. The individual is that person who synthesizes within himself the contingent singularity of particularity and the generality of the species.

The words 'synthesizes within himself' are very important. For every person is singular and generically general at one and the same time. The person is related to his singularity and to the concrete manifested forms of its generic generality (its immediate environment, its community, the postulates of this community) more or less as to ready-made data. The coming-to-be of the individual begins where the acceptance of the ready-made ends, and can be suspended – in *both* respects, it is important to notice. I may be dissatisfied with my 'fate' or I may be dissatisfied with 'myself' but that is not say that I am on the way to becoming an individuality. Refusal to accept the ready-made in ready-made fashion involves a reciprocal relationship between the individual and his world. Every individual entity forms, articulates his world, and in so doing forms himself as well. But not every one is motivated to re-form both this world and himself. When I am motivated to create myself and my world (and creation does not necessarily involve modification) to make my own capabilities objectivations, and to ingest into myself those capabilities and attitudes which have taken shape in those areas of species-

20

essentiality which are accessible to me – then and only then am I on the way to becoming an individual.

In step with the particularistic person's appropriation of the world and objectivation therein, continuity is generated. This continuity does not, however, greatly differ from man's organic continuity. The synthetic nature of the individual can again be seen in the fact that the continuity of his life is – at least partially – chosen. It is not a contingent relationship that subsists between individuality and its fate; in relation to the individual, fate is not external: it is *his own* fate. The more internalized the conscious synthesis between genus and individual, the more does fate become the personality's own fate.

When the individuality consciously relates to the species-essence, when he makes objectivation therein a motivation, he is at the same time relating to himself as to a species-being. Marx describes this as a general characteristic of the species-essence, and indeed it is, as long as the relationship to the self as to a species-being remains spontaneous. But the ideation of this relationship, its elevation to motive status, can only take place in the course of the organized coming-to-be of an individual.

We said that every person has self-awareness, as also awareness of appurtenance to species-essence. Only the individual has self-consciousness. Self-consciousness is self-awareness as relayed from consciousness of species-essence. Whoever has self-consciousness is not spontaneously identified with his self: there is a certain distancing between him and his self. He knows himself and he knows his natural endowments. He knows, or at least it is his desire to find out, which of his capabilities can be most harmoniously deployed with the species-essence, with development towards it, which are the most valuable. He does not cultivate those qualities (or at least not as a matter of priority) which are likely to promote most efficiently orientation in his immediate environment or his survival therein; he cultivates those which he regards as the most valuable, and at the same time tries to deploy the most valuable aspects of each capability, or those which are likely to be most rewardingly convertible. The Socratic edict: 'know thyself' is the first commandment in the organization of self-consciousness and the coming-to-be of the individual.

We shall return to this problem when analysing moral alienation: how and to what degree can the individuality do violence to its own particularity? For the moment, we shall consider only the individual's normal relationship with his own particularity. What can be said here is that, in the process of becoming an individuality, a human being consciously creates an arena for his own particular motivations: and, according to his system of values, he can redeploy them, regulate them – even, in the extreme case, reject them. But he cannot reject his own particular endowments. In the normal case, individuality raises its own particularity to a higher level; it operates with those qualities with which it was born, and with those capabilities which are naturally its own. Nor can the individual – again in the normal case – abrogate his own particular viewpoint. First and foremost, a man wants to find his place in the world, his own place, and seeks after a life which is reasonable for him, if not also 'happiness' (to use a cliché of traditional ethics). This was the rational core in the theory of 'enlightened egoism', so-called. Particularity and 'mute' (i.e. not yet conscious) species-essentiality cannot in any case be discounted, for there is no self-consciousness which has not to reckon with death – death which sets the term (admittedly a variable) within which the person can be active. In the extreme case, the individual can choose death, in which case death loses its purely natural character and becomes individual. In general, the fact of death is a natural frontier (both particular and generic) and individual, if at all, only in the manner of its reception. Were it not for the natural terminus set by death, the need for morality would not have arisen; because, if persons were not continually 'beset by time' the hot or cold war of particularity versus species-essence would never have been launched: eternity would have been at man's disposal for the satisfaction of all his desires and needs.

In distinguishing between particularity and individuality, it is of fundamental importance to differentiate between 'choice' (alternative awareness) and 'autonomy' (autonomous consciousness). I define autonomous choice as follows: when the individual chooses between alternatives, and places the imprint of his own individuality on the fact of choosing, on its content, its contours, etc. he is exercising autonomy. Ontologically, choice is certainly primary here: there can be no autonomous choice without choice, but there can be choice without autonomous choice. The alternative character of human action arises from the species-essence 'in itself'. Teleological intention belongs essentially to the human being, and applies not only to the end purpose of an act but also to all elements on the way leading to that end. In everyday activity such alternatives and alternative acts of choice arise in a literally endless sequence. As regards outcome, the majority of these acts of alternative choice are trivial in that the outcome, again in the great majority of cases, is a relative aim, and is

22

itself – from the standpoint of a different outcome – the object of a relatively indifferent choice.

Of course, not every act of alternative choice is indifferent from the standpoint of the outcome. Some acts of choice lead to erroneous outcomes; perhaps to outcomes which are in one way or another fatal for the individual. These provide the disasters of everyday life: I cross the road without looking and get run over. Thus, catastrophe has nothing to do with tragedy: catastrophe arises from an erroneous choice between alternatives, tragedy is the result of an autonomous choice and cannot be classified as 'erroneous'.

Every act of alternative choice is irreversible. From the point of view of the outcome, this is of no significance where choice is a matter of indifference, that is, where the situation is trivial. But there are also acts of alternative choice, lying far outside the radius of the catastrophes of everyday life, in which irreversibility of choice closes off whole areas of alternatives and affects the whole of the individual's subsequent fate.

Every fully developed individual is confronted at one time or another with 'indifferent' acts of choice, that is to say, acts of choice in which his individuality plays no part whatever. Again, from the standpoint of outcome, certain non-indifferent acts of choice do not go beyond the effective field of particularity: for example, choice of an alternative may *seem* to be indifferent but its unforeseen consequences may be disastrous; but this has nothing to do with the structure of my individuality.

But even where the wrong alternative has been inadvertently or fortuitously chosen, the situation arising from this mistaken choice will reveal who is an individual, the extent of his individuality and its nature. In such a situation, the man who is limited to his particularity weeps and laments and curses his fate; the individual, however, seeks ways of putting the imprint of his own individuality on the world that has emerged from the given situation. 'Misfortune comes to us all, it takes the astute man to turn it to profit', quipped Wedekind; 'prudence' is an individual property.

Where there is a choice of alternatives which are not trivial or indifferent with regard to their outcome, the individual not only chooses but chooses consciously in such a way as to realize his personality. This is not to say that realization of personality is the declared aim: this is a possible aim, but more often than not, this is not the main aim. Usually, it is with a view to concrete results, in the interests of certain values and impelled by consideration of them, that one chooses. Realization of personality may be a result, but by no means the only result – even on the plane of everyday life. When I give bread to the hungry, the outcome is that the recipient does not die of starvation, and the continuity of my own personality does not lapse. We say then that that choice is autonomous in which I choose 'according to the necessity of my own personality' (Spinoza).

Every man is born into a concrete situation and is therefore placed in a field of limited alternatives. Every act of choice between alternatives takes place within the more or less constricting rings of this delimiting field. Perhaps 'ring' is not a good analogy: the external field of choice is not only a restriction on autonomy but also its prime mover. It is this world that sets the problem, the task, the obligation. What obligation? 'Was ist die Pflicht? Die Forderung des Tages', said Goethe. All autonomy is therefore *relative* autonomy.

Responsibility for action always rests on the individual, whether the choice between alternatives be autonomous or not. The consequences of an action have to be borne; what Hebbel called 'the hour of reckoning' dawns. As far as the particularistic person is concerned, responsibility is external, which is why he feels that he can wash his hands of the matter since there is nothing he can do about it; for the individual, however, responsibility is 'internal' – it is not only responsibility but acceptance of responsibility. As I said above, for the particularistic person, fate is a sort of power floating in the air above his head, while the individual construes 'fate' as *his* fate.

We remarked above that practical wisdom, 'prudence', is a quality of the individual. Of course, by 'prudence' I do not mean a mental property in general, but rather a specific mental capacity which comes about exclusively as a result of achieving a measure of 'distancing' from particularity, and which becomes for the individual to some extent a 'sense'. It was the name Aristotle gave that capability which is directed towards finding the currently best 'mean', a central category of ethics, known in Aristotle's works as *'phronesis'*. The 'mean value' is a measure applied to the affects, and amounts simply to the evaluation, in relation to the given general norms, of how, to what degree, when, why, and for what purpose an affect is applicable. The individual must choose that procedure offering the best possible juncture of his individuality, the data, the general requirement, and the concrete situation – that is to say, in the light of the three factors (particular datum, general requirement and concrete situation) he must take the decision with the highest value input, and turn it into action. Clearly, we are here concerned with a disposition of the individual, with a specific synthesis of species-being (*Gattungsmässigkeit*) and the particular datum in a given situation; and it is also clear that such autonomous decisions remain within the compass of everyday life, or at least, can also be carried out within this compass. Aristotle postulates the accepted system of norms and obligations as a datum, and never even considers the idea (which could hardly have arisen in a polis society) of rejecting or transgressing these moral guide lines. He never goes into the question of how significant these situation choices are, and draws his examples from everyday life and from extraordinary situations alike. This special prudence – *phronesis* – is not present in particularity, since particularity wants nothing more than the mute prolongation of its self, in such a way, of course, that it does not come into open collision with the accepted system of norms: so that there can be no question here of that full relationship – spontaneously synthesized – with the situation, as in the case of the individual.

The emergence of individuality (postulating, as it does, a conscious relationship with species essence) and the development of individuality (in continuous correlation with the possibilities generated in the given society) are to be regarded as values. This is, of course, not to say that every individual is morally superior to particularistic persons. We shall return to this point in more detail later. For the present we need only point out that an individual may have a strongly developed *negative* moral value-component. In selecting his own fate, he may deliberately choose evil. When Richard III says: 'I am determined to prove a villain', this too arises from a projected and distanced relationship with species-essentiality and with himself. Richard despairs of the world's rottenness when he sees how his brothers make peace with the murderers of (his brother) Rutland, and, filled with a reflected hate and contempt for the world (*not* with a spontaneous lust for power) he begins to play with men as puppets. This is, of course, an extreme case. But it is not infrequent for persons to 'promote' certain particularistic affects from the status of spontaneous and adventitious attitudes to that of conscious designs: whereupon they direct their own fate, in the same way as do individuals endowed with positive moral value, and hold the spontaneous reactions of the self in check. The confirmed egoist also reflects his relationship with the species-essence in that he consciously rejects it as a motivation, and consciously selects one or another particularistic motivation, or simply makes his egocentricity the guiding principle of his actions.

If we have stressed the fact that individuality can be endowed with a negative or relatively negative moral value-component, this is not to say that the significance of such individualities in history is comparable with that of individuals positively endowed in the field of moral value. The individuality whose value-component is purely negative is exceptional, if only because such an individuality contains a double tension: on the one hand with the world whose norms, requirements and conventions, valuable or not, he rejects, and on the other hand with himself, in that he continuously and avidly 'purifies' himself of all his 'weaknesses' (including moral motivations). The morally positively endowed individuality can also be in a state of conflict with the world (and more often than not, is) but on behalf of the values of the world and of humanity. He may also be in conflict with himself, though this tension can be resolved *via* right action. We may compare the state of Richard III a few minutes before his death, when he loses himself and gives up his individuality, and the death of Othello, in which he finds and vindicates himself. The fact that individuality with a negative value-component often turns out to be null and void in moments of great tribulation, has tended to give the impression that in such cases we are in fact not dealing with individuality at all. This is what Ibsen was concerned to portray in the person of the button-moulder in 'Peer Gynt'. If the content of life is construed as 'overcoming the world' – whether because we hold it to be, as a whole, evil, or whether we merely wish to realize one or another of our over-emphasized and embellished motivations – and the world gets the better of us, this leads in the majority of cases to certain collapse. But this is not inevitable. The moral order of the world which Don Giovanni treats with such contempt (first and foremost, the moral order of the new bourgeois world) defeats him: but even in defeat he sticks to his guns and thrice refuses repentance. Ernst Bloch (thinking in this case along Ibsenish lines) denies individuality to Don Giovanni, whom he describes as *'il dissoluto'*, the profligate who merely repeats himself in all his adventures, and is incapable of promoting his individuality to a higher plane. If the individual whose value-component is morally positive is to be our yardstick, we shall have to deny individuality to anyone who has not yet developed to a morally higher plane, who lacks the capacity for catharsis of an axiologically positive nature. But this is not – at least not in my opinion – an anthropologically adequate yardstick. The moral individuality (as we can call the individual whose value-component is morally positive or relatively positive) has certain other anthropological character-istics which do not mark every individual: these turn upon the capacity for catharsis, and on whether, after catharsis, the de-velopment of the individual continues, and, if so, how. In the case of the individual whose value-component is morally positive, catharsis represents a discontinuity which is, in the long run, an integral part of continuity (cf. Faust). Where the value-component is negative, the individual is either incapable of catharsis or is destroyed therein, though exceptionally he may emerge as a new individuality (i.e. he begins afresh to form himself).

Reproduction of the person is a unified process. But it is a process in which choice between the interests and needs of particularity and the needs and values of individuality has often to be made.

I started from the assertion that everyday life is the aggregate of activities belonging to the self-reproduction of the person – the human being born into the given conditions of a given world; and we have also seen that, in history up to the present, particularity has been the subject of everyday life in the great majority of social orders and social relations. All the material wealth of the world has arisen from the activity of those who 'took things as they come'. Suffice it for the present to say that the 'person' of everyday life is a particularity which bears non-conscious, non-reflected species-essentiality in itself. It is my contention that this is the mark and token of the bodying-forth of 'history hitherto' on the plane of everyday life.

Exceptionally, however, integrations have come about in which individual reproduction has been more or less typically equivalent to the maturation of the individual – at times and in settings where the existence of the community itself demanded a personal relation to integration, that is to say, in democratic communities.

CHAPTER 3

The person and his world

The correlation between the person and his world is a historical question, and, as such, a question of history. It is a correlation which has been formulated in so many different forms in different societies, social strata, classes, that it cannot be described in any sort of philosophical generality without becoming schematized. In what follows, therefore, I make no attempt to deal even approximately with the full range of forms taken by this correlation and limit myself to a description of certain general tendencies.

(a) The person as class-unit

In the most general terms, we can say that in the 'history hitherto' of the human race, every person is a class-unit, that is to say, is the representative of humanity only in so far as he partakes in class possibilities, class values, class tendencies, and relays these in correlated form. The degree to which a person can be the bearer, the mouthpiece of species-essential development is, therefore, limited by the concrete structure of the social division of labour, and by the position occupied by the person therein. Not every person can become a representative individuality. The primary condition for this is that the class of which the person is an individual, shall be in one way or another, in greater or less degree, a 'historical class'.

History is the substance of society, since the substance of society is nothing more than continuity. Humanity's being therefore lies in its historicity. Here, however, we have to make a distinction

28

between the categories of 'history in itself' and 'history for itself'. History is 'in itself' if the continuity of a given socio-economic structure consists in its self-reproduction on the same level (e.g. the 'Asiatic mode of production' within its own petrified parameters); history is 'for itself' if continuity implies a continuous process of evolution of a given situation, whether this evolution is progressive, retrograde or both (in heterogeneous spheres). When we talk of 'historical classes' we are using the word 'history' in this sense. To be a maker of history as 'history for itself', i.e. to be a historical class, does not mean that the given class and its subjects necessarily take part in the making and guidance of political history. Thus the medieval peasantry – the serfs – were a historical class though its 'class subjects' did not make political history.

So, when we say that the individual is also a 'class subject', what this really means is that the historical nature of his class sets limits to the development of his individuality. Again, not every personal reproduction in a class must necessarily become individual to the same extent. There are classes in which personal reproduction implies the development of individuality – even if only in a relative sense. In other cases, it is precisely the necessity for individual reaction that is eliminated by the given class-existence. Of course, it often happens that the class demands reflected individual attitudes from its subjects in a certain sphere of existence, and complete conventionalization (or conformity) in other spheres. To a great extent, this depends on how individualities come into being, and on what type of individualities these are. It is, by and large, typical of the development of a class to demand in certain sectors reflected and distanced individual reaction of a kind which it discourages in other sectors. Philosophy and literature offer many illustrations and analyses of these questions, which are there treated as concrete problems. We may recall Hegel's analysis of Shakespeare's plays, in which he derives the greatness and the emancipation of Shakespeare's individualities from the fact that, in the period of feudal anarchy, there was no central power to prescribe the field of possible action open to the individual. (Here, of course, Hegel was failing to realize that to a very great extent the character of Shakespeare's heroes reflects not a feudal but a Renaissance field of action.) Or, we may take the example of cultural criticism in our own time, which turns on the problem of the de-individualization of the bourgeois personality *vis-à-vis* the possibilities of individualization created in the centuries of bourgeois ascendancy.

(b) Group and individual

I started from the premise that in the 'history hitherto' of humanity every person belongs to a class. In his everyday life, however, – and, in most cases, not only in his everyday life – the person does not relate directly to his class: the person does not appropriate his class norms, class requirements or the limits set by his class in this sort of direct relationship. Society's codebook is always relayed *via* concrete groups – units in which a 'face to face' relationship predominates, units, that is, in which the book of rules is always directly represented by people (people I know) and human relations (structuralized human relations). Of course, in this 'representation' a contradiction may lie concealed – especially where and when the 'group' is not the representative of a communal society. In such circumstances, what often happens is that the group confronts the person with the 'ideal' normative system of the society or class, a system which in society at large is transgressed every day of the year. Hence the phenomenon which is typical of certain circles, particularly in capitalist countries, that when the individual 'starts to live' i.e. leaves behind him the groups in which he grew up – family, school, childhood friends – he is unable to find himself in his new surroundings, and is sadly disillusioned or becomes non-viable.

The group plays a primary part, therefore, in the formation of the person's everyday life, in so far as it is in the group that the person appropriates his sociality. Nothing could be further from the truth, however, than to imagine that the group 'produces' norms and normative customs and that the norms and customs of society are composed of these engendered in the group. The true situation is rather the reverse. The group which indeed plays a primary part in the appropriation of everyday life, is not primary in so far as the creation of norms and customs is concerned. In this respect, the group plays no more than an intermediate role. And in so far as the group fails to discharge this intermediary function, the appropriation of the group norms and customs falls short of preparing the person for the organization of his daily life in general.

In which concrete groups, we may ask, does a man appropriate the skills and capabilities he needs for everyday life? Again, this depends to a great extent on society as a whole, and on the position the man occupies in the social division of labour. Let us take a few examples: family (in traditional societies always absolute and basic), village community, university life, the army, company of friends, house or apartment block, apprenticeship, etc. It is sufficient to list these for us to see that not every group is of equal importance in the individual's growing up process; and it is also clear that the person can belong to various groups, his development can be influenced or slanted by more than one group. The main tendency exercised by the group hierarchy is always determined by the structure of the society and by the position occupied in the social division of labour. Within these limits, however, the importance of the various groups in the life of the person varies rather widely.

From the fact that a person can belong to a wide variety of groups at the same time, it follows that affiliation to a group may be a product of chance. There are two reasons for this: the fact of birth does not determine affiliation, nor does individuality. The fact that one goes to school is a necessary consequence deriving from a given social structure (compulsory primary education); and exactly what sort of school is a function of the social and economic position of the parents. But exactly which actual concrete school I go to, and into which concrete class I am put – this is from the point of view of my 'being-born-into' and my development as an individuality, contingent. Thus, my affiliation to a given class group may be contingent. In so far as this chance element is overcome, in so far as my individuality can be organically, existentially and continuously (all three equally important) correlated with the given group, we can speak of a community and no longer of a group.

So much for the role of the group in the process of growing up into everyday life. But this is not all the group does. A sector of directly generic activity is unimaginable without the organized and stable structural unity of the 'face to face' relations we have mentioned.

The stimulating role of the group is, of course, not limited to the objectivization of species-essential capabilities but is felt in the case of the objectivization of other capabilities and skills which are claimed and cultivated by the group. A good football team can raise the game of each of its members; the individual grows into the group. Human life is full of such instances of 'growing up into' the group, and they are by no means limited to the coming-of-age period – on the contrary, they are characteristic of human life as a whole.

Where the value-input in group activity is uniformly positive, the same will be true of the 'growing-up' process. But maturation and skill-acquisition can also proceed on a very inferior level to the

31

detriment of essential human potentialities, and not infrequently we find a negatively orientated maturation into groups whose value-component is also negative – in other words, a process of degradation.

So far, I have considered two criteria of the group – the fact that one's affiliation to it may be contingent, and, secondly, the part it may play as an intensifier of given skills and capabilities. I now consider a third property of the group, one which follows from the previous two, and which I may put as follows: the whole man can never be related to one group only, or, to put it another way, a group (in so far as it is a group and not a community) is principially incapable of helping man to realize his full or even his main human potentialities.

Fourthly and finally: we can speak of 'the group' only if a 'face to face' configuration consisting of a certain number of people has some common function. Without at least one such common function – no matter how weakly delineated – there cannot be a group. The inhabitants of a house form a group only in so far as they exercise a common function in one or more respects, and if, in relation to this function, they find themselves in a system of formal and/or informal relationships which may be hierarchically ordered. The group is the lowest, most elementary and most primitive degree of social integration. It may gain special interest in so far as it sheds light on the properties, content and relaxation points inherent in other forms of integration, and indeed the group is only of interest to us in so far as it does so. Again, since the group is the lowliest form of integration, for this very reason it is a heterogeneous element within one and the same social structure. From this heterogeneous category it is impossible to derive the more homogeneous categories; from it, we cannot 'build up' homogeneous categories. What the group means for the individual, which heterogeneous group-formations are more or less significant, which are first or last in the group hierarchy, which are regenerate and which degenerate – to these questions the mere facticity of groups, their existence as groups gives us no answer; for this we must consider their place and function in higher social integrations.

(c) Individual and crowd

Before we turn our attention to such a high-level integration as the community and the person's correlation with it, let us say something about the relationship subsisting between the person and the crowd. The digression is necessary because the categories of 'person' and 'crowd' are often paired, in parallel with or to be replaced by the contrasted pair 'person' and 'society'. The first point to be made here is that while society, estate, nation, class, group and community are categories of social integration, homogeneous in so far as they denote various units related to social structure, the category of the 'crowd' is completely heterogeneous *vis-à-vis* these units. The term 'crowd' refers to the being-together of a certain number of people on the occasion of a given action, either as active agents or as bystanders. Action-together can arise fortuitously (e.g. fire breaks out in a cinema) just as bystanders can collect by chance (an accident). Again, either can be non-fortuitous, e.g. in the case of a demonstration. A crowd is, then, not necessarily characterized by identity of interests or function, as is a group; just as a group is certainly not necessarily characterized either by action-together or by super-numerary presence (group work can be successive). Neither group nor community can ever become a completely unorganized 'mass' as they are always stratified, or, at least, articulated; both in action and as bystanders, however, the crowd can be non-stratified and non-articulated. Not always, however: it happens, not infrequent-ly, that the community itself generates the 'crowd'.

In the case of mass action or reaction, the common features, aims and interests not only come to the fore in the crowd, but are reinforced and affectively amplified. What we are concerned with here is not group action, or only very rarely so. In group action, the group reinforces certain aptitudes and skills, incubates and deploys certain 'gifts'. In crowd action, on the other hand, the accent is not so much on the deployment and nurture of aptitudes as on the inflammation of affects. The power build-up in the inflammatory process ensures that the particular interests, require-ments, perhaps even the most personal considerations caught up in crowd action are effectively 'suspended'. (And not only the particular, but also those individual and generic interests which are not congruent with the intensified affect.) This does not necessari-ly mean that the crowd can be manipulated at will; it certainly cannot be so manipulated if it consists totally or partially of individuals, in which case the force engendered in mass action will carry the crowd along only in so far as it does not meet with the resistance of the individual core of action. If, however, the crowd is composed of individuals less well developed in the sense defined above (p. 23) especially of those who have no communal bounds or who have become schizophrenic in the effort to do what different groups ask of them, and who have become flexible in a morally negative sense – and if, into the bargain, the crowd is non-structured, then the chances of such a mass confluence being readily open to manipulation are greatly enhanced.

(d) Individual and community

Let us now turn for a moment to what is, from the standpoint of aggregate social structure and of the formation of the individual, the crucial integration – the community. As we have said already, the community is a social category in so far as it is a category of integration. But it is more than that. Various integrations (e.g. village, social stratum, group) can be communities but are not necessarily so. When it amounts to a community, and when not, depends on the concrete content of the integration, on the organizational type of its relations with the social aggregate and on the relationship between the person and the integration itself.

A community is a structuralized and organized group or unit stratum in which a relatively homogeneous system of values obtains, and to which the person necessarily belongs.

'Necessarily' here has two meanings which differ widely in regard to the social function implied. A community may be 'necessary' from the point of view of the social aggregate: i.e. a society in which the unit of production or of management – usually both – is the community, and in which the community forms an organic and indispensable component of the social structure. In such societies as this, the individual is necessarily 'born into' the community; the limits of his community are prescribed at the moment of birth.

A completely different part is played by communities which arise not as embodiments of essential social needs, but as derivatives of political action and/or individual development: that is, from a conscious wish or endeavour on the part of individuals to relate to the species-essence *via* a given communal integration, in situations where the community is consciously organized to operate on the species-essential level. The fact that such communities are not necessary from the point of view of the reproduction of the given society does not, however, mean that they are of no concern to that society. They are of structural help in the attainment of aims on the plane of species-essence, they articulate the individual self-consciousness of the members of the community, they set an example on the axiological plane, and, last but not least, they offer a way of life. The garden of Epicurus, the

34

community of Christ and his disciples, the Jacobin sects – these are examples of this kind of community drawn from widely varying societies. And of course it is quite possible for such communities to be formed on an axiologically negative basis – e.g. Fascist cells or gangs.

In what follows I shall limit my attention to those communities which are organized on a positive or relatively positive value-basis. Obviously, this limitation applies only in the case of consciously organized communities.

Given that we are dealing with organizational forms which are by definition 'necessary' in widely discrepant ways (the contrast being between a community or a group) it becomes questionable whether we are in fact entitled to work in terms of one single category. There seems to be no doubt, however, that, as far as our present inquiry is concerned, the business of carrying on everyday life, one category is enough. To support this conclusion, we have to consider other characteristics of the category of community.

First of all, we have to decide whether a given community is an articulated and structured group or stratum. In this context, 'structured' does not necessarily suggest a hierarchical structure: after all, non-hierarchical communities can be identified, e.g. the garden of Epicurus, as well as those which are hierarchically ordered. 'Ordered' here does not necessarily mean 'institutionalized'. We must also bear in mind that although a group may be a community, a community can be a unit comprising several groups, or can be a stratum. The community is therefore not necessarily characterized by the 'face to face' relationship; all we can say is that the community relationship is necessarily valid in 'face to face' formulations as well. (For Christians, the whole Christian *oikoumene* was the community. Within this aggregate, the community built on the 'face to face' relationship was the congregation of which the individual Christian was a member.) On a basis of fundamental units provided by 'face to face' communities is built up the community which sets aims and provides a relatively homogeneous value standard: the individual relates to these aims and to this system of values but his daily life-style is drawn directly from the basic units of the community.

'Organization' and 'unity' never amount to a formal criterion in the case of the community; what can be said is that the community provides an organized terrain for individual activity. The amplitude and the exact nature of this terrain depends very much on the type and content of the organization in a given community. (Some communities keep the person on a very tight rein; others thrive on the wide field open to individual initiative.) Further, the community provides terrain for the *whole* human person and his activities, for his lifelong activity, that is. The only relationship that matters as far as the group is concerned is that connected with the interests and the aims of the group. Whether one belongs to a community, and if so to what community, is expressed – must necessarily be expressed – in everyday life, in its whole organizational pattern and in its ethic. It is as a 'whole man' that the human person participates in the community.

From this it follows that the man who can in theory be a member of an infinite number of groups, cannot be a member of an infinite number of communities. Typically, the human person is limited to living his life within the confines of one single community. Membership of more than one community is, of course, possible, but in this case hierarchical preferences can hardly be avoided, and one community will by a natural process of gravitation assume a central position to which membership of other communities must remain subsidiary. This is a process which is spontaneous in natural communities, conscious in communities of adoption.

Every community has a relatively homogeneous system of values. If an individual infringes this system of values, he is harming the community. He cannot violate commonly held views in his everyday life either; communal man's house is not a citadel in which his behaviour is, to some extent anyway, beyond the scope of his status as a member of the community.

A homogeneous system of values does not necessarily mean a rigidly narrow system applicable to every individual case, nor does it mean a rigid hierarchy in which each value has its allotted fixed place. In 'natural' communities, into which the person is born, the value hierarchy is given and fixed by the community. For a person in the Athenian *polis*, it may have been a problem to know which action was to be described as 'courageous' and which as 'temperate', but there could be no doubt that the basic values were courage, wisdom, justice and temperance. From the standpoint of the *polis* community, whoever was intemperate or cowardly (in any of life's situations) harmed the community and was in conflict with it.

However rigid the moral code in any 'natural' community, the scale of values has never been worked out with uniform delicacy, nor applied with equal precision in all individual cases. It depends very much on the concrete community, which norms are kept in their generality to be applied in particular cases by the individual and which communities prescribe the exact manner in which the norms should be applied in these cases. For example, Christianity is much readier to prescribe the manner of application of its norms in the individual case than was the practice in ancient Athens. This means that not every fixed value hierarchy provides a uniform terrain for the person to build up his individual system of values, nor does it give equal opportunity for informed judgment, attention to individuality, prudence, etc.

I said above that every natural community has a more or less rigid hierarchy of values, though each such hierarchy leaves more or less room for individual variation in practice. With the growth of bourgeois society and a more dynamic social order, and the disappearance of 'natural' communities, fixed systems of value also vanish, both in practice and, as a result, in ethical doctrine. We have no space here to go into the consequences of this development. But it is worth noting that this is why the concept of 'happiness' (a central concept in antiquity, and, in the form of 'salvation', in Christianity) has progressively lost this central position from the Renaissance onwards; and this is why 'happiness' has been replaced by 'freedom' as the main target of ethics.

Since the communities of 'pure' (not communal) society are communities formed by persons voluntarily, the homogeneity of values here obtaining is determined by three factors: first, the purpose of the community, that to which the community is related; second, the circumstances in which it functions, and, finally, the degree of individual development of those persons who form the community, who enter into it. Hence, even voluntarily chosen communities may establish values and enjoin their individual observance in a way which curtails the individuality of the person to which they apply. And equally possible is the extreme case of the community in which the priority of the species-essential values functions as the only homogeneous community value, and it is left completely to the individual to decide how these values are to be realized in his own life. In this case, infringement of the community – i.e. infringement of its homogeneous value system – is identical with a way of life centred on exclusively particularistic interests. It is of course to be expected that here too the smaller community as the contractual and relational form, as a fundamental unit of the overall social *Gemeinschaft,* will have a formative role in the shaping of attitudes to life. It is up to the individual, however, to choose the concrete forms of life, the 'face to face' communal cells in which he wishes to realize the universal norms of a given universal community (even of humanity organized into a unity); that is, to choose any community likely to incorporate the overall species-essentiality, though on different levels and in different forms. There can be little doubt but that we must envisage the communities of future society as communities whose axiological homogeneity is close to this second type.

So far we have been speaking of the correlation between individual and community. We now turn our attention to the possibility of contradictions between them. The idea that human person and community could form contradictory categories was completely alien to societies based on the community. Typical of these is harmony between the person and the community: the person spontaneously accepted the communal system of values, and, in appropriating these, adapted himself to the terrain bestowed on him by the community as his permitted field of action. Persons centred on particularity tended to select that field of action (largely without prompting) which undiscriminating acceptance of the community's domain and norms offered them for the realization of their impulses, their needs, desires and interests. Loss of community meant loss of the conditions for one's existence. Expulsion from the community was the most severe punishment possible: in many cases it was enough to ensure the destruction of the expelled person.

Of course, even in community-based societies contradictions could and did arise between the person and the community. Expulsion (ostracism) was either the punishment visited on such a contradiction, or a threat which prevented it. Contradiction could arise for two reasons: first, if the person by reason of the over-active nature of his personality endangered communal equilibrium by lording it over others; and, second, if someone gave precedence to his particularistic aims (personal success, enrichment, etc.) over the aims and interests of the community, and began to regard the community as a means towards the fulfilment of his own personal aims.

In community-based societies, expulsion is a value-judgment. The expelled person is never exonerated even if the actual decision to expel him was an unjust one. The typical catharsis for the member of a natural community is return to, re-admission to the community, at whatever cost and no matter how much personal abasement is involved. In natural communities the expelled individual recognizes the community's right to expel him, even when he feels himself to be superior to those who expel him. It is for this reason that Socrates refuses to escape from prison, and accepts the verdict of the *polis* – death.

The idea that human person and community are contradictory

categories has grown up with the coming to power of the bourgeoisie. It derives from the conviction that any attempt to regulate the life of the person according to any homogeneous value system whatever, is an infringement, a derogation of individuality. It derives from the conviction that only the abstract commodity producer can be a true individual whose social character is realized only retrospectively on the market, *via* the mediation of the produced commodity. The concept of 'individual' coalesces here with that of 'individualist'. In his classical form, the individualist is that individual who believes that only self-realization and its effectuation constitute species-essential activity, and who therefore holds that the ego is the generally human: in other words, the absolute monarchy of personal individual development. But, if we take the social average as base, the annulment of communal 'alignment' guarantees nothing more than the cock-sure individualism of selfishness.

I am not advocating the Romantic standpoint – the belief that we must see the true potentialities of human development in the light of the now extinct natural communities of the past. All I am claiming is that the greatest and most important individualities of bourgeois society were precisely those who did not accept a world in which the community was null and void, but who saw the main prospects for personal development in the creation of selected communities – communities of a new type. Even in the earliest stages of bourgeois development we find such exemplary aspirations – the exemplary and ideal community circle formed by the protagonists of Rousseau's *Nouvelle Héloïse* in Clarens, and the fraternal collective formed round Lothario in Goethe's *Wilhelm Meister*. And in those less happy moments of history when it was no longer possible for the single individual to enter such a community, great artistic personalities were filled with nostalgia for the lost community and with a desire to find their way back to it (the late-comers Beethoven and Schubert, to take examples from the world of music).

Of course, the concrete contradictions between the human person and the community are not formulated in selected communities in the same way as in natural communities. There is no space here to specify these differences. Suffice it to point out that – since selected or elected communities most frequently exist alongside each other – what can and often does arise is re-selection of community. A catharsis may be expressed in such a re-selection and not perforce in return to a community (though this may also happen). From the outset, the person's field of action in a chosen community may be much wider than in a natural community (though in practice this is not always the case); and the individual is much more likely to leave his own imprint on the content of a chosen community and, what is more important, on its system of values as well. Accordingly, in a chosen community, ostracism of the first type (*vis-à-vis* the over-active individual) becomes meaningless and purposeless, and remains so even when it is still widely practised. The second type of ostracism remains operative, of course, and will continue to do so as long as communities exist.

(e) We-consciousness

As we have seen, the person's we-awareness develops along with his self-awareness. Only the inveterate egoist-individualist is devoid of we-awareness, but in his case this is not a point of departure but a result, the considered outcome of a way of life. With reference to the parallel development of self- and we-awareness, it cannot be denied that the affective force of particularity bears the main stress in the case of self-awareness. The 'we' component owes its most elementary gains in affectivity to the fact that the 'self' identifies itself with it. This is true, of course, not only of communities but of any and every integration, even of completely adventitious integrational groupings. With the disappearance of natural communities, persons often seek adherence to a group (whether consciously or not) on the grounds that they can thus prolong their particularity.

In the case of the person centred on particularity, we have analysed this particularity itself as a homogeneous category. But the various particular affects do not necessarily develop freely in their overall togetherness. Even in the case of those persons in whom particularity is maximized, some degree of self-control is necessary if they are to be viable in the world; self-control is, after all, nothing more than a restraint upon particularity in one or another aspect. A hierarchy is set up among the particularistic affects: the strength or weakness of inborn properties and the habitat in which these must be applied, decide together which particularistic affects are to be sacrificed and which not (spontaneously in the main) by the subject. In so far as they are connected, not with the process whereby the person raises itself to the status of 'individual', but with the simple act of restraining particularistic affects, these 'sacrifices' may often lead to 'complexes'. I agree with Bloch when he says that a *complex* is always generated by an infringement of particularity; the individual who is endowed with self-consciousness knows his motives and tries to fit his individuality to his obligations, in a way that takes the facts of his ipseity ('I am what I am') into account: as a result, conflicts may indeed arise – even with himself – but never complexes.

The simple suppression of particularistic affects (perhaps of inborn qualities also) – their inhibition – serves a double purpose. First and foremost, the interests of species-essential development. In the world of private property, of class society and of alienation, which for the most part produces persons centred on particularity, species-essential demands – like all social demands – can be satisfied only by the suppression or 'redirection' of certain particularistic affects or inborn properties. So, 'inhibition' becomes a fundamental aim of particularity itself: for particularity could not discharge its main function – self-maintenance in the world – if it did not go along with social prerogatives in the suppression of certain particularistic affects.

It is primarily morality, religion and law that ensure the inhibition of particularistic affects, their ordering in a hierarchy or their purposeful canalization. Yet the first two – morality and religion – invariably and not adventitiously are constructed on we-awareness. How is this so? The person sees the 'we' – whether it be an organic community, a selected community or group – as a prolongation or extension of himself. Accordingly, we-awareness is founded, not in the realm of ideas but very much in an earthly breeding ground. The person is part of an integration; the victories of integration are victories of the person, and when integration gains ground for its interests, particularity also flourishes.

Identification with the 'we', however, does not come about through the self assessing the possibilities of its gains and losses: we-awareness is spontaneously internalized. For the 'we', for the community – and here we are once again confronted with the contradiction inherent in particularity – the person is capable of the greatest sacrifices. To its content he can transfer his affects, relinquish his property and sacrifice his family. Not the least significant property of religion and morality is that they express this function of the 'we' which transcends particular interests. But we cannot say that we-awareness plus corresponding action would be in itself sufficient to ensure the transcendence of particularistic attitudes.

First and foremost, in the case of identification with the we , suspension of particularity is realized exclusively and alone in relation to one's own integration. My country is in danger: I

41

volunteer for the front. I am ready to put up with hunger, exhaustion, wounds; but when the enemy is defeated, I torture his men to death, rape his women and butcher his children – all of this has much to do with complete identification with 'we-awareness'.

We can even say that complete identification with 'we', with the actions of my community is precisely what opens the floodgates of my particular affects. I can thereby lose my moral understanding of and my discretion *vis-à-vis* those who have not carried the identification through to its limits. In the name of my community, I can give a free hand to my lowest instincts, feeling myself at the same time to be noble. What should be the execution of justice takes on the lineaments of vengeance.

Thus, 'we-awareness' and identification with the 'we' or joint action with it can, on the one hand, suppress the particularistic point of view, the particularistic inborn bent or affect; on the other hand, it can instill fresh life into them. At the same time – and again this is a motivation of particularity – such identification can simplify and facilitate orientation in the affairs of the world. For example, if I am a Hungarian, those nations are 'good' who like Hungarians, while those which are anti-Hungarian are 'bad'. What is 'good' is what is good for the Hungarians. These are very simple stereotypes, which anyone can apply for himself without special moral acumen, and which ensure that, in a given medium – in our example, the Hungarian medium – one may operate successfully, meeting with agreement and avoiding conflict, etc.

Furthermore, this identification can be a substitute for my own record: even if I have been notably unsuccessful in life, my country has been successful. Or, to put the reverse case – if I have been unsuccessful in life it is because the group I belong to has not been allowed to get on in the world.

But particular motivation takes part in 'we-awareness' in an even more intricate and more roundabout way. Once I have bound myself to a group or community, maintenance of identification with it, is, at the same time, defence of my life and of my conduct hitherto – that is to say, it is self-defence. Now if it turns out that the community with which I have identified myself is not worthy of such an identification, that its value-content is questionable, and so on – my particularity reasons that I have lived in vain: therefore I must cling to the identification and reject all temptations that might divert me therefrom (even by destroying the tempters).

What I have said by no means exhausts the possible forms that particularistic reaction may take. At least as frequent as those I have described is the reaction in which the person suddenly turns against the integration he has identified himself with, and what has been the object of his affection becomes an object of hate. In this case, he is defending his life by blaming the failed integration for all his mistakes – that is to say, he still identifies himself with it, but now in a negative sense.

PART II

The everyday and the non-everyday

CHAPTER 4

The heterogeneity of everyday life

(a) The objectivation of 'the whole man'

In everyday life – if I may use Lukács's terminology – the whole man takes part; or, to put it another way, everyday activities are those in which the whole man takes shape.

In itself and without remainder, everyday life is objectification. That is to say, it is a process in which the person as subject 'becomes externalized' and in which externalized human capabilities proceed to live their own lives detached from their human source; wave-like, they undulate onwards in their own everyday life and in that of others in such a way that, if only at second-hand, they merge into and blend with the current of history, and thus take on objective value-content. For this reason, we can say that everyday life is the basis of the current of history. It is from the conflicts of everyday life that the greater conflicts of society in the mass are generated: answers have to be found to the questions thrown up in these conflicts, and no sooner are these settled than they reappear to re-shape and re-structure everyday life anew.

Like every process of objectification, everyday life is objectification in two senses. On the one hand, it is the continuous process of the externalization of the subject. At the same time, it is the process whereby the person is continually being re-created. In the endless process of externalization, the person is shaped and objectified. In so far as its objectivations are uniform in rank, 'repetitions', the person reproduces itself on this same level; in so far, however, as its objectivations are novel, making landfall at a new higher level, the reproduced subject will also be on a higher level. In so far as the objectivations are incoherent, inwardly lacking a unifying principle, in so far as they are no more than 'accommodations', internalizations, in so far, the person is reproduced on the level of particularity; in so far as the objectivations are synthesized and bear the stamp of individuality, thus far the objectivation of everyday activity – on the level of the subject – is the individual. Objectification as continuous external-ization, and individuality as objectivation are therefore twin processes, indissolubly linked, mutually conditioning each other and borrowing from each other; perhaps we can more aptly speak of twin products of one and the same process.

I started by saying that everyday life is in its entirety objectification. It is objectification on one specific level – on the level of the 'ready-made world', that is to say, the milieu into which man is born, in which he must learn to manoeuvre and which he must learn to manipulate: the world with its ready-made collectivity, its integration, its ready-made customs, its tasks, judgments and prejudices, its emotional patterns, its education and technology, its serviceability, etc. When I say 'I love you' to someone, my emotion becomes external to me, it is set to work in someone else's individuality, and may transform its future course (whether my love is accepted or not) and at the same time it transforms my own individuality as well: the more violent the passion, the more extensive will be the changes wrought in the structure of my own individuality. A specific love (with specific emotional and moral content, with specific attitudes and be-haviour) is related to an objectivized world-order, to the erotic conventions of the age, its emotional expectations, and so on. The way I choose to furnish my home, arrange my garden or educate my children is equally an objectification.

I said that everyday life is objectification in its entirety. But this does not mean that every concrete everyday activity is an objectification and, even less, that all objectifications are on the same level, or have the same degree, let alone the same radius, of effectivity. Sleep, for example, is an indispensable biological ingredient of everyday life, but it is not objectification. Speech acts are more pregnant objectifications than gestures but different speech-acts imply effectivity of a different kind. The expression 'It's a nice day' awakens fewer ripples in space and time as a transmission of the uttering subject than, let us say, a proposal of marriage. It is quite impossible to divide the various types of everyday activity into 'objectifying' and 'non-objectifying', if for no other reason than that often how and to what degree a concrete action is an objectification depends on the given situation and the level of objectivation it is related to.

48

(b) Everyday and non-everyday thinking

Like everyday life, everyday thinking too is heterogeneous. The thought processes evinced in the various forms of everyday activity have this in common – they all arise from the facticity of the everyday. They arise, on the one hand, from the fact that heterogeneous forms of activity have to be co-ordinated and carried out in a relatively short time; and, on the other hand, from the fact that at different times, in different societies and in different classes these heterogeneous activities vary in kind, which means that the knowledge required for the appropriation and performance of these activities is also a variant. From the first of these twin facts arises the general structure of everyday thinking, from the second is derived the concrete content of everyday thought. Of course, not every form of knowledge can be made 'everyday'; not every form of knowledge can be fitted into the structural system of everyday thinking. Any form of knowledge which cannot be so accommodated remains professional knowledge and is not a necessary condition for the reproduction of a particular person born into a given society.

Everyday thinking as a function of everyday living can be considered as an invariant. Its structure, however, and its contents are variables, highly disparate in their rate of change. The structure of everyday thinking changes very slowly, and it contains completely stagnant aspects. Its contents change relatively quickly. But even these contents are prone to conservatism, inertia, if we compare everyday thinking with scientific thinking.

The inertia inherent in the content of everyday thought is dual in character. The duality arises from its close ties with the structure of everyday thought. Since the contents of everyday thought – as we shall see in due course – are embedded in a very largely pragmatic and economic structure, they are by definition inert vis-à-vis the products of thought which transcend the purely pragmatic. This transcending of the pragmatic may possibly come about in the *intentio obliqua* of science (philosophy),[1] in the discovery of problem complexes the cognitive understanding of which runs contrary to the anthropocentric experience gained in the pragmatic approach and the needs or interests of the everyday 'person', whether particular or individual.

In so far as the institutionalized or other objectivations which go beyond the everyday have been alienated, the pragmatism of everyday thinking appears vis-à-vis these objectivations as 'natural common sense', as the yardstick of normality. In so far, however, as these objectivations represent a deeper connection with the generic, the contents of everyday thinking appear as a system of prejudices; and 'common sense' acquires a negative evaluative imprint.

In pre-capitalist societies too there were certain spheres of objectivations requiring types of thinking which were not only in contrast with everyday experience, but which were in fact not derivable from it. This schism is characteristic of all types of thought – from ethics and politics to astronomy and physics – from the Renaissance onwards. The view regarding the relation of ethics to politics advanced by Machiavelli in *The Prince* offers solutions which no Socrates could derive from the everyday thinking of any everyday man. In his *Novum Organum* Bacon uses his theory of 'idols' to distinguish methodologically between scientific thinking and the pragmatized anthropomorphism of everyday thinking. In physics, Galileo promulgates the *intentio obliqua* not only through his discoveries but also in his polemics; and it is common knowledge that, since Galileo, modern scientific thought has run counter to everyday thinking. A similar process can be discerned in the subsequent development of philosophy: in his *Ethics* Spinoza rationalizes man's behaviour in its entirety, Hobbes, followed by Helvétius, reduces all human activity to self-interest, Kant proclaims the categorical imperative – all of this certainly transcends everyday experience. And the same goes for Marx's philosophy of history – the theory of alienation.

To recapitulate: by *intentio obliqua* we understand the content of non-everyday thought, a content which cannot be formed by extrapolating from and organizing everyday thought, related as it is to everyday experience, and purifying it of its particularity, its fortuitous character and its particularistic anthropocentricity. But this is not to say that the content of non-everyday thought formed *via intentio obliqua* has absolutely nothing in common with everyday life and everyday thinking. We shall go into this in more detail later; for the moment, it will suffice to say that the official rejection of the contents of everyday thinking as biased (and not only as confused), as bogus over-generalizations, presupposes the existence of the contents thus criticized.

We mentioned the anthropocentric character of everyday thinking. Here, 'anthropocentrism' is a shorthand expression for three separate categories which are present and usually undifferentiated in everyday thinking: these can be called anthropological-ness, anthropocentricity and anthropomorphy.[2]

'Anthropologicalness' means simply that in everyday life and thinking we cannot abstract from the 'thus it is' of our perceptions. This is not a fault of everyday thinking: this dependence on human perception is indispensable in everyday practice. We know perfectly well that the earth goes round the sun and that the sun does not 'go behind' the clouds – but our everyday activity takes its cue from the 'rising' and the 'setting' of the sun, and its 'disappearance' behind clouds, not from the astronomical facts. In order to perform the right actions, we don't even have to know as much as we do know. With the development of technology, more and more of the 'signals' informing everyday life are provided by science. But they can only become integrated into our everyday life and activity if our perception of them and our relationship with them are as 'anthropological' as in the case of 'purely' natural phenomena. Today, we use the alarm clock to waken us, not the sun. Instead of looking up to see whether the sun is likely to be hidden by clouds we turn on the radio and listen to the weather forecast: but this implies no change in our anthropological mentality. The anthropologicalness of everyday life and thinking is therefore equally effective whatever the state, advanced or backward, of the given technology; and it is equally effective, whether the subject – the person who lives everyday life – is a particularity or an individuality.

With regard to anthropocentricity we have to make one reservation. Everyday life is the direct reproduction of the 'person': hence, its teleology is relative to, correlated with the 'person'. I have to maintain myself: and my general questions concerning life are those that arise in connection with my own life, my own experiences. The 'anthropos' of everyday life is therefore the person who lives this everyday life. The anthropocentricity of everyday life is not directed to the same things as the anthropocentricity of philosophy, art and the social sciences. The intention of these is, in the first place, with humankind, the species (or with these integrations and creations in which humankind is incorporated). It may sound paradoxical, but, as far as species-being is concerned, everyday life is less anthropocentric than any other sphere.

In contrast with anthropologicalness, in anthropocentricity a significant distinction can be made depending on whether the subject – the person who lives everyday life – is characterized by particularity or by individuality. It is true that the everyday life of even the most highly developed individual is related towards his own maintenance and self-preservation; his other activities transcend the everyday. Since, however, individuality is characterized by the distance it has established between it and its own particularity, and since this distance is a product of intention towards 'humankind', the anthropocentricity of the individual, though still correlated with the person, contains a conscious relationship with human kind, the species.

As for anthropomorphism – the structure of everyday life (to be analysed in more detail later) encourages us to see the whole world as an analogy of our own everyday life. Precisely because of the analogical cloak with which we garb the pragmatic structure of everyday life, everyday thinking is often fetishist: it accepts things and institutions as they are, in ready-made form, and brackets off their origins. Art which depicts the origins of institutions and social relations, as well as the genesis of individuals, mostly provides an essential anthropomorphism, one raised to the generic level, in contrast to the local and provincial anthropomorphism of everyday thinking. If everyday thinking extrapolates directly from man's everyday experience, art sets a question-mark at this relationship; it transfers man's life, problems and conflicts into the life, the problems and the conflicts of a non-ephemeral 'whole'. In relation and in proportion to the whole, the provincialism and pettiness of the 'conflicts' experienced by man in his everyday life, are reflected. The lift to the generic plane (we shall return to this later) which takes place in the creation and in the appropriation-reception of a work of art is therefore anthropomorphic in that it safeguards what it rescinds – the anthropomorphism of everyday thinking. This is not the place to discuss the relationship between philosophy and the social sciences, on the one hand, and everyday thinking, on the other, but here again, in spite of the differences, the relationship could be mapped in the same way as that obtaining between everyday thinking and art. The situation with regard to the natural sciences – and to their forerunner, natural philosophy – is somewhat different. Not only do the natural sciences reject the analogical integument borrowed from everyday life; they reject altogether the projection of the human dimension on the natural world.

Of one ideological form alone – religion – can it be said, that the world-picture built up on analogy with everyday life provides an essential part of its content. The picture of the world received 'ready-made' from the hand of God, the whole idea of creation, depend on the anthropomorphism which is a characteristic of everyday thinking. This anthropomorphism, however, assumes different guises in different religions: in some, the world beyond is simply a reflection of our human world, as in *polis* religions; in others it may be profoundly spiritualized as in Christianity.

As I said, the anthropologism of everyday thinking is something no man can escape from, and the same goes for its anthropocentricity: though the anthropocentricity associated with particularity differs in type from that associated with individuality. My next question is: must everyday thinking be inevitably anthropomorphous in the above sense?

The answer must probably be in the negative. Men do not have to become scientists or philosophers in order to avoid the analogous projection of their experiences in their immediate environment and their everyday activity on to the world in general. If it were so, anthropomorphism would indeed be inescapable. There will never be a world in which every man can be an expert in all things, nor will there ever be a world in which one can cancel one's own everyday life while living it. In order to prevent anthropomorphism in the narrow sense from becoming the basic structure underlying everyday thinking, it is sufficient for us to have a general *Weltanschauung* which enables us to fit our own everyday experiences into the wider context of human life and experiences, human needs, and the intellectual level attained by mankind in our time.

Everyday thinking free of anthropomorphism is possible but – and this is a crucial limitation – only for individuals (in the above defined sense). Where life is limited to the narrow circle of particularity, anthropomorphism in the narrower sense is a necessity. As long as the majority of 'persons' in a society are particularistic, as long as everyday life can be carried on with nothing more than particularity in the role of subject, anthropomorphism in the narrow sense will be an indissoluble characteristic of human life. We may succeed in achieving a degree of de-anthropomorphization in our narrower specialist capacities; but in everyday life we go on thinking in anthropomorphic terms, and this anthropomorphism may indeed be projected onto other spheres of reality, in so far as these do not overlap with our narrower specialist interests. Everyday thinking is heterogeneous; and de-anthropomorphized, and anthropomorphic world-views and mental motifs mingle freely in undifferentiated fashion within its framework.

(c) Everyday life and social structure

We may start with a question: is it possible to read off, to discern from its everyday life and thinking, the social structure of a given period and, secondly, the stage which that structure represents in the generic development of the human race?

The social division of labour means that people lead very different everyday lives in a given society, their differentiation turning upon such factors as class, stratum, community, order, etc.; and this in turn means that from the everyday life of any one man, indeed of any one class, we cannot learn everything about the structure of the given society. The everyday life of the serf cannot fully express the structure of feudalism, any more than can the everyday life of the knight.

So, for the moment at least, the answer to our question must be in the negative; not only because of the division of labour but also because of the fact that a particular society is to be identified by its aggregate of objectivations and the relationships between them. The level of production and distribution, the degree of excellence reached in the arts and sciences, the structure of the society's various institutions and the types of human activity performed in them – from such data we can effectively read off what sort of society we have to do with, what it has to give mankind and what it may, on the other hand, take from us. It is clear that there neither is nor can be a society in which the generic objectivations are represented by nothing more than the aggregate of everyday lives.

On closer inspection, however, our initial 'no' turns out to require some qualification.

Persons are born into a given world, and it is the conditions imposed by this given world – at least in so far as their immediate environment is concerned – that they must appropriate and make their own if they are to survive. The production and distribution system that is internalized in their everyday life, the moral precepts and practices which become its inseparable paraphernalia, the role played in it by art and science, the nature of the art and science called upon to play this role – all of this tells us much about the structure of a given society. The generic development (or regression) of the species is also reflected in this everyday mirror, and can be to some extent gauged therefrom.

I said that the basic structure of everyday life and everyday thinking is relatively stagnant. This is not to say, however, that it shows no modulation, or that it is closed to the accretion of new elements, new prehensions: as I said, there is always the possibility that anthropomorphism in the narrower sense can be overcome. Do we not, indeed, learn much about society as a whole from the fact that certain individuals belonging to certain strata of society have, to a greater or less degree, the possibility of transcending the

54

everyday limits of particularity? For example, conversation (as we shall see later) as an adjunct to the business of everyday living, is by no means regarded as necessary by every stratum of every society; but we learn much about the degree to which a society has been humanized from consideration of the question to what degree and in what circles conversation has become a necessity. *Amour passion* has not always figured as a vital factor in everyday living; it is then all the more significant that certain ages have 'given birth' to *amour passion* as a vital factor – indeed, an obligatory factor in everyday life. And it helps us to classify a society when we see whether or not anything as basic as schooling has become an element in its everyday life.

Our main interest is not, however, in any new factors that may arise in the structure of everyday life and thinking, but in the transformation of the content of existing factors, especially the axiological content. This value-content can already be traced in the 'culture' of customs. How we nourish ourselves, what and how we eat, where we live and how we furnish our houses – in all of this, the humanization of the race finds expression.

But the best guide to the qualitative content of everyday life remains the formation of direct personal relationships between people. Fourier said that the history of the development of human values could be written from a study of the relationship between the sexes. Then again, one age will differ from another in the degree to which its social classes and strata had access to 'public life' in the course of their daily activities: or the degree to which their daily life was confined to 'private life'. Technical development is expressed in and by everyday activity in similar fashion: whether we eat with a wooden spoon or a stainless steel one, whether we travel by farm-cart or take the car, we are reflecting to some degree the state of contemporary technical achievement.

At no time in the history of man has everyday life been entirely unaffected by art: art has always had some kind of role to play. Much depends, of course, on *which* branches of art reach into the everyday lives of people, just as much depends on the quality of these works of art.

I must admit, then, that everyday life is not calibrated in such a way that we can read off directly from it the information we want about the structure of society and the level of generic development, and this remains true even if we deal only in terms of the general social average. At the same time, however, everyday life does have something to tell us about the structure of society and about generic development; and in fact, evaluation of the available range of possibilities in everyday life belongs to the 'reading-off' process.

My next question follows on logically from the first and concerns progressive development, the process whereby one society takes over from another and builds thereon, the evolution of values: do these find expression in everyday life? Again, I must give a qualified answer.

The concept of progress cannot be applied to everyday life in so far as it has been organized on particularity, and in so far as the average relationship between us and our world has remained constant. But everyday life has progressed in so far as the contents of everyday life, the contents of everyday activity have always to some extent expressed the development of the social aggregate. Were it not so, general social development of values would be impossible, for human history itself is built up on the everyday activity of myriads of human beings. The objection may be raised here that axiological development in everyday life is a contradiction in terms, since history can teach us no more than that some values evolve successfully while others atrophy: to this we answer that on the level of social structure, on the level of general social objectivations, the whole notion of 'development' is a contradiction in terms as well, since the successful evolution of values in certain spheres is accompanied by the atrophy of values in others. Whether efflorescence of values preponderates over their atrophy in everyday life or vice versa, in which arenas this takes place, whether or not efflorescence and atrophy of values affect the whole of society more than the everyday life of one or several social classes, and if the latter, which classes – answers to these questions will be factors in our description of a given society from the generic point of view as conducive or inimical to value growth.

(d) Homogenization

As I said above, one of the characteristic features of everyday life is its heterogeneity; it moves turbulently in a world of heterogeneous actions, it demands heterogeneous skills and capabilities. So, as I said, everyday life is something in which the whole man takes part. The norms and rules for action, the objectivations, among which the person acts out his everyday life, are heterogeneous as compared with each other. But this does not exclude the possibility of more or less homogeneous spheres of action and objectivations – on the contrary, it is their pre-condition; and we can say that the more generically established an objectivation is, the more homogeneous it becomes. The relationship to the most homogeneous of generic objectivations can be part of a largely heterogeneous everyday life, if the person is related to it in the framework of his everyday activity. For example, the legal system is a rather homogeneous objectivation; but our relationship with the law may be a vital factor in everyday life without its losing its heterogeneous character.

The mutual relationship between homogeneity and heterogeneity is also relative to the capabilities, inclinations, passions of the 'person' – which are themselves, in their turn, heterogeneous as compared with each other. The more developed the individuality, the more unified its activity in everyday life, the more do its capabilities and inclinations tend towards homogeneity – the homogeneous structure of the united personality. But none of this alters the fact that the various heterogeneous forms of activity call upon some capabilities and inclinations more than on others: which means, in turn, that even in the case of the most homogeneous of individuals, heterogeneity is an inseparable component of everyday life.

In spite of this shifting scene of relative relationships, we are entitled – following Lukács – to regard the process of homogenization as the category of 'emergence' from everyday life. In this sense, homogenization means that the individual is 'absorbed' in a given homogeneous sphere of objectivation, and concentrates his activity upon one single objective homogeneous sphere of action. In this case, the 'person' is always in direct and immediate relationship with the genus. His intention in the given homogeneous sphere is incorporated genericity, of which he does not have to be consciously aware. In this case, a man's activity is not only indirectly but directly also, a component part of general human praxis: from being 'a whole man' (to quote Lukács again) the subject becomes 'man-as-whole' – by which we mean an individuality who concentrates all his strength and ability on discharging a task within a homogeneous sphere of objectivation. The human activity which takes place in the process of homogenization is creation or re-creation.

Homogenization is the criterion of 'emergence' from the everyday, and – it must be emphasized – not a subjective criterion. Everyday life could not be reproduced without the heterogeneous human activities, and neither could the objectivation 'for itself' be reproduced without the homogenization process. The homogeneous spheres and objectivations themselves require homogenization for their reproduction. If a society has a positive legal system, then it also needs citizens who spend their lives or at least part of their lives 'working themselves into' the homogeneous structure of the law, to learn legal thinking. If a society needs natural science, it also needs individuals able to appropriate the homogeneous structure of the scientific disciplines, and learn how to 'operate' therein, thus bypassing both everyday life and everyday thinking. If a society needs deeds of a kind far surpassing run-of-the-mill ethics, deeds demanding virtues and heroism directly geared to a consciousness on the level of the generic, then it requires the presence in it of 'moral geniuses' who can raise their moral motivation to the level of moral objectivation.

In what follows, we shall give separate consideration to each of the generic objectivations – objectivations 'for itself' – which require the process of homogenization. For the moment, it will suffice to point out that the process of homogenization – depending on the specific homogeneous objectivation *vis-à-vis* which we are undergoing homogenization – may vary in extent, type and intensity. If then we try to set out criteria with which to assess this process, it must be remembered that these criteria are not all valid for all processes of homogenization, and that, even when valid, they are not all valid to the same extent.

So what are these criteria? First of all, the direct relationship to a homogeneous generic objectivation; secondly, the conscious relationship to it; thirdly, the active relationship with it. Next, concentration on one single task. The singleness may be literal (e.g. in the case of a work of art, its creation or its reception) but it may also have a wider connotation: it may denote concentration 'of a single type', or concentration 'connected with' a task. As for 'concentration', this may mean concentration of all human strength and capability, but it may also mean a degree of concentration as demanded by the given objectivation, allied with the simple suspension of other capabilities. A further criterion is the 'sifting' or 'screening' of particularity. Again, this may involve the suspension of all particular motivation (as in the case of moral activity on the generic level), it may be the suspension of a particular viewpoint (as in the case of artistic or scientific activity) or it may be simply the suspension of certain particular aspirations which run counter to 'being absorbed' into the given objectivation (as in the work-process). Finally, we must mention the criterion provided by the generalization of our personalities, our thoughts, our experiences, our aspirations, our capabilities. (Exactly which of these we generalize, depends to a large extent on the specific sphere on which our homogenization process is centred.) And here it must be pointed out that we may transcend everyday life without necessarily transcending everyday thinking; and, vice versa, ability to rise above, to emerge from everyday thinking does not necessarily imply leaving behind the intention of everyday life.

From all of this it is clear that the process of homogenization – depending on the objectivation and the degree of the homogenization – is indeed a *process*. And we cannot always label all the types of activity we engage in as either 'everyday' or 'non-everyday'. 'Everyday' and 'non-everyday' are ideal types of activity, and empirical overlapping does not impair the validity of the homogenization criterion.

CHAPTER 5

From the everyday to the generic

In what follows, we shall attempt to analyse in concrete fashion the relationship obtaining between everyday life and the directly and consciously generic activities. We take our starting point from the level of 'co-existence' between everyday and non-everyday activities and end up with an analysis of the sphere of objectivation 'for itself' so that we may scrutinize the undulations between the everyday and what is beyond.

(a) Work

So far, we have used the word 'work' in two senses: on the one hand it refers to a certain kind of everyday activity, and on the other it refers to a direct generic activity. And indeed both references are correct. The performance of work is an organic part of everyday life; the process, work-activity, is a species-essential objectification. Marx often uses two words to make this distinction: he calls the everyday activity 'labour', reserving the word 'work' for the species-essential category.

Those who construed 'work' as the concrete process of working could not, of course, distinguish between work as performance and work as activity. This interpretation of 'work' is very old; in Aristotle we find work construed as a purposeful human activity which we undertake to bring about a consciously premised end: a process in which tools, means to the end, are interposed between subject and object, and in which the human being creatively adapts to the object undergoing transformation, finally to create a new objectivation. Marx's innovation was not to analyse the process of work but rather to investigate the concrete conditions in

60

which a work process is carried out, how this is realized as 'work' for society in general and as 'labour' from the standpoint of the worker.[1] And Marx viewed with suspicion both Ricardo's failure to distinguish between work and labour and Fourier's neglect of 'labour' in his 'work as play' theory.[2]

What evidence is there that the process of 'work' is a social and species-essential activity which transcends everyday life? A first approximation may be seen in the fact that it is a process which creates a product which satisfies the needs of others. This is not necessarily to say that others do or will *de facto* use the product: but it does mean that they *can* use it. Under the conditions of commodity production the species-essential quality of work is realized in exchange; and thus all concrete labour is, at the same time, abstract labour in that it produces value – exchange value. But whether it happens indirectly, through exchange, that the social nature of work is realized, or directly, the work product must satisfy a social need, and it must still embody the socially necessary labour-time for its production. If the product does not satisfy a social need, or if the time spent on its production surpasses the socially necessary labour-time, we can no longer speak of 'work' but we can still speak of 'labour'.

Let us pause here for a moment. We have given one Marxian definition of the concept 'work', but any attempt to use this definition as a basis for classifying various social activities as 'work' or 'non-work' only lands us in confusion. The point is that the previously mentioned Marxian definition is concerned with 'work' in its economic sense, i.e. with production. This is after all the basic component in the concept of 'work', since the production of something is the *raison d'être* for work of whatever sort.

Let us try to refine our first approximation by relating the category of 'work' to the structure of the division of labour. From this vantage point, all the direct social activity, all the objectivation necessary for the reproduction of a given society can be regarded as 'work'. This amounts to a conditional endorsement of a conclusion which we drew from our first approximation – namely, that the term 'work' can properly be applied only to activity which is of use to others, in the sense that the function it discharges is indispensable for the given society, and that the manner in which it is performed corresponds to the norms and time-scales of that society.

This approximation from the sociological angle seems satisfactory enough but there is a snag. If the economic concept of 'work' proved too narrow for our purposes, this sociological version is too

61

wide. For, if we take it literally, we should be led to suppose that the king on his throne is also 'working', and that the upper classes were 'working' when they put down rebellious peasants. Our sociological grid is too coarse to distinguish between the activity of those classes which create the material goods of society, on the one hand, and those classes which make no such contribution, on the other.

Everyday experience is enough to show that this definition of work' casts the net far too wide. Our everyday understanding of 'work' is about as far removed as possible from the idea outlined above. To the question: what is 'work'?, most people will answer: 'what has to be done'. Neither everyday thinking nor everyday language makes a distinction, here between 'what someone has to do' and 'what someone is constrained to do'. We find a good example of this homespun wisdom in Mark Twain's *Tom Sawyer*: when the fence has to be painted – as an obligation – it is 'work'; as soon as the right to paint the fence has been traded, however, it becomes a privilege, even a game. The same fence is painted in the same way; the objective product of the 'work' is the same. In everyday thinking, work does not simply boil down to 'compulsion'; the concept also includes the reasons for the compulsion. Work then is 'earning one's bread', 'earning money' – that is to say, the activity whereby one supports oneself. Finally, 'wear and tear' plays a part in the everyday attitude to work: work is not simply that which has to be done, it is not done only so that we may survive, but it must be done regularly every day, in a given time, and this has an eroding and wearing effect on our strength and capabilities.

The everyday notion of 'work' can be seen as empirical, even fragmented – but it is not nonsensical. True, it fails to do justice to the economic and sociological content of the word, to say nothing of the philosophical implications. It does no more than state what work means *de facto* in everyday life. In some respects, this empirical description may conflict with the scientifically more reasoned concept, but by and large the two coincide remarkably well. 'Work is what has to be done' is the vernacular way of describing the objective obligation implicit in the social division of labour; 'earning one's bread' is simply another way of saying that production is always production for needs; while Marx also held that 'wear and tear' (of brain, nerve, sinew in the process of work) was a characteristic feature of work. The 'empiricism' of the everyday concept of work is due simply to the fact that 'work' is construed from the standpoint of 'labour'.

We proceed now to a brief analysis of the concept of 'labour'. As we have seen, everyday life is the reproduction of the 'person'. In order to reproduce themselves as 'persons', human beings have to work. That is to say, work is necessary for individual reproduction, and in so far as this is so, labour is an everyday activity. It could be objected that there have always been social classes which do not work. But the very reason why these classes could afford not to work is that, for the vast majority of society, work is and always has been an ineluctable part of everyday life.

So, when we say that work has always been an integral part of the everyday life of the 'person', we are really saying very little. Leaving contemporary Europe and America aside, we find that labour continues to be the main activity in everyday life. It is round about work that all other patterns of everyday activity centre and gravitate. To quote the Old Testament: 'men shall earn their bread by the sweat of their brow'. For a peasant boy, 'growing up' meant early adaptation to the work routines he would perform for the rest of his life. Most customs had to do with work, and most human relationships were cemented in and by work; marriage was contracted with an eye to work, and children were reared to continue that work; morality centred on work, and even most festivals were in one way or another bound up with work.

It lies in the essential nature of work that it is at one and the same time an everyday activity and an unmediated species-essential activity which transcends the everyday. In no way does it stand in any necessary relationship with its alienation. Other everyday activities may be alienated or non-alienated: thus, the relation between men and women can be an ownership or a property relationship – but it may also be a relationship between two free individuals, and whichever of the two it is, it remains part of everyday life.

However, it was not by chance that Marx used the concept of 'labour' mostly as a synonym for the category of the alienated work process. It is undeniable that work always serves the self-preservation of the 'person' and is always a structuring activity in everyday life: but this of itself does not tell us whether people enjoy their work or loathe it, whether they regard it as an arena in which they can exercise and develop their special talents or not. With the growth of capitalist society, however, the worker is deprived of the 'objects of production' and of its 'means of production' which are opposed to him as an alien social power. His own objectivized labour is an alien essence, a power which is independent of the producer; and while he produces more and more social wealth, he himself is more and more impoverished. Concomitantly, the work process becomes more and more alienated: 'as far as the worker is concerned, work is extrinsic, that is to say, it does not belong to his essential being' (Marx, *EPM*). As a result of this (and of the actual factory conditions analysed by Marx in *Capital*) work becomes an inorganic part of everyday life, a curse. 'Thus labour is not satisfaction of a need but a means to satisfy needs which lie outside the labourer' (Marx, *EPM*). And again

> The result is that it is only in his animal functions – eating, drinking and procreating, to which we might at most add putting a roof over his head and adorning it – that man (the worker) feels himself a free agent; in his human functions however he is no more than an animal (Marx, *EPM*).

That is to say, the work process remains one of man's basic species-essential activities: but, since work, as that species-essential activity which transcends the everyday, is alienated, the performance of work loses its quality as self-realization and serves only to reproduce the worker in its existence – or, to use our terminology, to support its particularity. The performance of work always creates and recreates the 'person's' life; but alienated performance of work only re-creates the 'person's' particularity. As the alienated performance of work, 'labour' is the performance of particularity, a part of the everyday life of particularity.

The intention to reproduce the life of a 'person' is present in all performance of work: otherwise, it could not be an integral part of everyday life. But the intention to reproduce the life of a 'person' is not identical with the intention to 'eat, drink and procreate'. Conversely, the fact that it is not restricted to basic survival activities does not by itself indicate a reduction in alienation. In modern society, the demands made by the productive worker are more and more complex and far-reaching, in keeping with his expanding standard of living – but these needs are not necessarily pointers to any equivalent expansion in individuality: they may indeed mark nothing more than an excess of particularity. As long as the need to possess things dominates the system of needs, particularity will remain the human subject of everyday life, and the performance of work will serve to support and nourish particularity.

Labour does not necessarily become less alienated when the worker enjoys his work. The science of 'human relations' has a way of fixing things so that labour looks more attractive – but what is eroded is the *awareness* of alienation, not alienation itself. Alienation of labour is not something that can be eradicated on the labour plane alone: rather, it depends on the transformation of society as a whole.

'Work' and 'labour' are, then, two aspects of one and the same process viewed from the standpoint of social reproduction or from the standpoint of the individual worker. But, though in general the terms 'work' and 'labour' have the same referent – they refer, that is, to the same act or performance – certain forms of activity may exceptionally be found in which one or the other component is lacking. The term 'work' alone (i.e. minus the 'labour' aspect) may justifiably be applied to 'social activity' which is not necessary for the reproduction of the 'person'. The term 'labour' by itself (i.e. minus the 'work' aspect) may be used when a given act of work appertains to the everyday reproduction of the unit-as-particularity or even to that of the unit-as-individuality, though its products never penetrate into the social bloodstream and never become generally and typically usable by others.

The distinction between 'work' and 'labour' was also of considerable interest to Marx, in so far as it concerned a communist society of the future. What 'work' would entail, what concrete form it would take, whether it would be simple or complicated – on such matters Marx changed his mind several times. Nor did he ever make his mind up definitively as to how the division of labour was finally to be set aside. As regards 'work' one line of argument dominates his thinking – namely that, at least as metabolism between nature and society, work will always be the domain of necessity. As to the prospects for 'labour' in a transformed society, Marx again changed his mind several times. In his youthful writings he seems to contemplate a constant rotation of jobs within the structure of the division of labour; in the *Grundrisse* he sees man as emerging from the production process; in *Capital* he foresees the rapid performance of given tasks (reduced to their simplest forms and taking up a minimum of labour-time) within the production process. Here, however, there is a constant factor: work becomes a vital need. It seems unlikely that the reasons which moved the mature Marx to regard work as a basic need, were the same as those which guided Fourier. In the *Grundrisse* his line of thought runs counter to the notion that unless man takes part in the social production process, his talents and potentialities are deprived of the opportunity for manifold growth and expansion. But to say that 'work becomes a vital need' means, *inter alia,* that if talents and capabilities are to be thus developed, it is necessary for a part of human life to be taken over by the kind of mental concentration, the conscious direction of physical and mental resources, which is characteristic of work (whether mental or physical). That work should 'become a vital need' is, however, not just a category of work *sensu stricto:* it is primarily a social-anthropological category. The fact of work 'becoming a vital need' betokens, first and foremost, the moral relationship existing between the free individual and labour. In the future as postulated by Marx, man will work because he cannot live without working: he will work, not because his particularity ensures that he cannot support himself without working, but rather because, as a free individual, he cannot reproduce himself without working. And in so far as this is so, alienation will cease as far as the individual is concerned – not independently of the way 'work' turns out, or of the concrete forms of 'labour', but not entirely dependent on these either.

The dual aspect of 'work' gives rise to three questions: (1) Can the active subject – i.e. the performer of the work – be purely particularistic? (2) Is everyday consciousness (awareness) in itself enough for the performance of work? (3) What is the significance of homogenization in the process of work performance?

As regards the first of these questions, we have first of all to be quite clear as to exactly what we mean by it. Put thus baldly, it requires no more than a simple 'no' as answer.But we started from the premise that every 'person' is at once particularistic and, as such, species-essential 'in itself': and in this connection we made it clear that we were thinking primarily of language and of work.

Species-essentiality 'in itself' is naturally a characteristic of all human activity in so far as this is indeed *human* activity. Work, language and custom share a common characteristic from which they draw their specifically species-essential content:[3] namely, that every utterance, every customary act, every job of work done, is a generalization. In all three instances man raises his particular endowments, wishes, impulses to a common level of generality, and in all three instances it is the objectivation sphere which gives the level of generalization: it is this which guides the 'person' in the process of generalization, that is, in the process of socialization.

If, however, our first question is construed as meaning – is a human attitude built round pure particularity able to bring forth a product likely to satisfy social needs? – then our answer must be in the affirmative. Of course, this does not mean that *all* work can be performed via a particularistic attitude (especially if we take 'work' in the wider sense connected with the social division of labour); but it does mean that a particularistic attitude has been enough to perform most of the work in human history hitherto.

It is true that in all acts of work certain human capabilities undergo a generalization which renders them species-essential. The more complex the labour process, the more competence and conscious control it demands, the more skill and talent it requires – the more do individual and particularistic capabilities become generalized into species-essential. Conversely, the simpler the work, the less the degree of concentration it requires, the more mechanical and monotonous it is in performance – the less are the particularistic capabilities involved capable of generalization, or, at best, of anything more than one-sided generalization; and the more likely to atrophy are the particularistic capabilities used in the work process. The possibility of generalization of the particular capabilities, on the one hand, and their degree of atrophy on the other, are very largely dependent on the position allotted to the 'person' in the given division of labour.

This is not the place to attempt an analysis of the division of labour or of its various types. But it is worth pointing out that the most one-sided generalization of work allied to the most radical atrophy of particularistic capabilities is likely to occur where there is a radical separation between the physical and mental aspects of one and the same work process, and where labour is extremely departmentalized.[4]

When we say that work, language and custom do not necessarily entail the transcending of the particularistic attitude, all this means is that a conscious relationship with the species-essential does not necessarily come about in us, nor does a conscious relationship with the particular self of the 'person' (otherwise, no life based on particularity could possibly exist). The generalization which is always inherent in work in no way militates against this: for, generalization here is of capability, not of personality: when I pause to consider before undertaking work of one kind or another whether I am capable of doing it, it is always of one or more of my capabilities that I take stock – strength, skill, experience, etc. – not of my individual personality as such.

Over and above the fact that work can be performed within the framework of a life centred round particularity, we have to remember that among the motivations underlying work those which are particularistic in nature are very common. This finds expression in everyday attitudes to work. For the most part, men have worked because they had to, to satisfy their basic needs – to

67

'earn their bread'. Their idea of heaven was *Schlaraffenland*, 'pie in the sky', where you didn't have to work for anything and where roast pigeons flew into your mouth. The man of property worked to augment his property: what impelled him was the desire to own things. The struggle waged for possession of the objects and means of work – land, means of production – the struggle for the work-places and for success is an arena in which particularistic motivations play a basic part.

This is, of course, not to say that it is only and exclusively particularistic motivations that come into action in the performance of work. There may also be moral motives: doing a good job, working precisely and impeccably, may be seen as a matter of honour. There may also be aesthetic motives: I may want to produce a masterpiece – an attitude which has not entirely vanished from the modern factory. But even when taken together, ethical and aesthetic impulses do nothing to change the essential nature of the particularistic attitude.

In this connection, another point is worth making. From the teleological structure of work it follows that in the process of working we are realizing certain of our aims: we 'succeed' in bringing forth that product which we have envisaged. Success is always accompanied by a feeling of pleasure – not only in work but in every walk of life, and it can act as a motivation in the sense that once we have experienced the feeling of success it will act, *inter alia,* as a spur to repeat the 'successful' undertaking. Chances of the pleasure of 'success' vary, of course, very significantly from one type of work to another.

Let us now turn to our second question: is everyday consciousness (knowledge) in itself enough for the performance of work?

If we are to give a rational answer to this question we must construe the word 'work' in the first sense: as the process of producing a product which can satisfy the needs of others, that is, as material production. For, if we take as our starting point the category of 'work' as delimited by the social division of labour, we shall end up with an endless concatenation of distinctions and confusions which are completely irrelevant to our present purpose. Having settled on our interpretation of 'work', then, our answer to the second question is simple: for the greater part of the work done in the production process, i.e. of material production, everyday consciousness (knowledge) has always been enough. We say 'the greater part' because the split in modern industrial practice between mental and physical work has meant that for part of the mental work-sphere – that having to do with the natural sciences – everyday consciousness and knowledge are not enough.

Given these provisos, then, what do we mean when we say that work has been normally performed with everyday consciousness and knowledge? In the first place, this means that in the performance of work there was no need to surpass or transcend the structure of everyday thought. (See the following section for an analysis of the structure of everyday thought.) Secondly (and this links up with our first point), the appropriation of work skills took place *via* a simple transfer of experience. Thirdly, work experience was broken up into separate, though associated, units which did not coalesce to form a homogeneous structure. And, finally, the conceptual apparatus in working was pragmatic.

We have to make a clear distinction between the question: is work, as 'labour', part of everyday life or not? and the question: does it or does it not require something more than everyday consciousness and knowledge for its execution? As 'labour', work is always an organic part of everyday life, whatever the degree of consciousness and kind of knowledge brought to its performance. Even today, the labour of the scientist contains an important aspect of everyday activity, though it is performed in a homogeneous objectivation divorced from everyday consciousness.

Let us now give a brief answer to our third question – what does homogenization mean in the work process? And here again, if the answer is not to be meaningless, we must understand 'work' in the first sense.

The process of work is also 'steered' by objectivation (by the work object, the tools) but not by a homogeneous complex of objectivations. This is not to say that the work-objects are not embedded in a sphere of objectivation; but there is no need of conscious relationship to the sphere as a whole in the work process. This is why the generalization which we perform in our persons when we work is simply the generalization of one or another talent or skill, never the generalization of the personality as a whole; nor is it the 'upward transfer' of the whole cognitive structure to another medium. The psychological aspect of homogenization is present: we concentrate all our efforts on performing the given task, and suspend all the instincts and motivations which might detract from concentration on this task. But we do not rise to the level of a homogeneous medium, nor do we relate in a conscious way to the species-essential. This kind of concentration may occur not only in the work process but also in play. In the work process, then, we perform a generic activity but

69

it is not a process in which 'the whole man' is raised to the 'man-as-whole' level.

What we are concerned with here then is a transitional type between the customary homogenization modes of everyday life (e.g. the sex act) and those types of homogenization which are consciously directed towards the species-essential (such as art). It is divided from the former, in that not need but the object and the means of forming it are conducive, and from the latter in that the object-referent towards which homogenization is directed does not require a conscious-reflexive relationship with it.

(b) Morals

In this section we need do no more than consider those aspects of morals which are of direct interest and concern in our analysis of everyday life.

Two points should be made clear at the outset. First of all, I do not regard morals as a separate or independent sphere, but as a human relationship which is immanent in all spheres. Secondly, morals is not to be regarded as an ideology. As we shall see, morals includes ideological moments, and ideology is projected or mapped on to it: first of all, these coherent theories which provide an overall interpretation of morals – ethical systems in the narrower sense; further, the moral codes, whether written or orally transmitted which set out the moral guidelines of a given society. It is these latter which play a crucial part in the organization of everyday life, though, in the case of individuals, the former are also not without influence. Primarily, however, morals is a practical relationship finding expression in action, and in the decisions and attitudes which initiate action.

Morals can be defined as the practical relationship of the 'person's' attitude and decisions to values and normative expectations. Since this relationship is a characteristic of every societal sphere, morals can be present in human relationships of all sorts.

The moral content of an action depends on several interrelated factors. These are: (1) the supersession of particularistic motivations; (2) the selection of those aims and those value contents towards which I raise myself from my particularity; (3) the constancy in such promotion commensurate with the given requirements; (4) the applicability of these requirements in personal situations and personal conflicts.

Let us take these four points one by one.

Basically, morality is the subjugation of particularistic needs,

70

desires and aspirations to the normative expectations of society. This subjugation may take many forms; in what follows we outline a few general trends. It may take the form of simple suppression of particularistic motivations and affects, whereby the content and direction of the suppression is entirely governed by a spontaneously accepted social order. Then again it may take the form, not of simple suppression, but of a gradual atrophy of suppressed particularistic needs while spontaneously accepted habits acquire customary status and take root. Or again, against the background of a spontaneously accepted social order, particularistic desires may be so channelled that they can be given full vent without jeopardizing survival in the given society. In all these cases we are dealing with the morals of the particularistic person. But the person may consciously distance himself from his own particularity, a relationship which allows him to articulate his particularistic motivations and talents in the light of his selected system of values – suppressing some and giving others enlarged room for action, which does not, however, vitiate or impede realization of the selected values. In the circumstances of alienation – as we have seen – the general and typical form of life is that built round particularity; and hence, in human history hitherto, morals have operated normally via the suppression of particularistic desires, ensuring their spontaneous atrophy or their canalization into more acceptable channels.

Society has always required the person to conform to its demands, to subordinate himself to it; but (with few exceptions) society was not interested in whether the person did this as a particularity or as an individuality – it was enough that the act of subordination took place. It is only from the standpoint of generic development that it is essential for the latter type to emerge and achieve continuity.

The simple act of subordinating particularistic affects and motives to the demands of the social order is, however, not yet morals; it is rather the indispensable pre-condition for morals. It becomes morals when the act of subordination is internalized and turns into a personal motivation: that is to say, when the external social expectation appears as an expectation made by the person upon himself – an expectation which is naturally, spontaneously or consciously, applicable also to others.

In relatively homogeneous and narrow integrations it has proved possible to arrive at a network of expectations applicable to each individual case of action. The emergence of more complicated social structures, heterogeneous spheres, strata, classes, etc. has meant that such a network of expectations is no longer achievable. It has become a social necessity to lay down elementary moral principles which individual persons can internalize, and which they can themselves apply in various spheres and in singular and unforeseeable circumstances.

Heterogeneity was, of course, only one reason for the emergence and development of morals. A second reason, to which I have already referred, lies in the fact that, with the formation of class society, the 'person' severs the umbilical cord linking him to the community, and becomes an independent entity (initially within the given community): so that a schism, even conflict, between particularity and the species-essential is the offspring of the age that sees this division. Precisely because the particularistic 'person' may have his own particular needs and aims which are not those of the given community, it has proved necessary to supplement the emergent legal structure with a system of morals no longer identical with the simple observance of customs.

If, then, we say that morals expresses the relationship of the individual person to the demands of the socio-generic normative expectations, we are emphasizing both poles of the relationship: the socio-generic normative expectations on the one hand and the personal relationship on the other. However much we talk about 'simple subordination' of particularity to the socio-generic normative expectations, the fact is that this subordination is not achieved without a struggle: man must 'master himself' if he is to meet the demands put to him and accepted by him. And however primitive (from the standpoint of individuality) the 'person' may be, the struggle with its 'instincts' will bear some trace of 'individualness' – if only because the particularistic endowments of individual human beings vary greatly.

A human being is born into a certain milieu which presents its unit members with a certain socio-generic system of normative expectations. It is very rare if not unheard-of, however, for this demand structure to be absolutely homogeneous. Later, we shall see that every society operates basically with two demand structures: one of abstract, and the other of concrete norms, which rarely coincide and whose discrepancies often sharpen into contradictions. Human beings, as we shall see, tend on the whole to follow, to be guided by the concrete norms, but they internalize the abstract norms as well, often failing to notice the discrepancies, not to say the contradictions between them. For every person, however, the possibility of detecting the discrepancy and of accepting, i.e. internalizing one system of norms while rejecting the other is within reach.

But when I refer to the 'selection' of a social norm structure as belonging to the essence of morals, I am not thinking simply of the discrepancy between abstract and concrete demand systems. The demand structures of different social strata – and of classes – differ among themselves. The possibility of choice between class moralities is open to the individual in any society that exhibits a dynamic development pattern. Born a patrician, one may opt for plebeian morals and postures, as witness the Gracchi.

In pre-capitalist society, divergence in moral attitude did not lead to the break-up of the value hierarchy, except perhaps in crisis situations. Society 'proper' (capitalism) has increased the chances of 'persons' to choose their own morals. The 'person' can pick and choose between the moral codes of various strata, or between concrete and abstract moral norms; but, more than this, he can internalize the ethical demand structures of bygone ages (available to him in the form of species-essential objectivations 'for itself' like art or philosophy) and, in the extreme case, contrast them with the moral norms of his own world.

So, when we assess a person's morals, we are not simply passing judgment on the extent to which that person has succeeded in internalizing the normative system of a given society, or to the extent to which he has been able to channel his particularistic motivations towards serving that system; rather, we pass judgment also on the value-content of the system of norms which he has decided to make his own from the field of choice open to him. This last proviso is important: choice always takes place within a narrower or wider field of possibility.

As a third property of morals I specified constancy. This is not just one value among many, but is related to 'strength of character'. What is subsumed by 'morals' is not simply the subjugation or canalization of particularistic motivations, nor a relative choice from among internalized values: it is of the essence of morals that it also subsumes the *continuity* of these processes. If I feed the hungry once in my life and ignore them for the rest of it – if I show courage on one occasion and never again, I am not 'holding my ground' and I cannot lay claim to being a truly moral character.

Finally a few words on 'applicative capacity'. I said above that the basic social function of morals is the application of the normative demand structure to individual cases. What does application mean here? It can mean simply subsuming the individual case under the general requirement. We act in accordance with the normative demand, and judge others in the same light. But since an infinite number of situations can arise, it is simply not possible to perform this subsumption without deliberation. It is up to the 'person' to find for himself what aspect of the general requirement applies to the given concrete situation, and how it applies. What is wanted in such situations is the 'moral sense' which Aristotle called *'phronesis'* – i.e. prudence.

The relationship between personal attitude and the socio-generic demand structure is expressed in these four factors: and all four affect the three main motivation fields in which personal action takes place – need, habit and knowledge. Furthermore, these three – need, habit and knowledge – are accompanied by affective processes, and these can play a part in all three motivation types. There is no doubt that, of the three, it is need that has the strongest affective base.

Need, habit and knowledge can all express the 'person' as built up on particularity, but they can also be the individual bearers of generic values as well. Here, the possible permutations and combinations are endless; but in every unit case – whether particularistic or individual – the three motivation types coincide in forming a structured unity.

The role of knowledge may require some further explanation. In the first place, if we are to regulate our own actions or pass moral judgments on those of others, we must be acquainted with the moral concepts and norms involved. And if we are to act properly in accordance with a given situation, or pass informed judgment on the behaviour of others in similar situations, we must be acquainted not only with the moral concepts and norms involved but also with the circumstances in which the given action is to take place. Further, in embarking upon any action we are guided by consideration of the consequences of our action as much as by our intentions. Of course, ability to 'reckon with' the outcome is not simply a question of knowledge: unforeseeable factors – the actions of others for example – can upset the most circumspect prediction. All we can safely say is that consideration of outcome in so far as this is foreseeable, plays a part in the assessment of the relation between moral intention and outcome, and is a factor in our moral posture. Last but not least, knowledge about the society as a whole, its values and tendencies, is a component part in the moral content of an action or a judgment.

When we deny morality a special sphere of its own and say that every action including a personal commitment has a moral content, we are not denying that actions can be performed by purely moral motivation. The whole of life can be morally motivated (I want to lead a decent, honest life, I want to be respectable, etc.) and the same goes for individual actions. It is rare, however, to find either lives or actions uniquely or homogeneously motivated; usually motives are very mixed: men do not want to 'be courageous', they want to serve their countries, win this or that battle, stand up for something, be successful, gain power – all of this in various combinations, and in the process they display courage. Juliet wants to be happy with Romeo – and the paradigmatic morality of her life and death is inseparable from this motivation.

We started from the premise that the primary ground-plan of morals is the subordination of purely particularistic motivations to the demand structure of society. Given this premise, it naturally follows that each of our moral concepts generalises the subordination of a particularistic motivation related to such-and-such an affect, need, demand or value. Courage, justice, moderation, generosity, unselfishness, charity – all of these express values which derive from the continuous and enduring subordination of one or more particularistic affect. At bottom, what do we mean when we describe someone as 'courageous'? Simply that some over-riding consideration has enabled him to disregard anxieties concerning his personal safety, his health or his property. Similarly, someone is said to be 'just' if he is not slave to his affections, habits or prejudices; he is 'temperate' means that he has subdued his appetite for pleasure and gain. Why is 'unselfishness' an asset? Because it involves taking account of the concerns, interests and desires of others, not just of our own. One reason why these moral concepts and axiological judgments run through the whole history of mankind lies in the fact that they are related to the basic function of morals. And this remains true even though certain moral concepts and virtues have varied greatly in importance in the normative codes of different ages and in the personal hierarchy of ethical norms.

'Selection' in the field of social requirement, however, is not primarily a matter of plugging in to a moral concept or concepts, but rather of the concrete content of such concepts. For example, 'loyalty' as a moral concept simply means that instead of deserting a cause, a colleague, a community for the sake of some momentary or long-term advantage, I should stand by them even in danger or defeat. But 'loyalty' in itself tells me nothing about what I am to do

75

if two rival loyalties – both genuine – confront me: do I show myself 'loyal' to a friend or to an ideal, to my family or to my country?

In denying the existence of moral conflict, Kant was concerned only with the basic element of morals – the subordination of the particularistic affects. And indeed, if there were no more to morals than this, if this were the total content of moral choice, moral conflict could not arise. There would be a choice between the particularistic desire and the moral norm, a choice which could not be described as a *moral* conflict, since the extra-moral factors are ranged on one side. It is undeniable that many such clashes occur in life, precisely indeed in everyday life; and here the categorical imperative makes itself felt. That particularistic motivations should be subordinated in the interests of some higher demand embodying generic-moral value, can be seen indeed as a universal maxim. What is peculiar is that most decisions whose moral content transcends the everyday do not in fact arise from a clash between particularity and the socio-generic demand structure, but from a conflict of disparate generic (species-essential) demands: their value-content may vary but this does not affect their status as value-concepts; they may incorporate differing ideals, but they remain socio-generic in status. These, then, are cases of moral conflict, for we are faced with a choice between courses of action, both of which have equivalent moral value-content. No appeal can be made to the categorical imperative; for, disparate though they may be, their value-content is of equal status, and the maxim of action can be equally universal if applied to either.

As I said, it is precisely in everyday life that supersession of particularistic motivation is most typical; it is here that the general rule 'don't give in to your desires' is most likely to be heeded. And the more particularistic the person, the more is this likely to be true. If I give something to a down-and-out, refrain from beating my wife, and put up in silence with my awful neighbours, these are day-to-day decisions and attitudes of a nature in which moral conflict proper plays hardly any part at all. It is this attitude which dominates everyday ethics along with adherence to the concrete normative structure, or in mutual interchange with it.

We started from the premise that moral concepts *per se* and *in abstracto* always represent supersession of particularistic motivations. To this we have now to add that what people are usually confronted with in everyday life is not moral concepts but moral judgment. Moral concepts are the aggregate summaries of a series of moral judgments. We do not learn what 'goodness' is: we learn that X and Y are 'good' because they help others; we do not learn what 'courage' is: we learn that X and Y acted courageously. That is, we do not receive moral concepts 'ready-made'; what we have at our disposal is rather the specific reading of a moral concept, a reading peculiar to the normative structure of a given class, stratum or community. Where a given normative structure and custom structure are contradictory, the contradiction will be reflected in discrepant or even contradictory readings of moral concepts, and equivalently in judgments based on these readings.

Every relationship of a moral nature has two sides: a subjective and an objective side (where 'subjective' refers, of course, not to 'subjectivity' but is to be understood as 'belonging to the subject'). I shall use Kant's terminology in describing these two poles: I shall call the subjective pole 'morality', and the objective 'legality'. (Use of Kant's terminology does not, of course, mean that I accept Kant's interpretation of the relationship between these two poles.) I shall reserve the word 'morals' to describe a relation in which 'morality' and 'legality' are concurrent and equally represented.

As we have seen, in so far as it has to do with evaluated relationships, every action has a moral content. A yardstick for this moral content is provided by the four factors we discussed above. These four factors characterize the relationship between the specific personal action and the socio-generic demand structure, a relationship in which the socio-generic demands function as norms. In so far – but only in so far – we can regard the moral content of the action as 'normative'. It is not necessary for this to be conceptualized as a norm in the individual mind: adherence to the norm can be spontaneous, and in everyday life frequently is.

Let us now investigate the two poles separately, i.e. in relative isolation from each other. The first thing to be said is that each pole is invested with 'normative' character, or, at least, can be so invested. In relation to the person, the demands of legality (divorced from morality) constitute an external demand (*Müssen*); the demands of morality (abstracted from legality) constitute an internal demand (*Sollen*). It has to be said, of course, that in no conceivable action is only one pole present. Action performed solely under external demand is, indeed, forced action – but there is no forced action in which personal assent or dissent, acquiescence or reluctance plays no part, however small. And action undertaken on a basis of *Sollen* alone is equally unthinkable. The individual person invariably draws all his values, his norms and his moral concepts, from that world into which he has been born. And even if he rejects the entire value structure of a given society, items of this society will inevitably have been internalized, to make themselves felt in due course in the demands of morality. There is, then, no such thing as action undertaken on purely moralistic or purely legalistic grounds. No doubt, either legality or morality may well *predominate* in one action or another; and we may find instances of personal conduct being continuously and consistently governed by either.

We can learn much about a person and about the world into which he has been born by observing which of the two – legality or morality – has the upper hand in his behaviour. An intensification of the subjective aspect in action invested with significant moral content is characteristic of historical periods in which the discrepancy between social and species-essential becomes explicit, and in which it is precisely the most highly developed individuals who take their stand on the side of the species-essential values *vis-à-vis* the concrete value-systems obtaining in the social systems they inhabit. These are the so-called 'moralists'. It will suffice to mention two examples from the history of philosophy to make this clear – Socrates and Rousseau. Both Socrates and Rousseau were, of course, quite well aware that the 'moralist' type is something of an anomaly, in that it is a reaction to a social situation which has deviated from the norm as they see it. Socrates' ideal was a *polis* in which one didn't have to be a moralist, and his career was a moralistic demo to this end. Time and again, Rousseau envisaged an ideal community in which there would be no need of 'virtue' because goodness – i.e. morals, not morality – would be within everybody's reach; and in *La Nouvelle Héloïse* he tried to portray such a community.

Internalization of the socio-communal demand structure is a mark of the process in which *Müssen* turns into *Sollen*. As we said above, in the case of a life centred on particularity it is typical for the 'person' concerned either simply to repress his particularistic needs or to direct them into 'permissible' channels. In contrast, the individual (in our sense) 'cultivates himself', nurtures those qualities which he regards as valuable, and distances himself from others. In the case of individuality, moral 'prudence' is much more fully developed, and precisely because of this, the individual is capable of greater pliancy in the adaptation of the overall demand structure to the individual case, his choice among conflicting demands and values is better informed, and he is more readily disposed towards the formation of an individual hierarchy of values. Exceptionally, the moralist may fit in here; indisputably he is an individuality in our sense, but over-concentration of morality by and for itself is as inimical to *phronesis* as particularistic custom is in its own way.

Conscience is the central category of morality. It is in the form of conscience that the socio-generic appears in the subject. Conscience is not a moral 'sense' and it has no necessary connection with spontaneity. Indeed, it is not by chance that most languages use a word connected with the category of 'knowledge' for this concept – *conscientia,* conscience, *Gewissen,* etc. Conscience can only function in the knowledge of good and evil: knowledge of good and evil is what becomes explicit in conscience. Not for nothing did Adam Smith call it 'an impartial judge': for the cardinal characteristic of impartiality is that it does not take the side of the particularistic. But neither will it take the side of those demand structures which deviate from the morality of the individual person.

Socio-generic demand structures confront the 'person' on two levels: those of abstract norms and those of concrete norms. Abstract norms fix the output of a continuous value development in form of imperatives or virtues; their more general validity resides not in the generality of their formulation, so much as in the generality of their content. Which is, of course, not to suggest that the demands expressed in the abstract norms are necessarily 'eternal validities'. The abstract norms appear on the historical stage in the form of the concrete demands of a given society, in the same way as the concrete norms do. Their abstractness is expressed in their continuity, their stability: often it is only retrospectively that it becomes clear which norms are susceptible of universalization and which are contingent, particularistic, embedded only in a specific system of expectations.

We appropriate both abstract and concrete norms in one and the same process. For all their abstraction, exhortations like 'be honest' or 'be courageous' are no different from many concrete cases relating to the specific manner in which honesty or courage is to be displayed. What is characteristic of everyday life is that we do not take account of the difference between concrete and abstract norms, which may even carry an implicit contradiction; and we appropriate the abstract norms only in so far as they make their appearance in the ranks of the concrete norms. Everyday life is, then, the field of operation of the concrete norms.

The concrete system of norms is indeed no other than the system of custom and habit which assumes (or may assume) the form of an imperative addressed to the person: in what follows, I shall refer to it as 'moral customs'. This is precisely what the abstract norm system is not: on the contrary, it hypostatizes certain values, which may indeed figure to some extent in certain customs or habits, but which are not totally subsumed by custom or routine morals. 'Thou shalt not kill' is one of the best known of all abstract norms – yet there neither is nor ever has been a social customary moral system which has abided by this norm: the demand structure of every society or social class has specified the cases in which one should kill. Thus, insoluble contradictions may exist between abstract and concrete norms. In what follows, I shall call the system of abstract norms 'moral obligations'.

On the ethical level, then, the contradiction between moral customs and moral obligations expresses the discrepancy between historically valid and universally valid values. In everyday life, as I said, we are not aware of this discrepancy; and one of the main characteristics of the transcending of everyday life on the ethical plane is that we become aware of this discrepancy. In this process of transcendence there is of course no question (or only very rarely) of the individual person taking the position of moral obligations against moral customs. What usually happens is that having recourse to moral obligations is one means whereby the 'person' forsakes one set of moral customs for another or chooses his own set; a means whereby he recognizes the relativity, the ephemeral nature of moral customs and seeks to replace them. With this conscious act of recognition – and its consequences – morals become once again an organic part of everyday life – only now it is the everyday life of the individual in our sense of the word.

The circumstance that moral obligations which we postulate as universally valid are held to be 'unrealizable' is but the expression of the self-alienation of morals.

What does it mean when we talk of a split between the concrete and the abstract system of norms? In the first place it means that value development on the species-essential level must be fixed in the most generalized, most abstract demand structures, and must bear upon itself the mark of unrealizability. Moral obligations embody mankind's most universal values as postulates which run counter to man's concrete existence and to the possibilities open before him, in that they are not directly applicable to this existence and to these possibilities. This must not be taken to mean that moral obligations are the 'good' which cannot be realized in the 'bad' world. Observing moral obligations in the world-as-it-is is

80

often inhuman and nasty. Who is to tell the starving man in the rich man's pantry that he is not to steal? Who dares to tell Hamlet that he must not kill the usurping king? The abstract norms, species-essential demands, do not and indeed cannot take stock of the concrete 'person' who lives in a given set of concrete conditions and possibilities, but remain sword-like suspended over his mortal head. And woe betide anyone who tries actually to live up to species-essential demands. In the first place he is courting death, for he can no longer move within his natural environment nor can he move that environment. He does endless violence to his own particularity, and also to his individuality, which relies for its nourishment on its mutual relationship with the order of concrete norms.

But is it only the system of abstract norms that is alienated? The alienation of abstract norms is only a reflection, a function of the alienation of concrete ones, that is, of moral customs. Societies do not have uniform systems of moral customs (though some degree of uniformity in moral customs is found in cases where a community integrates a given stratum). The class (or stratum) character of moral customs is in itself a sign of alienation.

What is more, even within the moral customs of particular classes, contradictions may arise: private life and public life present the person with differing series of demands, and so do political life and business life. Inhabitants of a class society dwell in a forest whose trees are commands, demands and prohibitions. In *EPM* Marx writes: the morality of political economy is gain, labour and thrift, sobriety – and yet political economy promises to satisfy my needs. The political economy of morality is the wealth of a good conscience, of virtue etc. But how can I be virtuous if I do not exist? And how can I have a good conscience if I am not conscious of anything? It is inherent in the very nature of estrangement that each sphere imposes upon me a different and contrary standard: one standard for morality, one for political economy, and so on. This is because each of them is a particular estrangement of man and each is centred upon one particular area of estranged essential activity; each is related in an estranged way to the other .... Moreover, the opposition between political economy and morality is only an apparent one. It is both an opposition and not an opposition. Political economy merely gives expression to moral laws in its own way (Marx, *EPM*, pp. 363–4).

In this passage, Marx is primarily concerned with the contradiction between moral obligations and moral customs; he does not distinguish between this contradiction and that inherent in moral customs themselves. For our purposes, the passage is of interest because of what it has to say about the alienated relationship which subsists between alienated spheres, and about the affinity which in the last resort exists between these spheres. The alienated relationship is expressed in that in the main we do not perceive, we are not even aware that we are internalizing totally disparate systems of values, which can happily coexist in particularity. The particularistic human being does not make a conscious selection between values – he just manoeuvres. He holds to those norms which appear to promote his chances of survival, and to this end he will suppress or rechannel his particularistic motivations. He closes his eyes to other demands, in so far, of course, as this does not jeopardize his tenure in a given milieu. He toes the line within certain limits. In the case of the particularistic person, the extreme limiting factor is public opinion. In the case of the individual (in our sense of the word) 'room for manoeuvre' is replaced by moral prudence, and therefore public opinion does not represent a limiting factor. The individual may even take issue with the 'invisible' particularistic motivation latent in public opinion, to the extent of – in the extreme case – endorsing as 'right' desires or actions which public consensus has decided are 'wrong'.

It must be added, however, that moral demand structures do not simply inhibit particularistic viewpoints and motivations: they have often been known to stifle the particular gifts and talents of the person, instead of enabling him to cultivate these. Often they have militated against species-essential values and feelings. The gods are athirst – for blood and for sweat.

We see then that morals in an alienated world are themselves always alienated. Does it follow from this that it is and always has been up to the individual 'person' to accept this alienation? And if so, are all individual 'persons' required to accept it in equal measure?

It would not be true to say that moral alienation has always been of identical degree in all historical periods, nor would it be true to say that it has always been homogeneous in type: we only have to remember that the split between moral customs and abstract norms, and the distancing from each other of component spheres of moral customs have not run in parallel courses. The person is born into a world in which morals are alienated in one way or another, in different forms and to different degrees. From one point of view, it is a situation which we simply have to accept. If when judging others we fail to take this into account – if we hold up abstract morality as an absolute and exclusive value *vis-à-vis* moral customs, if we espouse moral customs to the exclusion of abstract morality, if we take the side of moral customs or of abstract morality against the claims of particularity – we are acting as alienated beings to moral alienation. But it is in this respect alone that the individual person is required to accept alienation. Within these limits, it is possible for the person as he leads his own life, if not to do away with this alienation, at least to reduce it in some measure. The cardinal condition for this to happen is simply stated: we must recognize the contradictions, and we must recognize them as contradictions. In the business of living we must always try to identify the realistic possibilities for good action, and choose the best course among the various given conditions and relationships. It is clear that this sort of trans-alienated relationship with the alienated is only possible in the case of a relatively developed individuality – one who has been able to amalgamate his conscious relationship to the species-essential, on the one hand, and to his own particularity, on the other: and who has achieved a degree of separation in his relationship both to his particularistic motivations and to the social demand structure, including the moral customs. From all this it does not, of course, follow that every individual (in my sense of the word) can relate to moral alienation in this trans-alienated way. But certainly it is the individual alone (in my definition) whose relationship with the alienated can be in some degree non-alienated.

Everyday morals are as heterogeneous as everyday life in general. To begin with, the world into which we are born contains an infinite number of behavioural patterns and prescriptions. Observance of and adherence to these prescriptions is a requirement laid by the social milieu on all its members alike. In everyday life, the prescriptions are concrete in form: they specify individual behaviour with a high degree of precision. We must respect our parents, and this respect must be manifested in certain specific ways; we must go to church a given minimum number of times; there are right and wrong ways of courting a girl; insults are not to be taken lying down – there are socially acceptable ways of getting even. If the person is to survive in his milieu, he must be acquainted with these heterogenous prescriptions and he must on the average obey them. The word 'average' has two meanings here: on the one hand, the average person must toe the social line if this is to remain acceptable; on the other hand, every person must adhere to an average number of the relevant prescriptions if they are to remain valid. At the same time, in order to lead average 'respectable' lives in their milieu, human beings have to

83

do no more than achieve an average degree of adaptation to the prescriptions in force in that milieu. The content of the demand structure, in all its variety, need not be synthesized into a personal attitude, nor need it be articulated to form an independent hierarchy of values. All that everyday life demands of any one is the subordination of purely particularistic initiatives to the demands of moral customs in any situation where they are not coincidental. As I said above, this 'suspension' does not amount to the 'supersession' of particularity: particularity is not transcended, merely suppressed or inhibited.

According to Max Weber, every religious ethic which has developed beyond the stage of family piety and the prescriptions of magic 'is primarily determined by the two simple motives, that condition all everyday behaviour beyond the limits of the family, namely *retaliation against offenders, and fraternal assistance to friendly neighbours*'.[5] If these two prescriptions form part of every system of religious ethics, it is because they are organic components in the moral customs of everyday life: they are two 'primary norms' without which everyday life would not be possible. And, as will be readily seen, both stand in direct or indirect relationship with particularity.

The second of these – readiness to help a neighbour or even a passer-by (or vagrant) may be a simple reaction on the part of the particular person: it fits in with public opinion, and rarely requires 'suspension' of particularistic motivation. If my neighbour has no salt, I give him some of mine; if a tramp wants a night's lodging, I can find a warm corner for him. Of course, cases may arise in which particularistic motivations will have to be suspended, without, however, going beyond the anthropological structure of the particularistic person.

This is especially true in the 'frontier situations' of everyday life: where someone is exposed to danger, perhaps even mortal danger, and someone else risks life and limb in a rescue attempt. Unconditional help unconditionally offered in a frontier situation is a primary norm of everyday life, especially when it is not society but nature that threatens the 'person'. Help for those in peril by fire, flood, cold or starvation is part of being 'decent' according to the norms of everyday life. But action, perhaps heroic action, in frontier situations is still linked to particularity because it is guided by the norms of reciprocal expectations. This is evident in the light of the fact that in modern cities, where such things as fire brigades and specialist rescue teams are instantly available, and where people are all strangers to each other, the motivation of 'reciprocity' has been considerably weakened and frontier solidarity tends to be eroded. Not completely: at the sight of a drowning child someone will jump into the water, and a good Samaritan will pause in the street to tend a casualty. Indeed, the demand for helpful action in frontier situations has reached the statute books: for it now counts as an aggravating circumstance to leave unattended those injured in a car crash.

Let me repeat, however, that solidarity in frontier situations, however heroic, does not transcend the parameters of everyday life; and, at the same time (though not synonymously) it does not do away with life's structure built round particularity. Of course, it tells us something about a man, indeed it points to a not unimportant moral impulse – the degree to which he is capable of solidarity; but this does not tell us much about the 'person's' personal morality.

So far, we have been concerned with two aspects of the morals of everyday life. One of these is simple observance of custom, i.e. of behavioural prescriptions which, as we have seen, may be far from homogeneous as a set; the second, 'reciprocity' as shown in two primary norms: the norm of retaliation when wronged, and the norm of helping or rescuing someone in danger (a norm which applies primarily to neighbours, the poor and those who find themselves in 'frontier situations'). None of these factors requires supersession of the particularistic attitude. The relationship of the individual to the norms of reciprocity is itself individual. A defective individuality may often fail to obey the norm to rescue those in need; but this will be a conscious, a considered failure, not simply the act of cowardice characteristic of the particularistic 'person'. The moral individual is more likely to have doubts concerning the right to retaliate, to avenge oneself: Hamlet is a good example. Christianity tried to counter this concrete norm with an abstract norm of its own – 'turn the other cheek' – without much success, except in the case of moral individuals able to internalize the Christian norms.

We move on now to a third aspect. There are in everyday life certain basic and general norms, binding in every concrete sphere of moral customs without which everyday life would in fact be impossible. The four most important of these are: keeping a promise, telling the truth, gratitude and elementary loyalty. Repudiated as they are on numberless occasions, these four virtues nevertheless represent indispensable facets of everyday life, without which we would stand little chance of successfully navigating its currents. If we could not count on the average man being – on an average – as good as his word, if we could not believe that one good turn deserves another, it would be impossible for us to find our bearings in everyday life. In so far as these basic virtues can become problematical, this takes place not in the field of everyday life, but in their relationship to objectivations which transcend that terrain. No human community – not even a band of robbers – has ever found it possible to dispense with these basic virtues, if only in relation to their own members.

But even these virtues do not go beyond particularity. They apply with equal force to customs; they are likewise 'reciprocal' virtues like helping neighbours, members of one's family, etc. If I repay good with evil (as a general practice, not exceptionally) then I too must expect to be repaid in my own coin.

The morals of individuality, however, even in purely everyday life, rise above the level of practice as analysed above. The everyday morals of the conscious individual (in our sense) are not limited to adherence to the social demand structure, and the practice of the reciprocal virtues. Even if he does not homogenize the heterogeneous demands made by social custom, the individual is able to construct a value hierarchy, not only ranking one demand *vis-à-vis* another but differentiating hierarchically between the various applications of one and the same demand.

Every individual has his own moral physiognomy, worked out by himself. Its precise lineaments will depend very largely on the concrete value-content of the objectivation(s) with which it is correlated. It has to be remembered, however, that in general we can make a distinction between the individual and the so-called moral individual – by which we mean that individuality whose actions are *intentionally* invested with moral value-content. This does not simply mean that such an individual will undertake some action which has an objectively positive moral value-content: rather, it means that the very reason why he undertakes it is that he regards it as of positive moral value. We can say that the moral individual is inhabited by the moral imperative. His actions are not necessarily designed to be of universal validity (as we have seen, this is impossible in the case of conflict between species-essential values) but they are seen as susceptible of generalization on the moral plane.

We see, then, that the everyday ethic of an individual is in part at least nourished from the non-everyday. The criterion of the non-everyday is the property of, or rather, the tendency towards homogenization, both in the taking of decisions and in the acceptance of responsibility (the plane on which decision-taking is generated).

Homogenization in morals can be realized on more than one plane. Its criteria remain however the same, as in all kinds of homogenization: concentration on the given objective, subordination to it of everyday activities, even their partial or total suspension; concentration of all our capabilities on reaching the species-essential. Here again, to use Lukács's words, 'the whole man' becomes 'man-as-a-whole'. In taking a moral decision or accepting a responsibility which entails homogenization, we transcend our everyday selves; and from this standpoint it does not matter which sphere of our lives provides the terrain. When Juliet decides that she would rather die than marry Paris, the moral homogenization inherent in her decision is identical with that informing Brutus's suicide on the battlefield of Philippi. In fact, paradoxical as it may sound, we can say that moral homogenization – i.e. the supersession of everyday attitudes – is possible even in the sphere of everyday life.

The inference is inescapable: morals have no special sphere of their own, but are present in all spheres. That this should be so, is a property not so much of the various spheres of life as of moral homogenization itself.

In any homogeneous sphere, the process of homogenization lasts just as long as the person is active in that sphere: as soon as he leaves that sphere, the process of homogenization also ceases (the 'person' returns to everyday life). Where there is, however, no autonomous sphere, the starting-point for homogenization cannot take the form of entry into that sphere; and, equally, the content of the homogenization cannot be marked by sojourn in that sphere. As a result, moral homogenization, in the form which bears all the main indices of the content and function of this concept, is always momentary or instantaneous. The words 'moment' and 'instant' are, of course, not to be taken as units of temporal duration: all that is meant is that we must not imagine a gradual or continuous process. If when taking a decision I concentrate on the moral universality of my action, moral homogenization is at once entailed, irrespective of whether the decision is a political or a legal one, or simply one taken in the course of everyday life. Once the decision has been taken, however, its consequences have to be confronted: do I or do I not bear them? Where it is a question of an irreversible decision, consequences of course have to be borne *de facto* though they may be morally rejected: I can lament my fate, I can regret a decision taken on moral grounds, I can try to get out of it. Again, if the decision is not irreversible, there are consequences which *de facto* need not be borne. It is often less difficult to take a decision on the species-essential level, than to bear its consequences. Cases of 'disorderly repentance' are not uncommon: after an act of homogenization in which particularity has been successfully superseded, the 'person' finds himself unable to bear the consequences of his act either in his everyday life or in any other sphere, and relapses onto the moral level he occupied before the crucial decision. But if my decision to act in a certain way or to accept a certain responsibility – a decision induced in the 'momentary' locus of moral homogenization – is not merely objectively irreversible but subjectively also, then my whole subsequent life is transformed. My hierarchy of values is rearranged in the light of the moral values now discovered. To this moment of moral homogenization – a moment which retains its validity in the aftermath, a moment which separates a transformed 'after' from the 'before' – we give the name 'catharsis'.

Speaking of moral homogenization, I mentioned the suspension of the particularist view-point but said nothing about the content of the act of choice. It must now be stressed that a morally informed act of choice (i.e. an act tending to homogenization) very often comes about in the shape of a solution to a moral conflict. In such a moral conflict, not only particularist motivation clashes with some generic, species-essential demand but different species-essential values, different (but equally valid and equally internalized) norms confront each other. In such a situation it is up to the individual to seek generalization of his actions on the moral plane (i.e. to distance himself from certain norms and moral objectivations, and approximate to others) so that he may choose one among conflicting values, or differentiate among them to form a hierarchy. The extreme case of value-conflict is the tragic conflict which – if the protagonist carries through his own conflict to its own end – can also lead to tragedy. But it would be a mistake to imagine that moral catharsis can come about in tragic conflicts alone.

Two related questions remain unanswered. Firstly, are we not guilty of subjectivizing the difference between everyday and non-everyday morality if we regard homogenization as a criterion of the latter? Secondly, what is the species-essence towards which man is homogenized, if morals do not have their own specific sphere?

In what has gone before I have given a very general sort of answer to the first question, to which I can now add some detail. I said that homogenization is not a subjective but an objective criterion (even when there is an accompanying psychic impulse) since it is an indispensable factor in social activity, i.e. in activity taking place within species-essential objectivation: it is a demand with which these objectivations confront the 'person'. But moral homogenization has another – and decisive – function: the bringing about of moral unity between the different spheres. I said that the formation of specific moralities for different spheres was a symptom of alienation. What moral homogenization (which comes about in every sphere in the form and on the basis of moral generalization) does is to make explicit moral unity (i.e. in the long run, species-essential unity) in the specific alienated moralities of the separate spheres. How is this possible? Though morality itself has no sphere of its own, there is still such a thing as moral objectivation. The moral values – which incorporate the moral concepts, the abstract norms, the moral assessment of the affects, etc. – in their ideological form lead a relatively independent life, and as such regulate our actions and motivations. We could say perhaps that the moral concepts and norms form a quasi-sphere as the embodiments of the values attached to species-essential moral development.

In any sphere, moral objectivation is the motivating agent, though it may vary in scope and intensity from one sphere to another and from one individual to another. Every kind of homogenization has or can have a moral content, moral aspect: even if it is not itself a moral homogenization, and is not directly concerned with generalization of moral decisions. In every important political action, in every artistic or philosophical objectivation relationship to moral objectivation is invariably more or less present as motivation and (or) as content. We have defined the existence of specific morals attached to specific spheres as an index of alienation; we can now go a step further and say that the fact that specific spheres with varying moral content can exist at all is a consequence of that universality of morals which we have been analysing.

Every 'person' – even the most particularistic – has a relationship with moral objectivation, be this no more than spontaneous acceptance of a system of consuetudinal demands and primary norms. And accordingly it is not by chance that one of the most familiar forms of rationalization of particular motivations, of affects, is precisely moral rationalization. 'There was nothing wrong with me, but I got into the wrong set'; 'I have always been fair to those under me'; 'I've always done the decent thing by you but you've let me down' – this sort of ego-rationalization is a primary channel for the self-deception and self-justification that accompany particularity. When the individual is able to distance himself from particularity, he achieves moral distancing also: the moral individual does not shrink from applying the same criteria of truth and justice to himself as he does to others, and moral self-justification is something he can identify and combat.

(c) Religion

Religion can be defined as an ideal community, with the conceptual accent on both terms, 'ideal' and 'community', in equal measure. It forms a community in so far as it integrates and is invested with a uniform system of values, and creates a specific 'we-consciousness'; and it is ideal in two senses of this word. For one thing, it can run counter to the real communal structure of a given society, it can integrate communities built up on totally disparate material and social bases and heterogeneous integrations (different classes, social orders, nations); and on the other hand, it discharges its communal functions under the sign of the 'ideal' i.e. its character is 'ideological'.[6] This ideology is expressed in the consuetudinal systems which more or less govern human life and behaviour, but it is not necessarily institutionalized.

The relationship between the real and the ideal community may take very different forms in different societies and religions. In tribal societies, the two are often co-extensive. The ideal community may also be the form in which ethnic integration expresses itself, as in Judaism; it may be directed towards preserving a cultural community embracing several states, as in ancient Greece; and again it may be the ideological integration of the struggle against earthly statehood, as in early Christianity. The relationship between the ideal community and other integrations may undergo numerous and far-reaching vicissitudes in the course of history (e.g. Judaism, Christianity).

The 'ideal community' exists because it has a definite function to discharge in the reproduction of the given society. It cannot be dismissed by rationalism, as the savants of the Enlightenment tried to do; but neither can religion be dealt with by means of purely philosophical criticism, irrespective of whether such criticism endorses the value or exposes the worthlessnes of religious ideas and attitudes. Religious thought cannot be analysed in itself, in isolation; it can only be analysed in terms of its function as the basis and the vital support-system of the ideal community.

Within this functional field, however, the analysis of religious concepts is legitimate, indeed essential. For it is these concepts – concepts of the world, of man, of a God or gods, of the soul, etc. – which constitute the ideological nucleus of the ideal community, and which therefore hold it together. These concepts – which are mutually coherent, for the most part – are the collective images of the community, and adherence to them is an index of membership of the community: accordingly in what follows, we shall refer to them as 'collective images'.

Religion is a collective image which is based on humankind's dependence on the transcendental. The content of this ideology of dependence varies to a literally endless degree from one age to another and from one religion to another. One of the best-known examples is the creation myth. Here are a few more:

(1) The social order was created, as it is, by transcendental powers: or, to put it another way, the social order is as it is because transcendental powers wanted it that way, or allowed it to be that way. Max Weber gives a surprisingly lengthy list of variations on this theme. For example, the world is 'good' because God created it so; its estates embody justice (Brahmanism in fact roundly asserts that if we are born into a certain caste, it is because we have earned it in a previous existence). The converse is the assertion that the world is 'bad' because God is punishing us for the sins we have committed either as members of the human race or as members of a given people. A variant of this is the thesis that God is testing us by placing us in a world of evil.

(2) Our actions are directed or, at least, influenced by transcendental powers. Here again Max Weber has collected several variants: everything that happens is the will of God (or of the gods), so that a transcendental hand is guiding us in all that we do. We have freedom of action but only within certain transcendentally prescribed limits; or, we have freedom of action but divine powers thwart us, interfere in what we do, turn hostile towards us, etc.

(3) We have received our system of values from transcendental powers which have laid down our moral principles, and defined these as the 'good' which we are called upon to do. Failure to do so is therefore a sin against the gods. The gods reward us and punish us for what we do. The final reward bestowed on the virtuous is life beyond death, redemption, salvation (personal or collective), etc.

These three formulations of dependence on the transcendental are global in that they apply to all human actions; and consequently all actions are, in practice, motivated by them. In this way, the collective images of religion (along with their derivatory ontologies and ethics) imbue the average person in a class society and inform his behaviour in its entirety from his everyday activities to whatever consciously generic actions – i.e. actions on the species-essential plane – he is capable of.[7] In the case of consciously generic activity, religious ideology and its motivations function as the ideologies or the motivations of that activity; in the case of everyday life, they function, in general at least, as particularist ideology or as motivation. Human dependence on the transcendental is, then, common ideological ground in all the world's religions: but in addition many of them raise the claim to depict this human essence as human essence of the divine. Thus we find over and over again gods being born in human form, donning human shape, living out mankind's earthly calvary. This last motif is particularly important. No god expresses human essence as *human* essence simply by donning human form. No religion can imagine deity except in human form or, at least, endowed with human feelings; it is precisely the human essence that divinity is endowed with: creativity, love, foresight. Man's own potentialities are absolutized to become universals in his concept of the deity: total freedom, onmipotence. But man's particularistic reactions also reappear in the nature of his gods who are often jealous and spiteful.

What is of interest to us here, however, is the thesis that the gods share man's earthly lot. The Greeks and Romans believed that the heroic man could become a god, provided that he was sufficiently representative of man's species-essential struggle to deserve such a translation (Hercules); and they also envisaged gods who share human suffering as a result of their heroic action on behalf of humanity (Prometheus). In Buddhism, the figure of Gotama Buddha incorporates an analogous belief. The best example of all, however, is to be found in the figure of Jesus as presented in Christianity.

I cannot agree with Max Weber when he claims that the 'god becomes man' component in religion is simply a sop to popular need and popular imagination. Popular imagination is amply satisfied by the legend of the god who walks the earth displaying all of man's characteristics (including the most particularistic), without sharing his earthly lot. In these legends the emphasis is on marvellous deeds, miraculous escapes, superhuman feats. In the cases of Jesus and Prometheus, however, popular imagination is not a sufficient explanation. As I see it, what we have here is the repeated need to overcome alienation – the need for man's redemption to be seen as man's own work.

The most magnificent, in fact, the everlasting paragon of the religious imagination is the figure of Jesus, which, in its pure form, is the species-essential individual *per se*. As an individual he incorporates and bears within himself the human essence. The result is that the attractive force of the figure of Jesus goes far beyond the circle of those who 'believe in him'. Religion has created him, but his significance far outstrips the bounds of religion.

Jesus is *individuality,* but a god cannot become individuality by distancing himself from his own particularity. The Jesus myth gets round this by making Jesus representative of pure species-essentiality: he is devoid of particularity. This is not at all 'natural'. As I said above, gods created in the image of man often display man's particularistic qualities: they are vengeful and envious. Jehovah pronounced himself a 'jealous god', and it was jealousy that led Leto to have Niobe's children killed. Jesus, on the other hand, gives no sign of envy, vengefulness or jealousy. At the same time, as the representative of species-essentiality, as 'the son of man', he is supremely individual. He is individual *vis-à-vis* his time, and *vis-à-vis* the laws and customs of his time; he applies the divine and moral laws which he proclaims as valid individually (cf. the woman taken in adultery, the rich young man, Mary Magdalene). The manner of his death is also individual: he dies *his* death, a death which belongs to his destiny. It is his individualized species-essentiality that makes him an inexhaustible source of images for art.

Of course, the Jesus myth could not rescue Christianity from becoming itself a representative of religious alienation. The result was the strange paradox that as a codified religion Christianity has always been in stark contrast with the original Jesus myth. (This is beautifully brought out by Dostoievsky in the story of the Grand Inquisitor.) Christianity's striking regenerative capacity in the midst of changing social conditions is due not least to the fact that new departures, new movements are always attempts to 'return' to the original Jesus legend in order to confound its official representatives.

Religion is always the organizer of everyday life, and often its main organizer. Fundamentally, it is economic activity which governs way of life and rhythm of life: but it is religion *inter alia* that gives shape to the way and rhythm of life as dictated by necessity of survival. Even the most ancient religions known to us are already stocked with ceremonies designed to cover the natural summits of everyday life – birth, passing to adulthood, mating, death. Nor has any later religion shown any sign of relinquishing its hold on these ceremonies, to which a variety of social, ideological and ethical content has been added (baptism, marriage, sacramental burial). It is, however, not only these climactic points of life that are formed by religion, but our 'everyday' – in the strict meaning of the word as well. Judaeo-Christianity identifies the seventh day as the day of rest; working days are punctuated by prayers and chiming of bells. Before any sort of important undertaking, the Greek city-dweller turned to the soothsayer; the medieval baron or peasant sought the priest's advice. Even such mundane business as eating is regulated by religious ceremony. A congregational religion generates its own public sphere, whose members are instructed by general preachment or via allusions embedded in the canon how to live in accordance with the imperative and optative behavioural requirements. Religion as ideal community creates solidarity through ceremonies, both in time of peace and – very significantly! – in time of war. Religion plays a part in regulating economic activity, organizes charities, codifies and supervises observance of family 'duties' and even extends its field of influence to matters of personal hygiene and sexual behaviour. To live according to a given religion means then something far more than simply 'believing in it', accepting its dogmas or obeying its laws in a general way; rather, it means regulating one's life according to the demands made by the given religion, and in the pattern of its 'forms'. A religion which no longer shapes everyday life in this way has manifestly become a mere formality.[8]

The role of religion as a formative factor in everyday life is particularly tenacious in sexual matters. This goes also for non-ethical religions; sometimes this is realized, contrary to the customs and prescriptions of ethical religions, with reversed signs, e.g. in the organization of orgies. Common to ethical religions is the attempt to keep sexuality within the bounds of marriage (this to be applicable, at least in theory, to *both* sexes, in contradistinction to bourgeois practice). This is not to say that these religions are hostile to sexuality – an accusation which one could hardly level at Judaism, and most certainly not at Islam. All it means is that sexuality is obliged to take the form of marriage, whether monogamous or polygamous. The extreme case is found in Christianity, where – as Max Weber points out – virginity (again, of either sex) acquires charismatic value. Even in Christianity, however, virginity is seen as exceptional (which is precisely what gives it its charisma) just as readiness to do without worldly goods is exceptional. Christianity declared war not on sexuality but on unbridled, undisciplined sexuality, and on extramarital relations; further, however, and this is something which distinguishes Christianity from Judaism and from Islam, it is hostile to eroticism.

Why religion should have been able to retain this particular lever on everyday behaviour with such tenacity, is a question we cannot go into here. I can only hint at the fact that many such formative principles which were valid in mediaeval Christianity, turned out to be incompatible with economic and social change – particularly with the growth of capitalism. The church's rulings on money and money-based economy were simply swept aside as monetary economies took over. With the increased tempo of life, and the growth of modern industry (especially in urban settings), the daily visit to church became a meaningless, indeed an impossible requirement: and the growth of Protestantism saw its conscious and deliberate abolition.

In the organization of everyday life, its 'casting', the rule of religion was never absolute (if we disregard sectarian movements). In natural communities, in peasant communities above all, it had an invincible rival in the lay myth, the ancient lore of superstition and fancy that antedated by far the acceptance of any religious system. In part, this ancient lore was absorbed by religion, in part persecuted and suppressed. Religious autocracy was also threatened by the age-old lay system of customary morals and customary law which was able to hold its ground in so far as it could satisfy the economic needs of local communities. Between the codes of behaviour endorsed by this ancient system and those of organized religion there was no common ground. Other sources of rivalry to religion are provided by state legal systems, especially since the rise of the great nation-states, which take it upon themselves to exercise direct influence on our everyday lives; by the arts which disseminate a system of values divergent from those of religion; and finally by the growth (most marked since the rise of capitalism) of a scientific and philosophical ideology which has also penetrated into everyday life, and of politics totally divorced from religion.

We see then that the role of religion as an organizing factor in

95

everyday life is never unchallenged; but it must also be stressed that the role of religion is something more than this, in that it relates to other, consciously generic, activities. Often it acts as an intermediary between these activities and everyday life. The religious ethic transcends customary morality in that it prescribes internalization of moral principles; and, *via* the mediation of religion, general species-essential values can be internalized by someone who never leaves his immediate surroundings and never sees beyond their frontiers. Religion can act as a spur to political activity or to the formation of political views; it can help us to adapt positively in our everyday lives to a given socio-economic system (and this is what usually happens), but it can also open our eyes to the injustice of our socio-economic condition, and help us to get our values right and live accordingly. It provides a channel through which the arts are transmitted – to the people of the Middle Ages, for example, for whom church music was a profound experience which illuminated their everyday lives. It can provide a portmanteau ideology for the business of living: usually, one of comfort and solace, a reinforcing factor which tends to smooth out contradictions, but in certain conditions it can also fuel the fires of revolt. It can be an ideological force that induces men to 'step out of' their everyday lives, either *en masse,* as in the case of the Wars of Religion, or individually as in that of the 'knights of faith' (Kierkegaard).

The religions which exercise the most potent influence on everyday life are those which offer alongside the ideal community a real material community. These are primarily religions which are co-extensive with certain lay communities – nations or peoples – as whose ideological projection or mapping they appear. Congregational religions are also of this type. They attain their greatest influence as determinants of everyday life, and score most decisively over their rivals (where rivalry exists) if they allow some freedom of choice, e.g. the freedom to opt out; which is possible in so far as they are not direct constructs on the economic community, but rather form political, moral and ideological complexes. Thus early Christianity, the heretical movements, medieval Judaism and original Protestantism all controlled the lives of their adherents with extraordinary intensity. 'Official' congregational religions are doomed to lapse into conventional forms and to be forced, whether they like it or not, to share their controlling hand on everyday life with their rivals, where these exist.

(d) Politics and law

In the wider sense of the word, political activity is any activity which is performed directly with 'we-consciousness', and is directed towards defending or attacking any social integration wider than the family.

In the narrower sense of the word, it is always activity aimed at gaining or retaining power. Political activity is an organic part of everyday life only in so far as it figures in the simple reproduction of the 'person' in the position allotted to him under the social division of labour. From this point of view, discussion of political activity takes us further afield from the everyday than happens in the case of work, morals or religion.

Every social class or stratum has moral customs, just as it has – to some degree at least – a religion. But by no means every social class or stratum is politically active. Simplifying things to some extent, we can say that members of the ruling class or classes (estates) are always politically active, while oppressed classes, classes (estates) deprived of power, and women are politically active only in times of great social upheaval – war, religious war or civil war. From the rise of bourgeois society onwards, however, there has been no such thing as a class 'insulated' from politics. Political change affects the everyday life of everybody, and this is one of the main reasons why it has become an everyday necessity to be 'politically informed'. The desire for political information is not necessarily due to any desire to engage in political activity; rather it is usually a particularistic trait – we want to know 'what's going to happen', 'how can I avoid getting caught out', or 'how can I cash in'. Politics affect our everyday lives at a tempo which increases even within the confines of a single generation, and the need felt to be politically informed is an index of this.

It is a situation which can, of course, be politically exploited: and what is transmitted is not so much political information as political ideology. Political ideology has, of course, always existed, in that every ruling class (estate) of society has always been at pains to canonize its own ideology, legitimize its domination. In times and in societies in which political change was something that happened above the level of the masses and their daily lives, and in which the lower classes had little chance of being politically active, the ruling classes (estates) hardly felt it necessary to 'broadcast' their policies. There was no real need for political propaganda as long as tradition, convention and custom guaranteed the political slumber of the dominated. Menenius Agrippa tactics had to be used when the lower classes showed sign of restlessness, of following some sort of political line inimical to their masters, or of making up their own minds about something. *Pari passu* with the growth of bourgeois society and its campaign for politico-ideological hegemony the dominated classes – primarily the workers – begin to make their demands felt for political attitudes and an ideology of their own. One function of political ideology is to seek to deter those who are dissatisfied with their everyday lives from trying to change their lives, or indeed from imagining that their lives are worth changing. From this standpoint, the ideal is that men should stay within the confines of their customary everyday lives, and not seek to transgress these. That is to say, political ideology sets itself the task of conserving, of nurturing particularity.

In the initial stages of the labour movements, even if the struggle was entirely in the economic arena, things began to move beyond this appeal to particularity. At first, the areas in which the workers demanded satisfaction were particularistic in nature (bread, housing, shorter working week, etc.), but the means envisaged and used to attain these ends implied attitudes transcending the purely particularistic: social activity, solidarity, cultural enhancement and a capacity for debating and arguing their case. Thus participation in the purely economic battle gave the workers a new kind of everyday life, one not geared to particularistic demands alone; it was not fanciful of Marx to detect in these organized workers' movements the light of 'human dignity'.

Today, at least in Europe and the USA, a new relationship has emerged between the ideological content of the economic struggle and the everyday business of living. Participation in the economic struggle no longer requires particularity to be transcended, nor is there any social activity which depends on seeing society as a whole in an entirely new light. In so far as the labour movement wishes to transcend capitalism, it will have to postulate a new way of living whose groundwork will have to be laid in the movement as it now exists. Such a transformation can only be brought about with the help of masses who are imbued with the desire to overcome the particularity of their everyday lives, and to organize themselves in terms of a free association of individuals.

Even in its customary form, law has always and everywhere conditioned man's everyday life, in so far as it has limited the person's sphere of interested action to 'what is permitted'. With the growth of centralized government – i.e. in Europe with the rise of absolutism – law has come to play an increasingly important role in social organization; religion is pushed into the background, and so are the inter-personal relations which had previously gone to shaping everyday life. Today, it is impossible even to guess at the number of ways in which everyday life is shaped and conditioned by the state *via* its legislative system – from the punishment of crimes against property to the regulation of marriage and divorce and the custody of children, from compulsory elementary education to traffic control. As long as everyday life is, on the average, built on and around particularity, and is led in circumstances in which the close control of personal behaviour characteristic of natural communities no longer applies, it is inevitable that law will continue to partition this particularity, will continue to set limits to what is and is not allowed on a given plane of civilization, and to prescribe what is 'obligatory' (i.e. action which cannot be neglected).

(e) Science, philosophy and the arts

Science, art and philosophy are generic objectivations of human knowledge and self-knowledge. Both knowledge and self-knowledge are naturally part of general human practice, but as 'theoretical attitudes'. Initially, they grew directly from the everyday needs of given integrations; later, however, they acquired independent status as objectivation spheres in their own right, whose essential trait is that they no longer have any direct connection either with our everyday lives or with the immediate interests of integrations. The results of natural science are applicable to technology, though this is of fairly recent date; but natural science did not become natural science *through being* directly applicable to technology. Philosophy can become the ideology of one social class or another, and can play a part in 'fitting-out' the lifestyle of the 'person'. But it can only do so – it can only become an ideology and a life-forming factor – in so far as its content is not limited to the service of ad hoc ends; rather, it can articulate the vital concerns of a given age, a given social movement, by seeing them in the light of what humankind has so far achieved in the development of species-essential values: that is to say, its formative capacity is, indeed, to use Spinoza's words, '*sub specie aeternitatis*'. By means of the catharsis it generates, the work of art can have a formative effect on our lives, and in the same sense it can 'educate'. But again it can do this precisely

99

because it expresses the autognosis of human development, and because its *purpose* is expressly neither directly to affect people's lives nor to educate them.

These three forms of objectivation have, then, this property in common; but they differ in their relationship with the everyday, with daily living and thinking. In what follows, we shall discuss each of them briefly from this point of view.

The natural sciences comprise man's knowledge of the non-human world, including therein man's own physiology. From their inception, the natural sciences have aimed at de-anthropomorphization, even though this objective has not been totally accomplished. The essential brief of the natural sciences is to de-anthropocentralize, and where this tendency is lacking what we find is a philosophical-ideological view of nature. The more science de-anthropocentralizes, the further it moves beyond the possibilities open to man's sense perception of the world. What all this leads to is the inference that the natural sciences run counter to our everyday consciousness.

I distinguish four types of relationship obtaining between everyday and non-everyday thinking.[9] These are: *intentio recta*[1], which does no more than collect and order experience, the data of everyday thinking, and thus does not rise above its plane. Next we have *intentio recta*[2], which takes the data of everyday experience or everyday thinking as its point of departure, but 'raises' these to a level not given to everyday thinking. Using nothing more than ordinary experience and common sense, Socrates got an uneducated slave to derive the theorem of Pythagoras. But the causative verb is important here – Socrates had to prompt and direct the deduction process, because in and for itself everyday thinking is incapable of 'lifting' the structure of everyday thought and experience into a homogeneously scientific sphere. Plato said that philosophy originated in 'the sense of wonder' which not only fixes experience, things seen and things done, but which recognizes the unusual in the customary; that factor in everyday thinking which lifts it over and above the everyday. Thus, not only philosophy but every sort of thinking which is based on the second type of *intentio recta* derives ultimately from this sense of wonder.

As a whole, *intentio obliqua* runs counter to everyday thought; that is to say, it does not originate directly from the products of everyday experience and of everyday thought content. The entire body of modern natural sciences is built up on this sort of *intentio obliqua,* though experimental physics may still be conducted in terms of *intentio recta.*[2]

100

The difference between *intentio obliqua*[1], on the one hand, and *intentio obliqua*[2] on the other is the difference between modern philosophy and social sciences on the one hand and modern natural sciences on the other. In philosophy and social sciences what happens is that when a researcher has worked out a theory, using *intentio obliqua*, this theory becomes adequately understandable from the store of personal experience of life. This situation is a natural consequence of the fact that philosophy and the social sciences deal with society, with whose inter-relations, as revealed by scientific research, we come into daily, if fetishistic, contact. The natural scientist, however, – particularly the twentieth-century natural scientist – is more and more concerned with phenomena which lie totally beyond the scope of everyday life, though some of us may come into contact with them in our work, but even then only in highly specialized connections; accordingly, he cannot rely on his own everyday experience to help him in his problems. If we want to acquire even an elementary grasp of the theory of relativity, we have to rid our minds of empirical comparisons which are merely confusing. This is not to say that the translation of the concepts of modern natural sciences into everyday language is *per se* absurd – but, on the one hand, it is a *translation,* and, on the other hand, it expects the reader to make some attempt, however rudimentary, to cope with ideas which are remote from his everyday life.

The use of *intentio obliqua* in natural sciences always and necessarily involves defetishization (here we are disregarding ideological accretions forming round the interpretation of the results of modern natural sciences, accretions which may well be fetishistic in character, i.e. anthrophomorphic in one way or another). However, several ways are open to philosophy and the social sciences. Limiting ourselves to *intentio obliqua,* we can say that the theorist can raise, *via intentio obliqua,* the fetishistic facts of everyday life – including the concrete content of the fetishism of everyday knowledge – to the level of non-everyday knowledge, and mythicize thereby fetishistic being and knowledge into 'essence'. The converse process is also possible: i.e. using *intentio obliqua*, philosophy and social sciences may perform a *defetishizing* function. At their highest potential, philosophy and social sciences are grounded on the choice of such positive value-content that it makes defetishization not only possible but mandatory.

For scientific thinking to develop, everyday life too has to engender the requisite mental attitudes – *not* structures. *Intentio recta*[1] is certainly such an attitude, and I have already referred to

101

the 'sense of wonder' inherent in *intentio recta*. Lévy-Strauss asserts categorically that the taxonomies (especially of the plant world) which we find in the thinking of 'primitive' tribes, can be identified as a petrified thought-content which was an indispensable pre-condition of the so-called 'neolithic revolution'.[10] Ever since the emergence of scientific thought, it has never ceased to be 'fed-back' in more than one way into everyday thought. For one thing, it plays a part – admittedly, a very laggardly one – in the transformation of everyday thought, and is actively and obviously involved in the enrichment of its content. The conscious acquisition and relay of information originating in the field of scientific knowledge does not rise above the level typical of everyday need; but the content of everyday thought can be much enhanced by the injection of material deriving from the realm of non-everyday thinking. An investigation of the manner in which scientific theses (e.g. Darwinism) infiltrate into everyday knowledge, what ideological function they there discharge, and how they become 'commonplaces' would yield very interesting results.

Items of knowledge which have percolated down from a scientific seam of thought to become commonplaces, rarely lead a separate existence, independent of each other, on the plane of everyday thinking: their function is rather to combine to form a *Weltanschauung*. This function is nowadays consciously directed (e.g. in general education); and an encapsulated scientific world-view has an orientative function in everyday life, at least in Europe and America. The conscious amalgamation of such a world-view with collective images like morals or religion or with a conscious selection from among other competing world-views, is usually carried out, where and when it takes place, by those ideologies which are effectively active in everyday life. A superimposed scientific world-view could never win this terrain over by its own unaided efforts.

Somewhat apart from this, however, if not entirely independent of it, we have the practical penetration of everyday life in the form of technology as applied to our daily work or our surroundings (the lathe, the elevator, etc.) In this use, our relation to scientific results becomes part and parcel of the structure of our everyday life and thinking. It is true that we make more and more use in modern life of mechanisms which we are far from understanding; and this lack of understanding is compounded if we add thereto our ignorance of the physics, chemistry or mathematics underlying the mechanism. But this is only true in a relative sense, and there is an absolute sense in which it is not true. A medieval peasant did not have to understand the mechanical principles of the wheel in order to use one, or to repair it when it broke; and the twentieth-century citizen can switch on the light without knowing anything about electromagnetic equations. But as technology develops and penetrates more and more into everyday life, it comes about that more and more people have to know what to do when a fuse blows: and to mend it they need to know rather more about electricity than the peasant knew about mechanics. Everyday adaptation to the technological sector of modern life requires more scientific knowledge than at any previous time in human history. In fact, if the purely practical structure of everyday thought is to 'work' perfectly, its content must in part at least derive from the field of science. Between the feed-back of scientific thinking into everyday life and the use therein of applied science there is a far-reaching osmotic system which is reciprocal even where the former covers a much wider field than the latter.

The object of the natural sciences is not humanity; so that in the natural sciences man relates not to his own species but to nature. Is there a need in such activity for homogenization, for suspension of particularistic motivation? Is there any need for a conscious relationship with socio-generic values?

In one respect – that of knowledge – homogenization and suspension of particularity are unavoidable. I have to homogenize myself into the sphere of science, into the structure of a particular science; I have to generalize my knowledge in that sphere and structure. And in the process I have to suspend my everyday fetishized knowledge. The question is whether this conscious process of relating to nature is not conditioned by, or accompanied by factors deriving from our relation to purely socio-generic values. It is my contention that such factors do indeed exist.

To begin with, there is the search for truth, something which occupies the very highest position on the scientist's scale of values. In so far as the sphere of science is concerned, a scientist should utter no statement which he knows to be untrue. Often, rigid respect for the truth requires suspension or suppression of the scientist's particularistic interests – sometimes even of his otherwise valuable emotions or aspirations.

It does not require a dramatic clash of interests to highlight the cardinal position of truth in the scientific hierarchy of values; and the refutation of scientific preconceptions does not always require the scientist to sacrifice social status, success and even safety. It is a norm which applies to the most everyday cases too. A scientist who has just once announced the successful completion of an experiment which he has not in fact completed, or presented data as verified when they have in fact not been verified, is an outcast from the scientific community for the rest of his life; he counts not as a scientist but as a swindler. The moral virtue of trustworthiness lies at the very heart of the development of science.

But if we talk about the 'responsibility' of the scientist, of science, there is more to it than that. It is not just a question of work successfully completed, or of the contribution thus made to the development of humankind. The work of important natural scientists affects not only science; it has a profound influence on man's present and man's future, as certain natural scientists themselves are well aware. Szilard, Teller, and Oppenheimer are not different kinds of natural scientists; inspection of their theoretical work would reveal no such 'difference'. But there is a difference, and it lies in the fact that the three men had differing attitudes to the social use made of their scientific work: i.e. they differed in their attitude to social conflict (regarding the employment of nuclear weapons).

There is a third consideration. As we said, in the case of the natural scientist, the given scientific sphere guides the process of homogenization, and as 'man becomes whole' along with the generalization of knowledge, the supersession of everyday knowledge by species-essential knowledge ensues. But experience shows that, at least in the case of those scientists who break new ground, it is not simply mental activity and great ability that go to making this supersession possible. Most of the great natural scientists were also remarkable individuals. In the opening up of new domains of research, the development of new methods of experimentation, the adumbration of new results (excluding chance discoveries), there is a need for gifts of *character* and not only for the abilities normally adequate for activity in the given discipline to achieve the normal level of scientific knowledge. Strength of character, refusal to be discouraged by failure, civil courage, an open mind – i.e. not fettered by tradition – all of these are aspects and attitudes of character which mark the metamorphosis of personality into individual. New discoveries in natural sciences, therefore, often demand species-essential qualities, irrespective of the fact that neither in matter nor in intention is the research directly concerned with humankind. None of this, of course, applies to science which sticks to the beaten path, still less to those who merely apply science. But often it is precisely individual and moral qualities which decide, not that so-and-so should become a scientist, but on what level he will operate.

104

The distinction I make between the pioneers who break new scientific ground, and those who are content to stick to well-trodden paths, who are concerned with partial results – this distinction applies in the social sciences also. In contradistinction to natural sciences, the calibre of products of social sciences depends on two criteria. Only one of these criteria is the opening up of new research areas, the development of new experimental and heuristic methods. The second and intimately connected criterion is – in what manner, and how radically, can it discharge its practical function? For this latter purpose, particularistic gifts (activities) are not enough, nor are gifts on the moral-individual plane (endurance, courage, patience, etc.); what is necessary is, firstly, the exploration of an alternative embedded in the social reality, and, secondly, the shaping of the theory from the standpoint of a chosen value.

Even in purely 'professional' social sciences there is always an axiological component, a value choice: which is not surprising, given that social science is about human life. Withdrawal into 'professionalism' may be a defence mechanism and hence 'resistance' to negative ideologies; but mostly it is a kind of apologia, in that it views society as it exists, the *status quo,* as a datum, in the same way as the natural scientist views nature – he is concerned to investigate but not to change: at most, he wants to improve 'the way it works'. A social science which relapses into 'professionalism' is not necessarily more fetishistic than the consciously ideological one; in so far as it represents a retreat from negative-value ideologies, it can also express protest against fetishism. But when it views the structure of society and its workings as 'data', and takes this as its starting point, its hostility to ideology merely serves to strengthen the fetishistic everyday viewpoint by giving it scientific backing.

Probably only one branch of the social sciences plays no direct part in everyday life – that comprising such purely specialized subjects as ethnology, historical linguistics, etc.; though even here the ideologist may intervene by popularizing, i.e. inserting information from these specialist fields into everyday thought, with a view to furthering social fermentation.

Little need be said about the enormously important role played by the ideological social sciences in the formation of everyday life. The everyday mind has such a profound respect for science that even completely unscientific and axiologically negative ideologies will do all they can to provide themselves with a 'scientific basis' as proof of legitimacy (e.g. the appeal made by Fascist racism to all sorts of wild biological speculations). Science – both as natural science and social science – has an immense authority for the everyday consciousness of our age, and this authority can be used in an authoritarian way.

The penetration of everyday life by social 'technology' which is quite simply an up-to-date way of finding out how to manipulate people, is only in the formative stage. (It is, of course, only rather 'mild' forms of manipulation that need a scientific framework!). Today, scientific technological manipulation has extended its catchment area in everyday life to labour process and political activity. The fear is rather widespread that 'scientific-technological' manipulation will lead to the whole of everyday life having to 'conform' once and for all – indeed, that this cannot be long delayed. For myself, I cannot believe that these 'scientific-technological' methods will be decisive; manipulation can take place in other, more spontaneous ways, e.g. the consumer market, fashion, etc., and this is happening all the time. Nor am I convinced that people can be totally manipulated, whatever the means employed. Man has always shown himself capable of finding adequate ways of rebelling against any given form of alienation, so why should we assume that this will not or cannot happen in the case of 'scientific-technological' manipulation? But our contention that 'scientific-technological' manipulation is neither inevitable nor necessarily successful, does not alter the fact that it is up to social science and philosophy to use every means at its disposal to combat such manipulation, and to mobilize human beings in the defence of its individuality.

'Scientific-technological' manipulation, as it is today, has taken over all the negative functions of religion, without its compensating positive aspects. It 'fattens up' particularity and particularistic motivations, but promotes, or indeed, permits, only those particularistic qualities to flower which go to serve the interests of a given 'organization'. It prevents the person from taking a moral decision in ideological or political questions; it forms attitudes and ideologies which serve the *status quo,* without making it in any way questionable. It replaces the ancient myths with new ones – the myth of technology, the myth of the leader, the myth of the 'qualified professional'. It keeps an eye on our private lives, and either abolishes the 'private' sphere or subjects it to social supervision. Demands and expectations in whose interest certain sectors of particularity may be suppressed (so that particularity as a whole may be nourished) no longer represent, in any sense whatever, generic development, and are totally devoid of the

106

species-essential values they could and did retain in the case of religion.

Art[11] is the self-consciousness of mankind, and works of art are always bearers of species-essence 'for itself': and this in more than one respect. The work of art is always immanent: it depicts the world as man's world, as the world created by man. Its scale of values reflects mankind's axiological development: at the summit of art's scale of values we find those individuals (individual affections, individual attitudes) which have entered most fully into the process of species-essential efflorescence. To put it another way: 'survival' of a work of art will depend on its success or failure in reflecting this scale of values. In this way, the work of art is also mankind's memory; and if we can enjoy artistic masterpieces generated by the conflicts of bygone ages, it is because we recognize in these conflicts the pre-history of our own lives and our own conflicts.

In the process of creating a work of art, suspension of particularity is complete and without residue; the homogeneous medium of the particular art elevates the creating agent to the sphere of species-essence: his particularity has to be superseded, and the imprint of his personality has to be placed on the world of the artefact.

In the work of art – i.e. in the objectivation *sui generis* – there is equally no room for pure particularity, for particularity, that is, which has not been formed into individuality. And this goes not only for the particularity of the creator, but also for that of the characters in literature, painting, sculpture. It might be asked how, in that case, can we regard the work of art as a mimesis of life, since the lives of the innumerable human beings depicted in art are, in fact, centred round particularity? Our answer is twofold: first, that the work of art depicts particular motivation as well, as long as it is 'in its place', i.e. low down on the scale of values; and, second, that the work of art does not simply copy particularistic life, but rather individualizes it in terms of art. It is, finally, not only in the act of creation and in the work of art that particularity is superseded: it is also superseded in the act of reception. When we enjoy and 'appropriate' a work of art, we are lifted to the species-essential, like the creator of the work. It is for this reason that creative art can act as a moral purifying agent by inducing catharsis.

Art is an inseparable component in everyday life. This is not merely to assert (as we did in the case of science – see above, pp. 99–100) that the pre-conditions, the embryonic outlines of the aesthetic way of looking at things, are inherent in the heterogeneous complex of everyday thought; it is also to assert that aesthetic experience in some form or other, is always present in that complex. No social grouping, no way of life is known that is devoid of music, song, dance, and in which festivals and other climactic points of daily life are not accompanied by artistic performance in one form or another. Even where no distinction can be made between supersession to the socio-generic plane, on the one hand, and absorption in 'mute' species-being (erotic ecstasy in dance or music) on the other, there too is the specific homogeneous medium which acts as conductor to the supersession or the ecstasy. Art forms in which the scale of values is drawn entirely from socio-generic sources – legends, myths, fairy-tales, etc. – are continually gaining ground. The individual artist 'rises' out of this everyday but artistically supercharged sphere in order to fix in objectivation his own personal relationship to the species-essential. It is from works of art that we may most confidently surmise how and in what direction the individuality of a given historical age developed; and it is in its works of art that we may most profitably seek clues to such questions as – what sort of osmotic relations obtained between everyday life and the species-essential forms of activity? and, were these relations harmonious or fraught with contradictions? etc.

Art is therefore 'indispensable', to quote Ernst Fischer. At all times, people have sung while they worked, and love has always been expressed in song and poetry – indeed, human feelings in general have always sought an outlet in art forms. Again, it is from their songs and verses that we can best assess how people of bygone ages loved, rejoiced and sorrowed. People have always wanted to immortalize whatever seemed to them beautiful, holy or significant: and again we can identify what was beautiful, holy or significant for them by looking at the pictures they produced.

But does the suspension of particularity in the experiencing of art always take place on the same level? And are the extent and the intensity of this suspension of particularity dependent on nothing more than the profundity and the value of the work of art?

When we enter upon the enjoyment of a work of art, we come from our own privately lived and enjoyed everyday, we bring with us our own feelings and our own data-bank: but, most important of all, we come armed with the value-judgments and the ideologies of the society in and with which we have learned to live. This is what Lukács refers to as the 'beforehand' of the reception of the work of art; and it is this which will, in the main, decide what type of work of art is able to 'elevate' the observer (or listener, etc.) completely and without residue to the species-essential plane – the work of art which harmonizes with his previous experience of life, or the one which shocks by reason of its stark contrast therewith, the particular homogeneous medium with which the recipient resonates. It often happens that we are scarcely moved by an acknowledged masterpiece, while finding ourselves deeply disturbed and shaken to catharsis point by a much inferior work, which is, however, concerned with problems that confront us in our own lives. A picture may make a deep and memorable impression if it reminds us of someone we loved, a drama may move us because its protagonists embody our own conflicts, and music may further intensify an already emotional state. Spiritual take-off to the homogeneous medium is, therefore, far from being equally intense in all cases: but if it is abortive, if the spirit remains earthbound, then there is no real 'enjoyment' of the work of art, however adequate our intellectual grasp of it may be.

So much for the 'beforehand' of our reception of the work of art; the 'afterwards' of the experience of that work of art is equally many-tiered. The fact that a work of art may change my life and my relationship with the world, does not depend exclusively on the intensity of the experience, the degree to which I have been moved or disturbed. Direct translation of a cathartic experience to everyday life, or to life in general, is a very rare phenomenon indeed: and, it has to be added, rather more likely to happen in the case of 'uncultured' or 'illiterate' recipients than in the case of those who are habitually exposed to art and its products and who have become accustomed to 'being taken out of themselves' by a work of art. Artistic experience in the latter case is sophisticated: after it, the recipients return unscathed to everyday life, which is after all not the same thing as art. By itself, art cannot humanize life, but where there is a desire to humanize one's own life and the life of others, art can provide a yardstick, and it can provide emotional and intellectual support for the undertaking.

In *Economic and Philosophical Manuscripts,* Marx writes of the enormous evolutionary step forwards taken by man when he learned how to create according to the touchstone of beauty. However, 'creation according to the touchstone of beauty' is not necessarily the same thing as the 'work of art'. In the work of art, the world is always present, the work of art is always 'portrayal of the world': creation according to the touchstone of beauty does not necessarily involve this portrayal. But it is through the work of art as intermediary that beauty in its most highly concentrated form is transmitted to the world. The work of art is a human objectivation to which we are not related by 'utility'; its value lies not in its 'employability' but in something else, which has the power to awaken pleasure. Beauty of any kind partakes in art, in so far as it transcends the category of direct utility, even when the object or institution in which it is manifested is 'employable'.

The beauty of useful objects transcends pragmatism by awakening the affects and the feeling of sensual pleasure, and, in so far, unites with the species-essential values, though not necessarily with the *ideation* of these values: i.e. our relationship with this beauty is not the same as our conscious relationship with species-essential values. Beauty is heterogeneous, just as everyday life is. The farmer does not see the wheat undulating in his fields as 'beautiful' (as Chernishevsky believed) just because it is going to be 'useful' to him; the fact that he sees it as beautiful, 'experiences' its beauty, is a plus, a bonus over and above its utility: pragmatism is transcended. Of course, this is not to say that pragmatism is not found in the sense of beauty or runs counter to it: it is not a question of 'disinterest' but of 'above interest'. A painter may see the wheatfield as 'beautiful' not just because 'it would be nice to paint it'. A city-dweller may see the wheatfield as beautiful because it represents peace and quiet in contrast with the traffic at home – again, that is, for a reason which transcends pragmatism while not excluding it. In all these cases, one projects socio-generic values into nature, but in none of them does man's species-essential value-development emerge as a problem.

The spread of beauty into the totality of everyday life can be conceived of as a cultural value. But the 'enjoyment' of a non-pragmatic relationship to things as a general attitude in the everyday life of certain social strata may be the expression of the parasitical nature of that particular social stratum. Just when and why such a parasitism arises is an historical question (e.g. the aristocracy in the age of absolutism, or a section of our contemporary intelligentsia). And since the concrete historical function of heterogeneous beauty varies from one period to another and from one stratum to another, it is a problem that we have only been able to touch on in passing, on this very general level.[12]

Philosophy unites the functions of science and art: it is both the consciousness and the self-consciousness of human development. It is consciousness in so far as it always represents that level of species-essential knowledge which mankind has reached at a given moment; and it is self-consciousness in so far as its aim is always the self-knowledge of man and of man's world. Knowledge is presented as the consciousness of self-knowledge; and, for this reason the philosophy of nature too expresses self-knowledge. And conversely, philosophy is self-knowledge of humankind in so far as it conceptualizes the knowledge and consciousness of the historical period in which it is conceived.

The 'afterlife' of a philosophical work is a sort of middle way between the after-life of a work of art and that of a scientific discovery. On the one hand, it represents the state of human knowledge, and hence it is possible to take certain thoughts from the context of the whole work of a philosopher and build thereon, as on the basis of the accumulated corpus of human knowledge. Different thoughts expressed by one and the same philosopher can be built into widely differing systems of thought to give rise to widely differing questions and/or answers. On the other hand, however, philosophy is the self-consciousness of human development, so that in the sequel we relate to a work of philosophy in the same way as to a work of art. Every philosophical work is an individual whole (as is the individual art work). The extent to which a given work of philosophy serves as midwife for the conflicts of its day, and the extent to which this is coherently expressed – this is the prime source of our enjoyment of a philosophical work. And in so far, we do not study a philosophical work to see whether and how it can be built into our contemporary thought; rather, we seek to learn how completely, how profoundly and how coherently it summed up its own contemporary world.

Since philosophy carries out (makes manifest) species-essential conflicts, philosophical thought is always beyond everyday thinking, even when it is couched in everyday language or draws heavily on everyday experience – indeed, even when its declared purpose is to influence everyday life.

At the same time, philosophical activity is only possible via the suspension of particularity. In contradistinction to what happens in artistic creation, it is not only in the creative process that this is obligatory. The philosopher, like the artist, must be an individual, since every philosophical objectivation is individual. But that is not enough. Since the representative philosopher, at least, the ideal type of philosopher, has no option but to *live* his own philosophy, he cannot 'pick up' or 'lay down' particularistic motivation or its suspension, as the artist can. The philosopher has to be not only an individual but an individual who lives and creates on the same level. In so far, therefore, as his work is designed to

111

express species-essential aspirations in terms of their positive value-content, his whole life – including therefore his everyday life – must be an essay in living according to that value-content. His everyday life, in other words, must be a documentation of his philosophical position; and this goes, not only for the originator of a philosophy, but also – if on a somewhat lower level – for those who rally to his banner. If I am a Stoic, I must live like a Stoic; if an Epicurean, like an Epicurean. If I profess Spinoza's teachings, I must show myself worthy of that philosophy in my life as well. If I am a follower of Kant, I must continually lend an ear to the 'moral law within' and if I am a Hegelian I must gear my everyday life to recognition of necessity.

This last point is very important in so far as the 'penetration' of philosophy into everyday life is concerned. The non-philosopher rarely reads philosophical books, and hardly ever forms any sort of relationship with the coherent individuality of a philosophical work (as he may do with the coherent individuality of a work of art). This is so if for no other reason than that some preliminary training is necessary before a philosophical work can be intellectually appropriated. What primarily percolates downwards from a philosophy into everyday life is its world-view – its ideological core; and conceptual exposition is by-passed in favour of pointers to its political implications and its applicability to everyday activity. People who are always on the look-out for a general answer to their problems – on whatever level of abstraction – find this sort of thing irresistible. In the great days of the Athenian polis, philosophizing was a necessary component in the life of every citizen; it belonged to everyday life. But why was there a need for philosophy? In order that it should provide a de-fetishized world-concept to act as a guiding principle for political life, indeed for life in general, and the attainment of personal 'happiness'.

Following Ernst Fischer, we spoke of the 'necessity of art': we can take this a step further and speak, with certain reservations, of the 'necessity of philosophy'. Philosophy is necessary for every individual – all the more so if religion abdicates from acting as the transmitting agency of morals and ideology. It is necessary because humans want to know to what purpose they are living. Philosophy defetishizes man's world conceptually by showing us what sort of world we live in, and how to endow our lives with sense in this world.

We have seen how manipulative and technological science has begun to take over the negative functions of religion, leaving mankind deprived of its positive functions. The role of philosophy must be to excise these negative functions: the 'nurturing' of particularity, the substitution of authoritarian doctrines and conventions for independence of thought and action, the construction of world-views, of transcendental myths. In the place of all this, it must take over, develop and promulgate the positive message once transmitted by religion – conveying species-essential values for everyman in his everyday setting.

PART III

The organizational framework of everyday life

CHAPTER 6

Objectivation 'in itself' and 'for itself'

If we are now to investigate everyday life as, on the one hand, the territory *par excellence* for the appropriation of species-essential objectivation 'in itself', and, on the other hand, as the basis for species-essential objectivation 'for itself', we must first of all explain the use of these two categories. Of course, this is not the place for an exhaustive discussion of the philosophical concepts of 'being-in-itself', 'being-for-itself' and 'being-for-us'; and we shall say no more about them than is necessary for an understanding of the specific nature of objectivations.

'Being-in-itself' and 'being-for-itself' are relative concepts. In relation to nature, 'being-in-itself' is anything that has not yet been pervaded by praxis and cognition; and in so far – if we are dealing with the relationship between nature and society – we can regard the whole realm of praxis as 'being-for-itself'. In what follows, however, we shall be concerned solely with the social complex, and it is in this setting alone that we shall investigate these two categories. In this sense we shall be perfectly justified in speaking of certain spheres, integrations and objectivations as 'in itself' even when these are 'for itself' in relation to nature.

Human activity, human action, is always objectivized (as distinct from impulses, casual motivations which are not translated into action, dreams which are not directly objectivized, and which are incidental from the point of view of the development of the personality). But not every objectification is related to an objectivation. First and foremost, all objectivations are species-essential, in that they incorporate various types of species-essentiality. Secondly, they are not simply the consequences of

117

externalized, objectivized activity, but referential orders which are external in relation to the activities of the 'persons' who activate them while appropriating them. So, 'persons' must appropriate objectivations in order to objectify themselves under their guidance, or to shape these objectivations. At the same time, the objectivations can be appropriated by everyone: but not every objectivation can also be shaped by everyone on the same level. Crucial here is the difference between species-essential objectivations 'in itself', on the one hand, and species-essential objectivations 'for itself' on the other.

(a) Species-essential objectivations 'in itself'

The cardinal characteristic identifying social entities as 'being-in-itself' is that, without them, society would not exist at all: or, at least, a given social structure would not exist. This first aspect identifies an objectivation as species-essential 'in itself'. As society 'works itself out of' nature, i.e. when man begins to create his own environment, his own world, this happens by his bringing into being a unified though graduated structure of objectivation 'in itself'. This species-essential objectivation 'in itself' is the fruit of human activity, and, at the same time, the pre-condition of all human activity. The three different, if inter-connected, constituents of this sphere of objectivation are: tools and products, custom, and finally, language. The coming-to-be of man (i.e. his ascent from mute species-essentiality, which is conferred upon him like his particularity at the moment of birth) begins when he appropriates through his own activity this sphere of objectivation 'in itself'. This is the take-off point for human culture, and the basis and pre-condition for all objectivation spheres 'for itself'.

It is a property of the sphere of objectivation 'in itself' that though it is the teleological activity of human beings that activates it and modifies it, it appears nevertheless as an order which confronts each 'person' as 'given'. This is not to say that conscious human intention cannot play a part in its formation or articulation. In the case of language, examples of this conscious and intentional modification are rather rare (neologisms) but they are far from rare in work and in custom. At the same time, all constituents of species-essential objectivation 'in itself' are ontologically primary: none are relatively independent of each other.

The realm of the 'in itself' is the realm of necessity. If the freedom made possible by the 'in itself', by objectivation 'in itself' is to be realised, components other than the 'in itself', heterogeneous in relation to it, must be brought into play in the construction of social relations – species-essential activities 'for itself'.

(b) Species-essential objectivations 'for itself'

Species-essential objectivations 'for itself' are ontologically secondary. They are not necessary components of sociality. Many social structures can well be imagined as functioning without certain species-essential objectivations 'for itself' even though these are in fact present. Philosophy is a component in the classical form of the Athenian *polis*. But Sparta had no philosophy, nor did many other city-states and yet these were well able to reproduce themselves. Of course, certain social formations exist, and certain developmental levels exist within social formations, to which certain species-essential objectivations 'for itself' necessarily belong (for example, the natural sciences are a necessary component in advanced capitalism).

Species-essential objectivations 'for itself' cannot function otherwise than in accordance with the conscious human intention directed on and towards them. Indeed, they cannot come into existence at all without conscious relationship with species-being. They do, however, exhibit a certain capacity for development which proceeds according to its own specific laws. This is particularly true of the arts, but also of science and religion. This capacity is, however, no more than secondary and relative in nature, since these objectivations are essentially a response to questions thrown up as society develops, or at least a species-essential ideation of these questions. At the same time, every species-essential objectivation 'for itself' has, in its own ipseity, structural homogeneity.

All objectivations 'for itself' embody human freedom, and express that degree of freedom achieved by humanity at any given time.

The basis of objectivations 'for itself', their material and the propounder of its questions is species-being 'in itself'. Promotion to objectivation 'for itself', however, always entails a distancing from the 'in itself', its restructuring or, at least, its re-interpretation. In art, the particularistic personal is typified to acquire individual status; action intended to secure the realization of moral norms is related to, though distanced from, the mere observance of customary prescription.

Let me stress that the 'for itself' is not synonymous with

119

non-alienation. (In the same way, the 'in itself' is not synonymous with alienation). Science can be alienated, while language can become a basic medium for all human activity 'for itself'.

(c) The 'in-and-for-itself'

Integrations, political structures, law, etc. are objectivations both 'in itself' and 'for itself'. To what extent one or the other predominates in any given system depends very largely on the degree, type and grade of alienation. The more a social institutional system enables those who live in it to articulate their lives, the more will its objectivations tend towards the 'for itself' category. Here, as in all objectivations 'for itself' consciousness plays a leading part. As it is an essential property of objectivations 'for itself' that conscious intention should be directed upon and towards them, that they should represent human consciousness or self-consciousness, the 'for itself' component in the sphere of 'in-and-for-itself' is augmented *pari passu* with the growth and deepening of consciousness of social action directed towards the relevant spheres, and endowed with the capacity to act as protagonists in possible conflicts. In objectivations 'in-and-for-itself' the degree of the latter component provides a yardstick for the degree of freedom.

(d) 'Being-for-us'

'Being-for-us' is not an objectivation category: there is no species-essential objectivation which is 'for us'. 'Becoming-for-us' means that a state of affairs, a content, a norm, becomes internalized and reflected upon as adequate, and thus becomes practice. So we can say that the contents of species-being ('in itself' and 'for itself') are 'for us' if they offer an adequate, i.e. relatively truthful image of the world, and enable us to act in adequate, i.e. right fashion in accordance with it. 'Adequacy' has two aspects: (a) adequacy with truth content and norms, and (b) adequacy with the anthropological singularity of the actors.

The extent to which certain objectivations 'in itself' (the world of custom and habit) have become 'for-us' is reflected in the extent to which they are the objects of moral intention, and in the manner in which this moral intention expresses the dual adequacy: adequacy to the value content of the demands, and adequacy to the singular personality. It is therefore not by chance that the concept of 'truth' plays just as important a role in ethics as it does in cognition. The mute subsumption of our activities to the rules and norms of objectivation must always call in question the extent to which objectivations (customs, moral norms) are 'for-us'.

We know that the development of the personality is the process of objectivization into *subiectum*. And in the light of what we have said, we may now venture upon the assumption that the personality is objectivized into 'in itself' status in the particularistic person (let us recall that it is possible for particularity and species-being to coexist mutely); while, in the *individual,* the personality is objectivized into *subiectum* 'for itself'. But here, since it is a question of the 'person', of personal activity, the categories of 'for itself' and 'for-us' coalesce, or at least tend to do so. Taken together and at once, the maximum or near-maximum stage at any given time of the process whereby reality becomes 'for-us', plus the second concomitant factor – an advanced stage in the process whereby our human-personal nature becomes 'for-us' – unite indissolubly to constitute the personality 'for itself' – i.e. individuality. So it is not at all fortuitous that morals as the principial 'for-us' play a leading part in this process.

It must be added, however, that from the standpoint of the person, it is principially impossible for all 'items' of being 'in itself' or 'for itself' to turn into 'for-us'. At most, certain 'for itself' components can play a leading part in our actions, including those in the realm of daily life; and conscious relationship with species-being can likewise play a leading part in our relations with species-essential objectivations 'in itself'. From the standpoint of the person, therefore, reality cannot be constructed as absolute 'being-for-us': on the level attainable at any given time, including the future, there is always a datum 'not-for-us'. It is possible, however, to construct everyday life in general as something 'for-us' on the basis of the conscious-active relationship with objectivations 'for itself'. This what we may call 'conduct of life'.

Alienated everyday life is the realm of the 'in itself'. In it, the 'person' is guided by species-essential objectivations 'in itself', to which he has merely to submit. Non-alienated everyday life, on the other hand, is the realm of the 'for-us' which, let us repeat, does not mean that the 'for-us' level permits upward transfer to the species.

The 'in itself' aspect of everyday life is merely tendential: over and over again there arises the need to transform life into 'life-for-us'. These aspirations which are inseparable from human life become, *inter alia,* the bases for species-essential objectivations 'in itself'. These would never have made their appearance, were this need not covertly – often, indeed, overtly – present in everyday life, and active in generating the material – the problems, ways of thinking and acting – from which species-essential objectivations 'for itself' can grow and develop. No Great Wall of China separates species-essential objectivations 'in itself' from those that are 'for itself', or the particularistic person from the individual; and in the same way, no partition divides those everyday ways of acting and thinking which are directed towards species-being 'in itself' from those which constitute the bases for species-essential objectivations 'for itself'.

CHAPTER 7

Species-essential activity 'in itself'

As we said, species-essential activity 'in itself' provides an objectivation which is unified and yet articulated, in that it has three different constituent components: the first of these is the world of human artefacts, tools and products; the second is the world of custom and habit; the third is language. The various heterogeneous forms taken by our everyday activity are ordered and guided for us by these objectivations. This triple objectivation guides our activity as a whole: the three components are, however, functionally differentiated, in that each is specifically concerned with one or another human manifestation. This being so – and with the above proviso – we can say that implements (the tools and means of human produce) play a leading part in our material-manipulative activity, custom and habit control our attitudes and social postures, while language is primarily the medium of thinking.

It is primarily in species-essential objectivation 'in itself' (i.e. in implements and things, in systems of habit and custom, and in language) that human culture accumulates: their continuity is identical with the continuity of social life, and from them we can read off the average degree of development which a given social integration has attained at any given time.

At the same time, objectivations 'in itself' are also means – the means of reproducing any human life, i.e. the life of any 'person' or the life of humanity in any given period. 'Using a means' is equivalent to 'appropriation of its mode of functioning'; knowledge of a means is equivalent to knowing how it is used. I appropriate a word, a tool, a custom in so far as I know how to use it in the right situation: i.e. properly, in the way for which it was designed. And I cannot hope to grasp the meaning of ancient tools, customs, word combinations, unless I can understand how these were used in the given culture. As Malinowski writes,[1] translation from a primitive language into a modern one is possible only if the translator knows the culture in which the language was a component, and understands the situations and ways in which it was used.

As I have already said, the three constituents of the objectivation 'in itself' cannot be divorced one from another. The use of implements, the handling of objects and work itself go to condition the system of customs and habits: by which we mean not simply those social habits which prescribe time, place, content and form of work, but the work process itself, since the most successful ways and means of working are handed down, wholly or partially, in the form of custom from generation to generation. But language also belongs to the work process, since not even the most primitive tasks can be performed without the transmission of linguistic information of one kind or another such as words of command. According to the well-known legend in the Bible, it was the confusion of tongues that put paid to the tower of Babel: without a common linguistic medium, the work simply ground to a halt. Malinowski describes a very simple work process – a 'primitive' tribe's method of fishing – which is performed according to very detailed and highly organised customary rules, and in which language plays a decisive part on several heterogeneous levels – not only in words of command and their acknowledgment, but also in technical instruction and in the oral reaction to success or failure which is as much a part of the process of fishing as technical commands. If we approach the problem from the standpoint of custom, we get the same result. First and foremost, most customs are expressed in speech, or can at least be translated into speech. For example, as a purely speech act, prayer is a custom. If I give up my seat on the bus, I accompany the action with the words, 'would you like to have my seat'. At the same time, purely social customs – or at least most of them – are relayed through the intermediary of objects. Prayer, to use the previous example, usually takes place before or towards an object which is symbolic. In the bus, I relinquish the place in which I was sitting: i.e. custom here relates to the use of an object. And we may recall such everyday examples as putting on one's clothes or eating. As for language, speech itself is a kind of activity which man has to learn to manipulate just like any other form of activity. One function of language is to direct the use of tools (objects) and to assist in turning that usage into practice. Language is always linguistic custom. On this point, Wittgenstein writes: 'Following a rule', providing information, issuing an order, playing a linguistic game – all of this is habit (customary rules, customary institutions). Hence, it is practice if we 'follow a rule'. And hence we cannot follow a rule privately or 'on our own'.[2]

Thus, species-essential objectivation 'in itself' – even though we distinguish three components in its make-up – is a unified relational system, and, at the same time and indissolubly, a unified system of means.

Objectivation 'in itself' provides ready-made schemata for persons entering a given society, who order and collate their experience according to the relevant schemata. The same objectivation is characterized by a relative inertia with regard to capillary motion and change. Change is continually being brought about in the given objectivation system via new experience, new demands, needs, new methods of production and distribution; novelties and innovations in fashion catch on, and even the structure of language is, up to a certain point, subject to change. Objectivations 'in itself' act as a conservative force, however: appropriation of the schemata of the given referential system inhibits certain new experiences and can in various ways slow up the actual process of change, the formulation of new ways of thought, etc.

Every form of species-essential objectivation 'in itself' has objective signification. This signification is identical with the social function of the item, that is, it is identical with its own use. The 'signification' of the plough is that we use it to turn over the soil; if we bow to someone, this signifies greeting, respect, or, in the extreme case, subservience. In so far, signification is not only a property of language, but of the other two constituents of species-essential objectivation 'in itself' as well. As the example of bowing shows, a custom or an implement can be polysemantic just as much as a word: that is to say, polysemy here refers to the several social functions which the custom or implement may discharge, the different functions in which it can be used. Leontiev writes: 'man finds a ready-made, historically formulated system of significations which he appropriates, just as he appropriates implements which are the material embodiment of these significations.'[3]

The meaning of a word is one and the same thing as the function discharged by that word in the language it belongs to. In language, meaning can appertain to what does not materially exist, what no longer exists and what does not yet exist – a meaning which is based on apprehension of the latent or potential properties of things and processes. Materially, there is no such thing as 'the devil': but it is a meaningful word in so far as it exists in the social consciousness. The Deluge is as meaningful as the Last Judgment. Of course, an ancient implement retains its intrinsic meaning, but – since we no longer use it – this can become 'meaningful' for us only if we make an effort to reconstruct its erstwhile use, and this is something that only thinking in a specific language can do. In the same way potential material meaning appertains to a new piece of machinery which, for the moment, exists only in the engineer's head, but – in so far as we do not yet use the machine and it fulfils no function – it acquires social meaning only when the engineer presents his completed plans in oral or written form. Along the time axis, therefore, the meaning appertaining to the elements of thinking in a language covers a much wider spectrum than is the case with systems of material objects or customs.

A similar relationship obtains between language and the other two spheres of special-essential objectivation 'in itself' in the spatial plane. Language transcends space, and provides us with a way of knowing things and acquainting us with customs which we cannot appropriate, in that they are not 'our' things and customs. Whatever can be thought or imagined becomes invested with meaning for us by language.

We described everyday language as the primary objectivation of everyday thinking: which is certainly not to say that it is *exclusively* in language that thought is presented. Thought is presented in *all* forms of action. Here I take the word 'action' in Leontiev's sense, according to which any form of activity can be described as 'action' if the motive of the activity can be differentiated from its object. In this sense, only man can be regarded as a thinking being. Unmediated unity of motive and object cannot have the potential of *generalization*. (It can, of course, have that of abstraction, which pure perception also possesses to a large extent.) What we have said is of course not to be taken as meaning that *all* human action (activity relayed or mediated through thought) is based on the disjunction of motive from object. In higher types of human action (to be discussed later) the unity of motive and object reasserts itself, though in this higher stage it is reflected rather than direct; mediated, that is, through thought. This latter unity characterizes or can characterize conscious activity directed

126

towards species-essential being without intermediary, and its incipient germs in the process of everyday life.

I said above that every generalizing objectivation – i.e. every action – is at the same time an objectivation of thought. We can therefore assert that our tools and our customs are just as much the embodiments of human thought as our languages. In work, the process of producing an artefact, the personal and the species-essential capabilities of a man are objectified according to certain norms (a point we shall take up later); and if there is no general-normative embodiment of these capabilities, the artefact will have no use-value. Bare observance of custom is also the generalization of an attitude – the generalization of personal feelings, impulses, initiatives, accompanied by alignment to a social norm and the appropriation of this alignment. The use of things and customs is just as much a mediated activity as the use of language.

It is clear then that action is always at one and the same time thought, and that the objective result of any action is, in this sense, a product of thought; but we are still faced with the question – does language have a preferential role to play in the coming-to-be of other, i.e. non-linguistic, objectivations in the material world and in the system of customs? The answer is that it does. Not only because neither of objects nor of behaviour is generalization possible without language (for, as we have already seen, neither can language function except in situations where tools and implements are produced and used, and in which a customary system obtains) but also because it is precisely language that guides thinking in other forms of objectivation. This is a specifically human characteristic, and a main criterion of the coming-to-be of the human being. Vigotski claims that in the animal world, intelligence, on the one hand, and pre-linguistic skills, on the other, develop along quite separate paths. The intelligence possessed by the higher animals (apes, for example), is not expressed in any special proto-linguistic capacity, but rather in extraordinary manipulative skill. In the case of other animals (including less highly developed ones), proto-linguistic forms of communication – signs, etc. – are fairly elaborate, but these animals are weak in intelligence in that they lack a high degree of manipulative skill. In the case of man, however, manipulative skill and language have developed conjointly in unitary form; and this is why language is the mentor of thought in all forms of manipulative activity as well.

In certain actions, of course, objectivation takes place without language – as a direct realization of thought. If I wish to repair an implement and succeed in doing so, I solve a problem: I think without an accompanying use of language, without even internal speech. At the same time, problem solving becomes socially generalized only when it is communicated. 'Communication' here can, of course, be purely demonstrative: but the 'demonstration' contains of necessity communication, some sort of speech, not only in the shape of an explanatory text or a set of instructions, but also in feed-back, questions, etc.

From 'thinking' in this wide sense we may distinguish 'thinking' in a narrower sense: a procedure analogous to Lefèbvre's two categories.[4] Lefèbvre distinguished both phylogenetically and ontogenetically between what he called 'repetitive' and 'inventive' praxis. 'Inventive' praxis generates novelty (both on the generic level and in personal life) while 'repetitive' praxis is no more than the reiteration of schemata elaborated by previous generations, or of practice which has already been appropriated by the person. In adopting these two categories, however, I construe them in a different sense from that of Lefèbvre. By 'inventive' praxis I understand not simply the generation of novelty but rather any activity which is at the same time the solution of a problem – the *intentional* solution, that is, construed as acquisition of experience, broadening of opinion, the taking of decisions. And 'intentionality' is here taken not in the narrow sense – that of the solution being present in my mind, 'envisaged' before praxis – but rather in the wider sense, i.e. as meaning teleological activity in which intention is central to action and is itself formed and articulated as the activity proceeds.

Thinking, in the narrower sense, belongs to the realm of inventive praxis. I use 'praxis' in a wide sense, to include mental activities directed towards the solution of purely theoretical problems. I shall therefore use 'repetitive thinking' to mean thinking in which activity of some kind, which has been engendered at some time by an act of inventive thinking, is now spontaneously practised; while by 'inventive thinking' I mean thinking used in the *intentional* solution of problems. Clearly, there can be no such thing as purely repetitive thinking, just as there can be no such thing as inventive thinking which is devoid of repetitive components. Thinking – especially as applied to wide areas of everyday life – is an amalgam of the inventive and the repetitive, with one or the other predominating at different times.

Actions, speech acts, usages, manipulations, related to the

sphere of objectivation 'in itself' are, functionally, equivalents, irrespective of whether they arise as a result of inventive or of repetitive thinking. When I jump over a ditch for the first time, I may feel that I have consciously solved a problem; later, I jump the ditch a thousand times quasi-reflexively without any conscious thought at all – but it is really immaterial which process leads to the performance of the action: functionally they are equivalent, in that in either case I cross the ditch. As soon as we go beyond the plane of species-essential objectivation 'in itself', however, this functional equivalence ceases to obtain. It is easy to see why this should be so in the case of objectivations 'for itself'. A work of art produced by a routine and purely repetitive process cannot be the functional equivalent of a work of art generated in the process of the creative solution of a problem. As regards morals, the dialectic of intention and consequence can only arise and obtain if there is no functional equivalence between repetitive and inventive praxis (thought). If I say that I 'know' someone, I may mean simply that I can place him in one or another ready-made sociological slot – or it may mean that I seek to know him as an individual by identifying his ipseity, that which characteristically differentiates him from others; and my treatment of him, my behaviour towards him will vary accordingly – i.e. functional equivalence will here again be abrogated.

Let us repeat that repetitive thinking is still thinking, though the cogitative process is greatly abbreviated. But not every action (including mental action) requires inventive thinking, or does so except in very small measure. We would simply not be able to survive in the multiplicity of everyday demands and everyday activities if all of them required inventive thinking. Gehlen is perfectly right when he says that disengagement is an indispensable pre-condition for man's continued activity – i.e. acting in such a way that he is freed from the necessity of thinking inventively, and can act spontaneously without any conscious thought at all. If as a child I have used inventive thinking to learn a language, I can simply 'use' it in later life without stopping to reflect on the correctness of the grammar, the syntactical constructions and the use of vocabulary.[5] The fact that any sentence we formulate spontaneously can be both new and unique – in the sense that it has never been uttered by anyone before, the creative aspect of sentence formulation, can only be explained by assuming that the flow of speech is entirely spontaneous: that is, it becomes repetitive. Repetitive thinking and praxis can be seen as disengagement in that our capabilities are thus liberated so that they can be applied to the solution of tasks which can only be tackled via inventive praxis (or thinking). It is true that thereafter solution of these tasks can also become spontaneous and routine. But not ad infinitum. As we have said, in the last resort, the *raison d'être* of 'discharging' (via the appropriation of cognitive activities which tend to become repetitive) is to free us for the execution of such tasks and the acquisition of such experience, as can only be approached through inventive thinking (praxis). Repetitive praxis or thinking creates a sphere of spontaneity or immediacy which comes into existence through mediations both on the generic and on the personal level, and which serves as a basis for further mediations.

The fact that it serves as a basis for further mediations has several implications. Firstly, repetitive praxis and thinking enable us to do things in a relatively shorter time than would be possible with the use of inventive thinking. This represents a real saving in time. It also entails an accumulation of practice, thanks to which we can do things with greater accuracy. Repetitive praxis or thinking also enables us to do more than one thing at a time; several repetitive activities can be pursued in parallel. Inventive action can also run in parallel with repetitive activity. The conscious division of labour among the senses can also come about.

Since repetitive praxis (thinking) is spontaneous (that is to say, it absorbs mediation by immediacy) repetition functions smoothly where activity or thinking can be subordinated to a general schema. Hence, all repetitive praxis or repetitive thinking is a generalization – but one in which we do not have to follow through the whole of the generalizing process. In the main, thanks to our appropriation of a socially inherited general schema, we can dispense with reiterating the generalization process – but on the basis of such socially inherited generalized schemata we then proceed to erect further generalized schemata constructed from our own fund of experience, from our own thoughts and activities. Before using knife and fork we have to master the technique which derives from the nature of tools and the customary usages we have inherited. But people do not all hold their knives and forks in the same way: and in any one particular case, the generalized form of a personal way of holding and using these implements will be imprinted. The looser the unity between society and person, the more latitude there will be for personal variation in custom or for purely personal habit. But whatever the quantity of personal habit and personal variation in custom, this in itself tells us nothing about the individuality of the person. Very many of those who are given to custom variation and personal idiosyncrasy, are in fact particularistic persons; it is not in the practice of a habit that a person's individuality emerges, but in the content of that habit and in his relationship to it.

Repetitive praxis and thinking form, then, a necessary and cumulative basis for human action and thinking. However, as this is a generalization which is devoid of a generalization process (since it is spontaneous and immediate) it can and usually does induce a certain rigidity in human action and thinking. Repetitive praxis (or thinking) is constantly on the attack, and can encroach even on terrain which is, if optimum results are to be achieved, rightly the province of inventive praxis and thinking. It can and very often does render us slow to recognize what is novel, and to identify the problems inherent therein. In problematic situations – i.e. in situations where inventive thinking is called for – we often try to get by or make do with repetitive thinking. As we shall see, this can lead to the catastrophes of everyday life: more than this, it can also impede the development of the personality.

It must now be made clear that the subsumption of our acts and thoughts to general schemata is not the only form of mediated spontaneity. There is in addition another type of spontaneous thinking which is often at cross purposes with, or runs counter to, pure subsumption: the sense of singularity. If this sense were not, up to a point, built into every person, the catastrophes of everyday life would be unavoidable. This is a psychological fact which has cognitive value in everyday life (and not only there) and it is customary to call it 'intuition'. Intuition is then just as much a product of the accumulation of experience, and just as much the spontaneous manifestation of cumulated experience in the actions and thinking of the person as are repetitive praxis and thinking. As a derivative of personal experience it becomes part of the personality. But precisely because it becomes part of the personality it can be called upon and brought to bear in unforeseen circumstances, when one is surprised or taken aback, in any 'out of the ordinary' situation. Since intuition takes shape and develops through the medium of the personality, it is, like repetitive praxis and thinking, primarily mediated, the only difference being that in the case of intuition it is not personality that is subsumed under generality, but the solution of a concrete situation that is subsumed under the structure of the personality.

The most primitive form of intuitive thinking is the quasi-reflex. Examples can also be drawn from the realm of higher types. In *Die Eigenart des Aesthetischen* Lukács speaks of tact. Tact is indeed a product of accumulated experience, but there can be little doubt that its roots lie not in repetitive praxis but in personality: nor could appropriation of social custom, however intensive, generate tact. Again, tact is a necessary addendum to polite custom. However successfully a man may have acquired social manners, without tact he remains 'uncouth'.

In no way – as regards its essence – does intuitive thinking in general differ from tact. What we are dealing with here is the capacity built into the human cognitive structure to recognize new and unexpected phenomena (something which repetitive thinking cannot do) to 'sniff out' the nature of a problem in cognitive terms (without this, inventive thinking cannot get off the ground), to be suddenly sensible of something that is ostensibly commonplace as strange and inexplicable, and to be fascinated by it. Let me repeat: this is also a secondary growth, the product of a mediation (the personality as it develops mediates the experience) and it makes its appearance spontaneously, without any process of intentional thought. Deprived of intuitive thinking, man would perish just as surely as he would if deprived of repetitive thinking. He would be unable to scent danger, detect possible threat in the unknown or get to know his fellow creatures.

Intuitive thinking is not generalizing though it is based on generalizations (this is why intuition represents a necessary completion of rigid generalization). It is precisely for this reason that I have described its full cognitive value as limited to everyday thinking. In scientific thinking only what is generalized is known. Here too, intuition has a role to play but exclusively as the take-off point for inventive thinking. What is intuitively known must thereupon be generalized, step by step, via arguments: otherwise it will remain on the everyday cognitive level and never be absorbed into science or philosophy.

So far, we have been considering repetitive and intuitive thinking; and a few words may now be in order on the different types of inventive thinking. As I have said, this is the thinking used in problem solving. But we have to understand problem solving in a rather wide sense. It includes problem-solving in the narrow sense – i.e. when the problem is consciously formulated and considered: how best to bridge a stream, why I've stopped being friends with someone, what sort of future I plan for my child and how I acquaint it with my decision, etc. But it also includes appropriation of new thought or a new way of thinking, the consolidation of new experience, the acquisition of a new way of doing something, even the conscious fixation of new information.

But let me repeat: there is no fixed partition between inventive and repetitive thinking, since the wide field of everyday thinking and praxis contains a greater or lesser admixture of each. Thus, repetitive praxis and thinking are not simply the basis for inventive praxis and thinking but also the framework for heterogeneous creative activity and modes of cognition.

CHAPTER 8

The common properties of species-essential objectivations 'in itself'

The common properties of species-essential objectivations 'in itself' form the basis for everyday life-activity and provide a framework for its make-up. This is because appropriation of species-essential objectivation 'in itself' is the minimum necessary if a person is to sustain his existence, support himself, in a given social setting; and strict adherence to the norms thus generated is, up to a certain point, obligatory on every man, as otherwise he will simply be non-viable and perish. Analysis of the common properties of species-essential activity 'in itself' is therefore tantamount to analysis of the indispensable ground structure of everyday life and thinking.

Here we must make one reservation. It is true that everyday life and thinking are necessarily built up on the framework provided by species-essential objectivations 'in itself' and can only develop in such a framework; but everyday life and thought *as a whole* cannot be reduced to this framework or derived from it. Primarily, this is because there is more than one way of relating to this framework; and, secondly, because appropriation of this framework and its translation into activity open the door to completely different types of activity and of cognitive attitudes, and liberate the various forms of creative and inventive thinking and praxis, even within the framework of everyday life.

With this proviso in mind, let us now investigate the common properties of species-essential objectivation 'in itself' which serve as a basis for everyday life and thinking.

(a) Repetition

Species-essential activity 'in itself' is reiterated activity. A single action is not customary action; an object fortuitously handled once does not thereby become an object invested with concrete signification; a word uniquely uttered is not a word. So, it is not simply a question of our actions having to fit, *via* more or less elaborate mediation, into general social praxis (which is true of any and every social activity); rather, our actions must be repeatable, and are in fact repeated in their own 'thus-ness' by anyone.

All three restrictions are equally important. In clarification of the category of 'thus-ness' we may recall that the signification of a species-essential objectivation 'in itself' lies in its function. Therefore, in the repetition of a species-essential activity 'in itself', 'thus-ness' means that the activity is repeated in its own concrete function. The conditional conjunction 'if', for example is not 'repeated' by being repeatedly pronounced, but by being used repeatedly in its proper function – that of introducing a conditional clause. Bowing is not 'repeated' by simply bowing the head a number of times, but by doing this in its proper function – i.e. as a sign of greeting, respect or deference. The same motion may indeed occur in other circumstances (e.g. in athletic exercise) but it is then not part of the system of customs.

The rigidity of 'thus-ness' of norms belonging to species-essential objectivation 'in itself' is a historical variable. For example, in the earliest stages of 'work', the same stone could serve as hammer, chisel, ammunition for a sling, etc. Now that these functions have been clearly differentiated, and a specific tool is manufactured for each, this *ad hoc* usage has vanished from socially necessary work (production). It still appears, however, and frequently, in other types of work. If I want to drive in a nail and can't find the hammer, I make do with any object hard enough. In relation to tools, however, we can say that both in production and in consumption 'thus-ness' has gained ground. Exactly the opposite is true of customs. Customs in the modern world are looser, the connection between a custom and its ostensible function is less and less rigid, and the manner in which functions are fulfilled is more and more personal.

Repeatability, as I said above, is repeatability 'by anyone'. This means that for appropriation of species-essential objectivations 'in itself' only those capabilities are necessary which any healthy person can bring, more or less efficiently, to the task. Needless to say, not everyone will succeed in appropriating all the activities relating to all items of objectivation (for one thing, the division of labour rules this out), though in principle one could. Again, appropriation of species-essential objectivations 'in itself' requires little or no specialist training (none for customs, for language only in the special case of writing, none for learning how to handle objects, and for work only in the more advanced stages of the division of labour – especially if 'working' calls on artistic ability or scientific knowledge).

What is 'repeatability' from the standpoint of the 'person' is 'repeatedness' from the standpoint of the objectivation. A type of action appertains to species-essential objectivation 'in itself' only if it is repeated many times – that is to say, if its recurrence belongs to the essence of its existence as objectivation. Repeatedness is the basis for repeatability.

(b) The 'rule-character' and normativity

In the context we have been discussing (repeatedness as the basis of repeatability), we could cover only one aspect of the fact that species-essential objectivations 'in itself' provide action with rules. Rule is rule 'aligning with something' or 'referring to something'; its observance is taken for granted, that is to say, only failure to observe it is significant. (Violation of a rule varies in significance from one objectivation to another, and this is a problem to which we shall return – here I mention it only for the sake of completeness.) It was for this reason that Wittgenstein compared the rules of speech to those of games. The comparison is not entirely apt. Species-essential objectivations 'in itself' considered *as rules* can be appropriated by the 'person' only through practice – i.e. by repeating them; other rules (e.g. those of games) can be learned *before* they are applied.

The 'rule-character' not only marks the 'taken-for-grantedness' of the observance of rule but also its binding validity as well. In this respect, species-essential objectivations 'in itself', as the crystallized structures of norms and rules mapped out by repeated activity, have normative character. Discussing morals in Part II of this book, I pointed out that custom functions as concrete norm. But the ready-made world of things and objects which we have to use also imposes norms on what we can do in it. In this sense, the world we have to use is indissolubly linked with the normative functions of custom. We live in houses, we wear clothes, and it would be very difficult indeed to make any precise distinction here between the rules relating to the use of objects and the norms relating to custom.

We know that the normative character of species-essential objectivations 'in itself' is directed towards their functions. To observe the norm is tantamount to discharging the function. We know that 'thus-ness' is also related to the function, i.e. to the formative aspect. From this it follows that observance of the norm is not a 'point' but a 'field' function. I am observing a norm when I discharge (reiterate) that function which resides in the specific property of the species-essential objectivations 'in itself'; but I can discharge this function efficiently in more than one way, that is I can observe the norm in more than one way. Thereafter, which actions take root in me, and which yield ground to others, is not so much a matter of chance but the product of another structural property of everyday life – its economism – which we shall come to in due course. The extension of the field of the norm is not static, and it varies widely from one objectivation to another (it varies within them as well). Let us take the use of language as an example: in the case of a language whose word-order is fixed, violation of that order is at the same time violation of the normative field; but there is no such norm in the case of a language whose word-order is not fixed. The normative field is also dependent on the goal of an action. A blouse made for me or one for my daughter can discharge this function, but the same blouse cannot become a marketable commodity if it fails to reach an average level of a commodity 'blouse-norm'. In the first example the field is wider than that in the second.

Whatever its size, large or small, wide or narrow, the normative field always has a limit set to it. Using Ferenc Jánossy's terminology[1] I shall refer to this as the 'critical limit'. Its locus is given as the point where the expansion of the field begins to inhibit fulfilment of the function itself – that is to say at the point where action no longer corresponds to the norm. There can be all sorts of reasons for transgression of the critical limit, which usually, indeed in a large percentage of cases, happens inadvertently rather than by design. The chance element can arise from external causes (the intervention of unrehearsed and unforeseen factors) and from internal causes accompanying them (total or partial failure of intuitive abreaction, or inhibition of repetitive praxis and thinking). This is when the catastrophes of everyday life ensue. However, transgression of the critical limit may also be intentional: as in conscious suspensions of repetitive praxis and thinking, which may be prompted by all sorts of motivations and which may vary widely in value-content. If I am in more than my usual hurry I may go through a red light; anger may make me break something, or be rude to someone. Only in the case of language use can there be no intentional transgression of rules or norms – in speech acts where the linguistic formula fixes a custom, it is the custom that is being consciously transgressed, not the norm of language.

The observance of species-essential objectivations 'in itself' – seen as rules – has then a force-field; and this is in itself enough to show that the ontological basic factor of human activity – its alternative character – applies also to species-essential objectivations 'in itself'. In this case, the object of the alternative is not discharge of the function itself, but the manner in which that function is discharged.

(c) The sign system

As the bearers of reiterated communication, the species-essential objectivations are also systems of signs. Here we must make a proviso. The three kinds of species-essential objectivations 'in itself' do not form systems of signs to the same degree, nor do they do so in the same manner. Accordingly, it is only approximately true to speak of 'common properties' in this case.

Let us first see what is meant by 'sign'.

Only what has signification can have a 'sign' – at least on the level of everyday thought and praxis. The connection between signification and sign relates not only to those objectivations which embrace signification. Our everyday concepts of nature are enough to identify the signification of natural phenomena, at least from the standpoint of human praxis. Here too the sign is a function of the concrete signification both in space and in time. As far as the peasant is concerned, a build-up of cloud has no independent signification but is a sign of the approach of a natural phenomenon which matters from his point of view, and which guides much of his activity – heavy rain. Hence, he has learned to distinguish very precisely between clouds which are unlikely to produce heavy rain – which are therefore not signs of a gathering storm – and those which generally do bring rain, and which can therefore be interpreted as signs of approaching storm. In this case, there is a causal connection between the sign and the signified. In the case of a stone, the function of the sign is discharged by those properties of the stone which signify the uses to which the stone can be put: thus, colour, for example, is not a sign if it is devoid of significance in so far as the job in hand is

138

concerned. Phylogenetically and ontogenetically, the recognition of properties which do not act as signs postdates the recognition of those properties which do.

As Quine[2] points out, children learn to distinguish between a ball and a cube long before they can distinguish a red ball from a green one. This is simply because the shape of the ball is a sign of its use, while its colour is not. This is, of course, not to deny that colour too in certain circumstances can function as a sign: the green cherry indicates its unripeness, hence its inedibility: a red cherry indicates its readiness to be eaten.

As is the case with all human objectivations, the sign function inherent in species-essential objectivations 'in itself' differs from that attributed to natural phenomena in that it is intentional: it is not a property independent of man that becomes a sign for human praxis. Breaking the dishes, hitting someone – these are signs of anger: a smile is a sign of friendship, receptivity, etc. In the case of human beings, we can speak of the intentionality of signs even where, to all appearances natural phenomena alone are involved. Thus, moaning is usually the sign of mental or bodily pain. Weeping indicates grief; but it can be the sign of happiness or it can be hypocritical; in the first case, the sign refers to one signification, in the second case to many. So we regard these signs as intentional since the alternative character of activity applies to them also. We can grit our teeth and bear pain in silence (a posture which will itself then become the sign of pain); we can hold back tears, in which case facial expression becomes the index of grief. It is very rare for a sign to be a pure reflex-expression.

Here we have to stress that the concept of 'metacommunication' unites heterogeneous elements on a basis of superficial similarities.[3] It reduces to a common denominator such disparate items as the report of a starting pistol (which is not a sign but a signal), the nod of the head indicating assent (which properly belongs to the customary system), gesticulation (which as an individual trait does not belong to the current of custom inherent in species-essential objectivation 'in itself'), etc. For our purposes it is extremely important to distinguish between sign and signal, and between signs proper to species-essential objectivation 'in itself' on the one hand, and signs of no more than personal significance on the other.

The problem which presents itself when we make the distinction between sign and signal is primarily one of conventionality. In a wide sense, every sign is conventional in so far as we all understand it or can understand it. Historically, however it has developed independently of the will of persons or groups of persons, even when – as in the case of language – there is no causal connection between sign and signification. It is true that a concrete custom can be 'introduced', and, in a narrower sense, can be created by agreement (e.g. the introduction of a national coat-of-arms). But the creation of a custom by agreement can never be arbitrary: it has to be closely integrated with the established system of custom. The preconditions for the introduction of a new national coat-of-arms are (a) the existence of the custom of having a coat-of-arms, and (b) general intelligibility of the symbols used in the new one.

A sign cannot, therefore, be explained in terms of the simple relationship 'one sign-one signification'. A sign is a sign only by virtue of its belonging to a complex, and only thereby does it carry signification. For example, the sign-function of a word does not arise only because the word refers to things or events or actions (which could also generate signals and not signs) but because it comprises those contexts in which the word is customarily used and the contexts in which the word could potentially be used – the totality of the function which the word discharges in the given system.

The signal, however, is conventional in the narrower meaning of the word. At any time we can agree conventionally to stop at the green light instead of the red, to start runners in a race by means of applause instead of a pistol shot, etc. Exactly which convention we settle on is largely an arbitrary decision; and if that decision is in any given case less arbitrary, this is due less to the objectivation order we have inherited on the social plane, than to such considerations as: is the conventional signal readily observable? is it convenient? is it concise? etc. That is to say, the signal is or can be isolated. Language can also serve as a signal but as an articulated sonic complex rather than in its true linguistic function.

It has long been realized that language and custom share common properties; and Saussure was the first to suggest (in the *Cours de linguistique générale* ...) that language and customary signification systems should be studied together – a proposal to which we owe the new discipline of semiology. Exactly what role the world of material objects plays in a signification system, however, is a question to which very little attention has been paid, except perhaps in so far as symbols are concerned.

The sign is the bearer of the functions discharged in social activity; i.e. it carries a signification. The sign is inserted, accordingly, only where the signification of the signified cannot be presented directly. In most cases, the signification of the world of objects as means of production, consumption or manipulation, is presented directly, and therefore the world of objects requires no objective signs. Where, exceptionally, the signification or function needs to be labelled, this is done not by means of an objective sign, but *via* heterogeneous sign-systems (e.g. instruction leaflets, directions for use, etc.).

The world of objects is, however, an important signification system in so far as it transmits and mediates the meanings of customs. By this, I am not suggesting that every sign mediating the meaning of a custom is a thing. There are at least as many purely lingual signs, and signs expressed *via* a bodily gesture or movement. Thanking, bowing, showing respect, praying, chatting, giving way to elderly people – these actions either require no mediation *via* things or very little. At the same time, we have to remember that the mediation of a sign *via* a thing is not tantamount to the sign-function of the thing. If I raise my hat or wave my handkerchief, these actions involve mediation by a thing, which does not, however, function as a sign. The hat is not the sign of 'paying respect': the sign is the gesture of lifting the hat. The handkerchief is not the sign of bidding farewell, the act of waving it is: I could replace the handkerchief by simply waving my hand, or by saying 'goodbye'. The object itself functions as sign if its material existence, its 'thus-ness' refers to the signification – if only to the signification of a custom.

The fact that someone has a palace, the fact that it is that sort of palace – the fact that someone else has a hovel, the fact that it is that sort of hovel – these facts act as signs. They are not simply signs of richness or poverty but of the customs of certain social strata or classes; they signify the class to which the owner of the palace or the hovel belongs, and the custom structure to which he adheres. Clearly, both palace and hovel are susceptible of individual variation in habit and taste: but again, only within the limits of the normative order, the system of rules – within the critical limit. In this respect, the critical limit is a variable in time. In the Middle Ages, for example, dress was fixed by custom, and if a high-born damsel donned peasant clothing she was overstepping the critical limit. With the growth of bourgeois society, it became more difficult to make inferences from clothes. But the prescriptive norm and the critical limit have not ceased to exist though they may have shifted. It is not done to wear your bathing suit in town, nor does one stroll about in broad daylight in evening wear. One still dresses up for the ceremonial occasion, black is still the

141

sign of mourning, shorts suggest holidays (especially in summer), etc. Formal and informal clothing cover our bodies in much the same way; but it cannot be said that they have the same connotation.

What is clear is that these things (objects) have not acquired their social meaning and function as signs independently of their material propensity. Large and imposing public buildings could become signs of the power of a Renaissance city because their material nature bespoke durability, they stood out from among other buildings, they caught the eye of the stranger entering the city, they provided a suitable surface for aesthetic expression, etc.

The great majority of objects as bearers of meaning are signs, not symbols. Clothes, houses, silverware on the table, the closed door, a ruin – all of these have a sign-function, but not necessarily a symbolic value. The expression 'symbolic value' goes to show that the symbol does not simply relate to meaning, but always to value or to a complex of values; it is the linguistic or material representation of these value-complexes.

Of course, value can be negative (*Unwert*) as well as positive. The symbol represents this value which is usually reflected and sanctified by tradition. It does not *present* – as the sign does – but *represents*. And precisely as a result of its representative nature it is not simply part of an objectivation structure, nor does it acquire its meaning from the use-function it discharges therein: rather, it is from the idea which it represents. A worn-out dress is not the same dress, but a tattered flag is the same flag.

Of course, a symbol can be of personal-individual value. A lock of the beloved's hair can have symbolic value for the lover, though it will have no value of any kind for anybody else. At the same time, unlike the pure sign, the symbol can, in art, attain the level of species-essential objectivation 'in itself'. Once it has been elevated to the aesthetic sphere, an object represents – i.e. it becomes symbolical. In poetic usage, a word has not only meaning but symbolic value as well.

I have stressed that in everyday life and everyday thought custom-signs and word-signs have no symbolic value; but this is not to deny the presence of symbols in species-essential objectivations 'in itself'. Sacramental and votive objects and actions (customs) are imbued with symbolic value – e.g. the altar, communion; and so are objects which embody integrations, and some of the customary actions related to these integrations – e.g. coat-of-arms, blood-brotherhood, etc. The words we use may also have symbolic value, particularly those which have entered the vocabulary of everyday life from the realm of myth, e.g. Eros. Some words may function as signs and have symbolic value which can be recognized from the context in which the word is used (cf. 'spring' and 'the Spring').

The appropriation of species-essential objectivation 'in itself' is therefore always *pari passu* the appropriation of signification systems.

(d) Economy

Economy is a common property shared by the various moments in species-essential objectivation 'in itself'. It is crystallized in the objectivations themselves, and is manifested in their appropriation and in relations with them. Economy always relates to the given aim (the given function). The species-essential objectivations 'in itself' (all their elements) are so articulated as to require, in the discharge of their functions, the minimum exertion and the minimum input of inventive thought; and, further, that their functions be discharged in a minimum time relative to the aim of these functions. Here, we put equal emphasis on minimum effort, minimum input of inventive thought, and minimum duration (always remembering that this is in relation to the given aim or function). It is worthwhile pointing this out since these factors are not always in mutual harmony; as types of objectivation activity vary, so may one or another factor 'take over'. (The relationship between the three factors does indeed vary in all objectivation moments, at different historical periods.)

A load is less heavy if we carry it properly; a movement is quicker if we have practised it. No inner compulsion is felt in the work process to choose the more difficult way, no value attaches to choice of the more difficult; if such a choice should be made, it would be motivated by considerations lying outside the species-essential objectivation 'in itself', considerations of a moral, religious, political or aesthetic nature.

The lack of any need for invention (inventive thinking) has in itself economy-value. Often, however, absence of any need for inventive thinking is sufficiently powerful to outweigh all other factors making for economy; and as a result the overall degree of economy involved in producing or using an object is actually reduced. We tend to fight shy of 'swapping abilities' though by doing so we could perform our habitual actions more efficiently: the flight from taking thought becomes an inhibiting factor. Fear of a spell of inventive thought, however short (which is also an

143

ergonomic device), can be a conservative force. The flight from inventive thought, the attraction of routine, represent an ergonomic force which is normally stronger in the customary world of social norms than it is in the production of objects or in their use.

The way in which the appropriation of customs is economized, depends to a great extent on whether a given custom relates to objects or an object, sets preconditions for human interaction, or regulates interaction itself. In the former two cases, what we said about the use of things applies with equal force: the aim is to do something with the minimum effort, in as short a time as possible, with a minimum recourse to inventive thought: which is exactly what we do in repetitive praxis. In the third case however, the key factor is the category of minimum recourse to inventive thought, so much so that observance of the custom is very largely time-consuming, and may, as far as the pure function is concerned, actually demand surplus effort. From the standpoint of the person, therefore, economy in communication customs is saving of thought, not of movement; the ergonomic aspect of a custom is that it is accepted and practised without reflection, i.e. 'naturally'.

The degree to which language is or is not 'economical', is a constant source of dispute among linguists. According to the 'convenience theory' of Curtius, language always seeks the most economic way of functioning; against this, Leshien and Sievers point very pertinently to the many grammatical properties that have no real function in linguistic usage: many languages appear to be overloaded with superficial complications. My own view is that the situation with regard to language is more intricate than it is in the case of custom, since of all species-essential objectivation 'in itself' language has the most extensive functional field; what is ergonomically efficient from the standpoint of one function, may not be so from that of another: and what may act towards simplification in one function may act towards complication in another.

But it is not by chance (as Saussure believed) that language comes into being as sound, i.e. as spoken language: rather, this is a consequence of the economy of language, though other factors play a part. The fact is that sound can fulfil the most heterogeneous functions with a minimal expense of energy. As for the structure of language (and of individual languages) we must go along with Jespersen when he asserts that – in spite of the differences which cultural and social antecedents have generated between languages – all languages tend towards simplification, i.e. towards linguistic economy. Jespersen supports his thesis by pointing to such factors as the following: (a) in general, formulas tend to get shorter and shorter, (b) there is a tendency for the memory to be less and less burdened with many special formulae, (c) derivations tend to become regularized, (d) syntax tends to crystallize towards eliminating irregularities, (e) language tends to become more abstract and analytical, and thus increases its combinatorial power, (f) recapitulation of grammatical agreement becomes superfluous, (g) fixed word-order ensures unambiguous understanding. To sum up: 'The evolution of language shows a progressive tendency from inseparable, irregular conglomeration to freely and regularly combinable short elements.'[4]

Grammatical structure itself tends towards economy: i.e. towards formulations which, given the manifold uses to which language is put, can be appropriated as simply and spontaneously as possible. The same tendency towards economy is found in the case of sound clusters which are difficult to pronounce: these are smoothed out in spoken language *via* assimilation as it tends towards ease and rapidity of delivery, though they may be retained in the written form of the language.

The case of speech acts which discharge certain concrete functions is more complicated. Because of the communicative nature of language, custom and social manners play a very large part in speech. If I feel thirsty in company I do not simply utter the word 'water!' though this would be the shortest formula. I use some such formulation as 'Do you think I could have a glass of water?' or 'Could you please give me a glass of water?' But this is only an apparent departure from the economy rule. The fact is that the expression 'Could you please let me have a glass of water' has a quite different social meaning from the exclamation 'water!'. The meaning of the exclamation 'water!' is not immediately clear: the speaker might be thirsty, but equally he might be feeling ill. The longer formulae are not simply in accordance with accepted standards of courtesy; they carry social connotations which differentiate them from the shorter formulae which exist alongside them.

(e) Situatedness

The foregoing example brings us face to face with another problem – the fact that certain items of species-essential objectiva-tion 'in itself' are strictly bound to certain situations. In the case of language, internal speech (speaking to oneself) forms an exception: internal speech is not 'situated'. But this is because when we speak to ourselves we are using language not as a means of communication but as a vehicle for thinking, and thinking is not necessarily bound to any situation (though it may be).

As regards the world of objects we have to make a further proviso in this connection. It is not in communicative situations that the great majority of objects play a decisive part, and the same goes for the uses to which these objects are put: hence, they may not be attached to interactional situations. As far as objects are concerned, situatedness is only relevant if the objects or implements are signs of customs, or if customs are observed in the relationship obtaining with these objects or implements. If a table is properly set with all the cutlery to hand in the correct positions, the fact that one of the diners uses only the spoon has to be explained in specific terms of uncouthness, discourtesy or simply a desire to make oneself conspicuous. At a picnic, however, it would be quite 'natural' to use the spoon as an all-purpose utensil.

As a general rule, every custom is bound to a situation. Learning to observe a custom means, in fact, learning in what circumstances it is valid, in what situation it can be applied. Greetings and salutations differ with time of day; we do not behave in church as we do in school; we do not talk to young people in the same way as we do to old. Cultures differ in the degree of meticulousness by which customs are 'broken down' according to situation, and the point at which the individual transgresses the field of norm by mistaking the situation, varies. But all cultures 'break customs down' up to a point by linking them to situation.

The tie between speech and situation is the most radical and, at the same time, the most multi-functional. The use of language as speech is meaningful only in the context and the situation in which it is uttered. A word which has more than one meaning can be used with impunity because the situation in which it is uttered (i.e. the context, or the specific part it plays in the speaker's situation) identifies one of the meanings as the correct one. The same words 'I love you' may be used by a child to its mother or by a man to a woman, but the meanings are quite different. We can divide sentences into two categories depending on the way in which they are situated; into 'occasional sentences' and 'standing sentences'.[5] 'Occasional sentences' are understandable only when bounded to a certain situation. If someone walking along the street suddenly cries 'Clear off!' we may have doubts about his sanity. 'Your hands are dirty' can only be uttered rationally if we are speaking to someone. Words like 'How?', 'Why?', 'You don't say!' are understandable only as reactions to something already said. If I look out on a June morning and say 'It's not raining', this immediately makes sense since it has a function in the given situation (I don't have to take my raincoat). But if I look out on Budapest on a June morning and say 'It's not snowing', this does not make sense, since the possibility of snow in June in Budapest does not arise.

The bonded relation between word and situation in a 'standing sentence' is looser and it is different in nature. I can say 'Peter visited Paul yesterday' or 'Budapest is on the Danube' in any situation. And yet even these sentences are situation-related in a wider sense: the 'situation' being presented by the norms of social and personal custom. If during a conversation about the weather, I suddenly announce 'Budapest is on the Danube', people will be surprised to say the least. And if I inform an acquaintance of mine who knows neither Peter nor Paul, that Peter visited Paul, the reaction will be the same. Since the purpose of communication is to induce in others either assent or dissent, there is no point in uttering a sentence which cannot produce either: not even if the sentence makes sense, in itself and apart from the situation.

It must be emphasized that situatedness is a property which is characteristic not only of species-essential objectivations in itself. For example, political and moral decisions are also bonded to situation. There are, however, important differences. Violation of situatedness leads, in the case of species-essential objectivations 'in itself' to irrational action or utterance, and in some cases to the catastrophes of everyday life; but this is not the case with political or moral decisions, where violation of situatedness is not necessarily irrational. Again, while observance of situatedness of norms in the case of species-essential objectivation 'in itself' says nothing about individuality as such,[6] in the case of political and moral decisions identification of situatedness (i.e. doing the right thing at the right time in the right place) is a mark of personality. Finally, while in the case of species-essential objectivation 'in itself', situated action becomes a function of repetitive praxis and thinking, in the case of other types of activity, identification of and application to the situation is normally performed by intuitive and inventive (sometimes purely theoretical) thinking.

CHAPTER 9

The special properties of species-essential objectivations 'in itself'

So far, we have considered species-essential objectivation 'in itself' as a unified structure: that is, we have been concerned only with the basic tendencies common to all constituents of this objectivation. But the three main constituents of such objectivation – things, customs and language – have their own special properties, which are in themselves heterogeneous. In what follows, we shall consider these special traits and offer a brief analysis of the internal differentiations of each species-essential objectivation 'in itself'. This analysis is not intended to be exhaustive; indeed, I restrict myself deliberately to those factors and aspects which are of immediate relevance to our present purpose – a comprehension of everyday action and thinking.

(a) The world of objects

When we speak of our 'relations with the world of objects' what we really mean is 'relations with humanized nature'. Every object and every successful act of manipulation of that object afford proof of man's power over nature. We must nevertheless distinguish between objects as (a) means for the satisfaction of our needs (means of use and means of consumption) and (b) as means of production. The distinctive utilization factor is often built into the ipseity of the object, but by no means invariably. One and the same implement may serve for both production and consumption: but implicit in these different uses is a difference which is of both social and personal significance. It is socially significant because, by using means of production, we enter the social division of labour; and our success in handling the means of production is a measure of our success in filling the place allotted to us in the social division of labour. Our successful handling of the means of consumption, however, has little to do with our place in the social division of labour. Of course, this is no more than a relative independence. Those belonging to certain social strata often do not know how to make proper use of means of consumption which are customary in other strata: often indeed they cannot even understand what these articles are for. Since the rise of capitalism, the historical tendency has been for us to be able to use more articles than we can produce. This is not to say that human universality is convertible into the act of manipulating and using more tools. This is indeed a factor in universality, but only one.

The fulfilment-value of the use of means of consumption is always private. This is not to say that the use of these means is itself private. As we said above, the use of means of consumption is determined by custom and tradition. But usage that is socially normative serves the satisfaction of private desires and needs. We learn to practise both the production and the consumption of cigarettes; but while the latter aims at the satisfaction of a purely private need, the former serves a social need. The fact that the borderline between the two is not always clear-cut is not significant.

From what we have said it follows that the normative principle implicit in means and implements (the field of the norm) is not uniformly intensive and extensive in the use of means of production, on the one hand, and means of consumption, on the other. As a general tendency, we may claim that the normative field is narrower when the implements are being used as means of production than it is when they are being used as means of consumption.

It has to be added that the norms governing the satisfaction of private needs may be intensified by other social expectations, and their field may be narrowed. For example, I can very well satisfy my private needs, in the case of hunger, even if I don't know how to use a fork and knife properly: but this is only true if I am on my own. If others are present they would look askance at my lack of *savoir-faire* and so I am constrained to remain within the narrower field of the normative activity: this way, I avoid the catastrophes of everyday life.

It is, however, in the relationship between use (of means) and the development of human capabilities that we see the greatest difference between tools as means of production and as means of consumption: or, between the use of an object as a means of production and its use as a means of consumption. The point is that in the case of consumption what I appropriate is a meaning already given to an object (i.e. a tool) in so far as I use it appropriately, i.e. in accordance with its functions. In this sense, I construe 'consumption' as the appropriation of any meaningful object in which the key role is played by the relay of social meaning (or social import). (Learning how to use a flag is equivalent to appropriation of the social import inherent in the flag.) In appropriating the representation of an object, therefore, man does not bring anything really new into being – for the most part, not even new objects but certainly never new meaning (i.e. an object invested with new meaning and capable of new functions). But when we use things as the means of production, the essence of what we are doing is bringing new things into being. These may carry the same significance as objects already existing; but they may also be invested with new meanings. The work process not only brings into being single things that do not as yet exist, but also, in the process of history, an ever-increasing number of novel types of object and of implement: things which have never before existed, and which accordingly are invested with new meanings, new functions and new uses. This is why inventive thinking cannot simply be seen as a relatively brief developmental stage preceding repetitive thinking in the work process. On the social average (i.e. not in every case) and as a general social tendency (not in all societies to the same degree), the work process continually renews inventive thinking. In the mere use of things, man (as person) can only realize himself *via* moral mediation. In the work process (creating new things via the use of things), however, he can up to a point realize himself – i.e. he can objectivize his personal capabilities – even without moral mediation. It does not follow that this is something he can do in all circumstances. Even if we disregard the alienation factor, it remains true that not every type of work affords the requisite possibilities for this.

In the use of things (by which we now understand *both* types of usage) we have to do with a dual feed-back. This dual feed-back divides the world of material objectivation from the structures of everyday custom and from language. Nature and society together endorse our activities as successful or disown them as unsuccessful; and this goes for all our activities, from pressing the lift button to removing a goose liver. In contrast, the customs governing social relations and everyday language continue to function with only social feed-back.

150

This dual feed-back has an inner affinity with fulfilment-value. Fulfilment-value is simply the satisfaction of a need, or, to put it more accurately, our own self-assertion in the satisfaction of a need. Human needs are heterogeneous and are interposed by society with manifold mediations. For example, a social custom may satisfy a certain need by hampering or annulling the satisfaction of other needs. That is to say, the function of custom *vis-à-vis* needs is ambiguous; and fulfilment-value is often coupled with non-fulfilment. Speech can also be a means of satisfying a need, but functionally it can also be a means of preventing that satisfaction.

It is a property of the world of objects (means) however, that by virtue of its essence it is need-satisfying and invested with fulfilment-value. Directly or indirectly, it is precisely the *aim* of work to produce use-value: that is to say, to produce objects and implements which will satisfy needs. Every object (every means) is for something: it satisfies a need, and when it fails to satisfy that need it loses its signification. Nor is there any ambiguity in the way in which objects satisfy needs. In no object is there implicit the means for preventing the satisfaction of some other need, or satisfaction by means of another object. If I refrain from using some object, this happens *in spite of* the signification and function of that object, and for reasons (of morals, health, etc.) which transcend the use of objects.

The importance of fulfilment-value in the case of the mere utilization of products in everyday use is clear; and it is equally clear that the supply of such products is, in the final analysis, the aim of the work process. But does this hold good of the work-process itself? Can we speak of fulfilment-value in the case of the labour process, the activity of working?

Satisfaction of need in the human case differs, *inter alia,* from that found in the animals, in that, for humans, satisfaction of a need is at the same time the realization of an aim. Hence, realization of an aim can be in itself a human need. Successful action in the use of nature is the simplest and the most contradiction-free form of successful teleological positing. In itself, creation is always an unconditional success. When the corn ripens, when we make a hammer, we have scored a victory. Success of this rudimentary nature is very rare in the realm of purely social action, occurring only in extreme cases. What is a success from one point of view may easily be a failure from another. Again, success can be a basis for further human activity which, in the event, may make the original 'success' very

151

questionable. But, if success achieved in work forms a basis for new activities, this need not in itself detract from the successful nature of the original work. Like the objectivized forms of man's purpose, the results of work are principially invested with fulfilment-value, even when – because of the concrete nature of labour – the activity itself is not invested with any such value.

The fact that even successful work has, in so far as the labour process is concerned, no fulfilment-value, is primarily due to the alienation of labour. In expecting work to become a necessity of life under communism, Marx was also looking forward to the inclusion of fulfilment-value as a component in the process of labour.

(b) The world of custom

The world of custom is much more elaborately differentiated and stratified than even the world of objects. The nature of its strata depends very largely on such factors as: what sort of content is regulated by any one stratum, how wide is the field governed, how pressing is the social need or interest dictating the degree of governance etc. The primary customary norms of social coexistence are those with the smallest, most intensive and most stringent fields. They may have a moral value-content; they may also be morally neutral. The concrete forms as manifest may vary from one historical age to another, and from one social stratum to another, but all such manifest forms express in essence one and the same social interest. That certain human needs have to be satisfied not in public but privately in a specially designed location, that we greet each other as a sign that communication is about to take place between us, that specific wear is donned for ceremonial occasions, that human bonds are ritually solemnized: all of this, however varied in concrete usages, serves the same social function.

However colourful, plentiful and manifold the spectrum of concrete custom-types in which the primary custom-norms manifest themselves, it has to be repeated that they all serve the same function: all regulate the most general preconditions of societal life. It is because of this that they are found in all historical ages and throughout all social strata, even though they may take different ritual form.

It is worth stressing here that a rite is not itself a custom: it is the concrete form taken by a custom. Of course, a custom cannot be 'generally' observed except in the form of a rite. The rite belongs to the custom. It is important, however – especially in the case of the primary social custom-norms – to distinguish between custom proper and rite; if for no other reason than that rite often becomes loosely defined (e.g. a variety of rites may express one and the same custom) without a corresponding relaxation in the prescriptive force of the custom. Church wedding gives place to civil wedding, religious funerals are replaced by lay funerals: that is, the rites change, but the age-old tradition built into societal life – that these events are culminating points of everday life – is retained intact.

Characteristic of the primary customs regulating societal life is the fact that the intensity of their observance varies only very slightly from one person to another. One consequence of this is that, in essence, observance of a primary custom regulating societal life (and of the rites subsumed by it) tells us nothing at all about human personality – no more than we can learn from the fact that someone can drink from a glass or use a knife and fork.

Gross breach of these primary customs, however, is senseless. If someone decides that from now on he will ignore everybody, or go about naked, he will be rightly regarded as abnormal. He is not expressing his personality thereby, but demonstrating irrationality. At the same time, it is not at all irrational if one does not observe custom in certain *concrete* cases (e.g. if one fails to greet certain people). In such cases, breach of the custom amounts to proof of the custom's validity in general, and to proof of its validity for the person who fails to observe it in particular: since the very reason why he withholds a greeting from a certain person is that greeting is a sign of respect – and respect is something he is not prepared to show in this particular case. (Language knows no such 'exceptions'. Any senseless sentence indicates breach of the norms of language.)

From the primary custom-norms of societal existence we have to distinguish particularistic customs. These regulate the lives and actions of people living in certain integrations and certain strata, and are consequently the manifest forms of the interests, aims, axiological systems and ideologies of a given integration. The regulative prescription affects contacts within the given integration, and also contacts between integrations. In itself, the world of particularistic customs is extraordinarily complex and heterogeneous. At random we might mention such examples as religious customs including religious ceremonial, customs within an estate, customs belonging to institutions, etc. The rites associated with the elementary customs of societal life often assume shape as particularistic customs: that is to say, they belong to the system of particularistic custom.

Particularistic customs and custom-systems are distinguished from the primary customs of societal life first of all in that they always have a greater or lesser degree of ideological content; hence, their observance and the manner in which they are observed invariably express a relationship to the values obtaining in a given integration, whether this relationship is spontaneous or conscious (reflected). That I should address people with whom I wish to communicate is not in itself an ideological act: but it becomes ideological when I address one group as 'My Lords, Ladies and Gentlemen' and another group as 'you lot'.

In the case of the observance of particularistic customs, the amplitude of variation in intensity can be very large, and this variation factor can reflect personality, particularly the moral personality. The intensity factor in the observance of a particularistic custom type is in fact an index, the manifest form of the extent to which the person has become identified with his own integration, and the extent to which he has internalized its values and its ideology. Duels can be fought as a mere act of ceremony, as a choreographical act, but they can be fought to the death as well. On the whole, the tendency is for identification to be esteemed in proportion to its intensity in any given integration, though here again concrete cases can be found where intensity of identification is regarded by public opinion as 'hubris'.

In the case of particularistic custom, we can learn much about a personality, not only from intensity of observance, but also from the manner in which the observance is practised. One reason for this is that these customs are not primary but complex systems which can engage the personality structure in several modes and from several angles. A number of particularistic customs relate not to any specific type of interaction but to behaviour in general – a way of behaving which is adhered to in the most heterogeneous situations ('a perfect gentleman').

From the particularity of this custom-system it follows that at any given time different customs are valid for different people. While it is a breach of custom for a man to weep, women can weep as much as they like without transgressing their own custom-norms. As long as social structures and their integrations are unassailed, the intensity of particularistic custom is in no way threatened by this division of labour, nor is the need to identify with them. When structures and integrations begin to weaken inwardly however, plurality of customs will turn out to be one intellectual and emotional source of decrease in intensity of observance and of the infringement of custom.

We now come to what is perhaps the most striking difference between the primary customs and the particularistic customs: the fact that infringement of the latter is not necessarily nonsensical or irrational. This is true not only in individual cases of infringement; these, as we have seen, are not infrequent with regard to the primary custom-norms as well, though here they take place against a background of recognition of the general validity of the custom-norms. Total infringement of a particularistic custom goes to show that the infringer no longer recognizes the validity of the given custom. A decision to refrain from greeting people in future is a nonsensical gesture. But when Corneille's Polyeucte decides that he will no longer do sacrifice to the ancient gods, this is very far from being a nonsensical gesture. It is an expression of the fact that he no longer recognizes the divinity of the ancient gods, and that he denies the beliefs and the ideology expressed in the sacrificial ceremonies. He has accepted another ideology and another system of customs – those of Christianity. Due to this property of our relationship with particularistic customs – the possibility of denying their validity – there is a radical distinction between the custom system and the world of objects and language, that is, the other two constituents of species-essential objectivation 'in itself'. Since the particularistic custom-norms are by definition ideological in character, their infringement carries an even more unmistakably ideological stamp. Of course, this does not apply in cases where a particularistic norm is infringed although its validity is not questioned (that is, where the infringement is due to desire, pressing need, cowardice, etc.), but it does apply when it is infringed deliberately, when I 'give notice' to the content (values) expressed in such customs.

I am going to term the third type of customs 'conditional customs'. One can define as conditional all those customs which are indeed characteristic of a human grouping or of a relatively large number of human beings, but observance of which is not a *sine qua non* for the person who has to occupy a duly allotted place in the social division of labour and live therein according to the relevant norms. They include a large number of customs which cannot be infringed in principle: they can only be observed – e.g. superstitious customs. If I count the corners of the room before going to sleep so that my dreams may come true, if I touch wood to avoid bad luck,

I am observing customs which are allied with certain superstitions. But if I refrain from counting the corners of the room or fail to touch wood, I am not infringing any customs.

There are, however, certain conditional customs which can be infringed. These are local customs, customs relating to narrow integrations, etc. Failure to adhere to the rules of a masonic lodge can lead to expulsion of the offender: though he can remain very much the man he was before expulsion, respectable nobleman or a burgher.

This is the most heterogeneous group of customs, so much so that we cannot hope to sketch even in outline the relationship obtaining between personality and customary behaviour (degree of intensity and manner of observance). Suffice it to point out that in the case of the custom-types belonging to this group, this relationship shows an extraordinarily high variance factor, so much so that we are often confronted with singularities. It is clear and easy to understand, however, that total rejection of the customs in this grouping is as rational and intelligible as it is in the case of the particularistic customs. Here, I should like to point out, however, that classification of a custom as general (i.e. belonging to primary societal life) or particularistic or conditional, is very far from being rigid. One and the same custom can be particularistic at one moment and can be promoted thence to the level of primary social customs; just as a particularistic custom may be demoted to the level of conditionality. Many a religion has seen its sacred ceremonies demoted under the pressure of successor religions to the status of conditional customs or superstitions.

In the unbelievably vast number of conditional customs and their global expansion, we can, however, detect something of a general principle – the 'contagious' nature of custom formation. Custom helps man to find his way about the intricate structure of human activity; it lends framework and form to everyday life (often aesthetic and moral in content), and these factors lead to an enormous proliferation of customs. No group, however small – even a group of friends – is without its customs, its traditions; and no group is too small for infringement of its customs and traditions not to be attended with certain consequences for the infringer's relationship with the integration (if not always for his personality).

This is the place at which we must touch briefly on the problem of personal customs. If we are to cope successfully with the heterogeneous activities of everyday life, we have to be able to count on 'order', on 'regularity'. The objectivized forms of this regularity are provided by social-general or special systems of custom. These determine not merely the specific forms action is to take, but also a kind of 'life-rhythm'. We get up in the morning, have lunch at noon and eat dinner at night – in their tempo-setting regularity these factors amount to 'disengagement' in Gehlen's sense. But if custom delineates the rhythmical framework, a very big part in the concrete shaping of the life-rhythm is also played by the anthropological 'thusness' of the person. The slow or clumsy person takes longer to perform certain socially necessary activities than the fast or skilful person does. Over and above this, personal properties and needs have a far-reaching effect on the manner in which customs are observed, the special forms taken, the allocation of time thereto, etc. Personal custom-variants arise within the framework of the general custom as observed, but these cannot overstep the critical limits set to the field of socially valid customs.

Personal customs serve to regulate a person's life only within the framework characteristic for that person. 'Personal' here will only very rarely mean 'practised by no one else'. Even if someone has the custom of bathing every day in the Danube during the winter, he and we can be reasonably sure that someone else is spartan enough to do the same. The personal aspect of a custom does not derive from its singularity but rather from the fact that it is not related to any valid and socially objectivized system of custom, or to the collective images prevalent in this or that circle. Suspension of personal custom is therefore never infringement of social norm. At the same time, personal custom does much to characterize the personality of the individual person, just as does infringement (or, more accurately, suspension, discontinuance) of personal custom. And even though the singularity of a personal custom does not consist in its being shared with no one else, it remains true that the system of personal customs as a complex, and the relationship between this complex and the objectivized system of social custom, are unique. No two people share exactly the same structural system of personal customs.

The primary meaning of 'habituation' is 'formation of repetitive praxis'. It is the sphere of species-essential objectivation 'in itself' in relation to which we *have to* develop repetitive praxis – otherwise we perish. But this is not to suggest that habit is no more than the appropriation of species-essential objectivation 'in itself'. In a wide sense, 'habit' means the 'becoming natural for us' of certain types of action, of decision-taking, or behavioural attitude, of thinking: their practice is no longer open to question, as they have become coherent parts of our personality. We can become habituated to acting honestly, to being outspoken, to lecturing, to thinking mathematically: we can even become habituated to not giving in unconditionally to whatever schema of repetitive praxis and repetitive thinking happens to present itself. In so far as this is concerned, Gehlen is right when he asserts that in the human world there is no firm dividing line between *Antrieb* (urge, drive) and *Gewohnheit* (habit, habituation). A characteristic index of the process of developing an individual personality lies in the fact that personal habits far outstrip those appropriated with the world of custom.

(c) Language

In Sapir's words, language is a 'perfectly homogeneous medium'; and this homogeneity is what distinguishes it both from the world of objects and from the world of objectivized custom. What Sapir means is that the entire culture of an age is expressible in the language of that age; that language, like any homogeneous medium, homogenizes within its own medium activities and spheres of all sorts, however heterogeneous, and, again like any homogeneous medium, leads, guides man in the given culture. Wittgenstein did not accept this concept of language as a homogeneous medium as his theory of 'language games' shows. However, the various language games which Wittgenstein describes do not constitute specific homogeneous media, but are simply functions of one and the same homogeneous medium. These functions never occur in isolation (neither historically, as we saw in connection with Malinowski's fishermen nor in any given speech situation). There can be no situation in which language consists exclusively of commands, just as it can never be pure expression of emotion or pure constatation of fact.

At the same time, I agree with Rhees[1] when he points out that use of language does not simply mean use of sentences and syntagma, but rather the use of these components *according to their meanings*. And meaning, let me add, is indeed tied to situation but not to one type of situation only. Rhees rightly points out that the language game which consists in giving commands is not really 'language'. Animals can also be taught to react efficiently to words of command. People can be taught to respond automatically to whole Greek sentences which they do not 'understand'. Understanding comes about within language as a homogeneous medium; language becomes humanly understandable when sentences and syntagma are related no doubt to situation but are grasped within a homogeneous medium: more precisely, within life as a whole which the medium homogenizes.

Everyday language is the homogeneous medium of everyday life, whose heterogeneous spheres it either does or can homogenize. As is well known, language can also be the homogeneous medium of various species-essential objectivations 'for itself'. The professional terminology of scientific language homogenizes scientific thinking; the language of poetry does the same for poetical ideas and attitudes. As a basic tendency, we can say that the closer the thought (and hence the associated behaviour) of any given discipline is to everyday life, the closer will its special language be to everyday language. The wider the gap between a science and everyday knowledge and experience, the more its linguistic medium is likely to contain formulations (e.g. the symbols of mathematics) which are not to be found in everyday language. It is my belief, however, that – precisely because our everyday life and thinking provide the basis for all species-essential objectivations 'for itself' – there can never be a total break with everyday language.

The homogenizing function of language is synonymous with its function as the conceptualizing agent of everyday experience. This is not to say, of course, that it is only thoughts that can be expressed in language: whatever is thinkable can be expressed, and this goes for feelings and perceptions just as much as for ideas – though not in exactly the same way. There is a difference, in fact quite a wide area of difference, but this is a very complicated question which we can do no more than touch on here. What interests us here is the 'just as much as': we can say this because there is no dividing wall between our perceptions and feelings on the one hand, and our thoughts on the other. Our feelings are always reflected feelings and most of our perceptions are reflected perceptions; and our ideas (we are talking of everyday ideas) are never fully detached from perception (our everyday concepts which Vigotski calls 'pseudo-concepts' always contain a 'pictorial' component, to some degree at least), just as our everyday judgments and pronouncements always have affective concomitants, even if not an affective content. Accordingly, it is too one-sided if we approach the question of the conceptualization of perceptions and sensation only or primarily from the standpoint of the persuasion that the rich concrete content of our perceptual and sensible world is discarded in the conceptualizing process precisely because of its generalizing nature: Schiller's words (quoted *ad nauseam*) '*Spricht* die Seele, spricht die *Seele* nicht mehr' are usually brought in here to clinch the argument. From the standpoint of our human essence it is at least as important that it is only with the help of language, – language as intermediary – that we can be aware at all of these feelings *in concreto*. I can only be 'in love' if the concept of 'love' exists, I can only suffer from a 'headache' if I know what 'head' is and what local pain is (as distinct from general discomfort); and we could not appreciate colours if language did not provide us with a differentiated concept of colour. In saying this, I am not denying the validity of the problem raised by the Schiller quotation. In what follows, however, we shall find that what we have to do with here is not a specific defect or shortcoming in language, but rather a property (inability to grasp the singular) which language shares with all species-essential objectivation 'in itself'.

In the heterogeneous complex of everyday life, then, everything is thinkable and therefore capable of homogenization in the medium of language. 'Everything is thinkable' is tantamount to saying 'everything can be said'. Of course, there are many obstacles in the thinkable/sayable equation, but these obstacles are not due to the limits of language. We say one thing in public and something else in private, and there are things that can be thought but which it is preferable not to say (magic cultures, in which words and things are often identified, are particularly rich in norms specifying words that must not be uttered).

As the medium of conceptualizing thought, language has one specific property which distinguishes it radically from the other two constituents of species-essential objectivation 'in itself'. The manipulation of things, the observance of custom, – each of these is invariably direct objectifying activity. Work completed in one's head may well be the pre-figuring, the prelude to work – but it is not that work itself; imagined adherence to a custom may serve as a declaration of intent – but it is not in itself observance of that custom. In the world of things, as in the world of custom, objectivation must be *de facto*.

In the case of language, however, we cannot disregard the existence of 'internal speech' i.e. talking to oneself. Historically, this is a later development, coming after the emergence of language as a medium of communication with others. Anyway, Vigotski has shown experimentally that in the development of children, talking to oneself is a relatively late development: at earlier stages, language is always vocal, serving either a communicative function or as accompaniment to such activities as problem-solving (egocentric speech). As a product of internaliza-

160

tion, internal speech is probably generated under the influence of two factors. One of these is purely social – the need to conceal one's thoughts from others; the second has an economic function. Internal speech demands less energy output than normal utterance (for example absence of articulation permits of radical abbreviation). Vigotski also considers that a need for abbreviation makes itself felt in vocal speech as well: if part of a sentence will serve for the whole without impairing the sense, truncation takes place. (This sort of thing is very common among close friends and acquaintances, who 'know each other's thoughts'.)

Internal speech (talking to oneself) is not preparation for speech (as thinking about action is preparation for that action) but speech itself; and it follows the norms of vocalized speech, albeit in an abbreviated form. Internal speech, it must be stressed, is not directly objectified. If I say a sentence over to myself silently and then utter that sentence, the objectivization process takes place in the second case, i.e. in the utterance: the anticipatory inner speech is only indirectly engaged in this objectivization (in as much as I shall probably express myself better, more clearly after silent rehearsal). Even so, this is the extreme case. It is usual for no more than a few variants to reach the objectivization process from the highly intricate complex of internal speech: most of whose components remain on the level of wishful thinking or passing fancy. It can indeed happen that certain scraps of inner speech – conversation with oneself – may reach objectivation *via* a multiple series of mediations (even if they are not actually enunciated); for example, *via* constant repetition, in human personality, or in simultaneous or subsequent action. But an infinity of thoughts pass through the human brain which will have no effect either on the personality or its actions, and which will fail to reach the communication chain in any shape or form whatsoever. There is a difference of responsibility between internal speech and vocalized speech. The more a thought, an opinion, a feeling of mine interpenetrates the communication chain, the greater the responsibility I must accept for it. In the case of internal speech there is no need for the public act of recantation as there may be in the case of speech act, and in the case of activities characteristic of the other two types of species-essential objectivation 'in itself'. A badly made article is scrapped, thrown away, an ill-chosen word calls forth an apologetic 'I don't mean it that way...', if I am guilty of bad manners I beg someone's pardon, etc. None of this applies to internal speech.

It remains true, of course, that the content of internal speech (in

161

so far as it can be retained and recalled) is available for public utterance at a moment of our choosing. If our masked selves contained nothing more than the subconscious, the subsequent (*post festum*) conceptualization of our covert thoughts, desires, etc. would be principially impossible. But it is a general fact of everyday life that we can conceptualize our hidden thoughts, desires etc. and later – i.e. in other circumstances – objectivize them. ('Two years ago, I thought it was all over between us.')

That spoken language itself is a direct objectivation – this is a proposition that hardly needs amplification. Wittgenstein was right when he said 'words are also deeds'.[2] The fact that the objectivation may be significant and intensive, or insignificant makes no difference in this respect, and this goes for every objectivation in the sphere of 'in itself'. The specific gravity of 'It's nice today' is quite different from that of 'God damn and blast you'. One and the same utterance may be significant or insignificant depending on situation: saying 'Goodbye' is one thing if I'm going away for a fortnight's holiday, and something quite different if I am leaving for good. The key point is that, like everything else I may do, the words I utter 'resonate', wave-like, to a greater or less degree, from their point-source outwards; on the one hand, in the objectivation itself (in language which resides in human speech and may thereby be transformed) and, on the other hand, in the totality of heterogeneous life, of which language is the homogeneous medium.

We took as our starting point the fact that language lacks a differentiating stratification such as is found in the other two constituents of species-essential objectivation 'in itself'. This is, of course, not to deny that language has a variety of functions. But we cannot appropriate one or another of these functions in isolation (as we can, for example, in the case of things: we can learn how to handle things without being able to create these things; and we can appropriate certain customs while consciously denying the validity of other customs). Appropriation of language means exercising it in all of its functions.

We have been talking about language in general, disregarding the fact that there are many different languages. In this we are, however, justified, since all languages have the same functions; and I am bound to agree with Chomsky when he writes: 'The deep structure that expresses the meaning is common to all languages, so it is claimed, being a simple reflection of the forms of thought.'[3]

Language is the only species-essential objectivation 'in itself' in which the primary semiotic system has been reinforced by a secondary system – writing. As I said above, Saussure and his followers have asserted that the development of spoken language is fortuitous in that any other system would have served just as well to carry out its semiotic functions. (Schaff goes so far as to claim that originally language was sign language, i.e. a language of gesture, and that spoken language is a later development.) But, whether we consider the actual course of human development or the functions now actually discharged by language, we have to conclude that spoken language is *the* natural semiotic system. (Gehlen comes to the same conclusion on anthropological grounds.) Not only because vocal utterance produces signs with the minimum of effort, and is primarily more economical than any other semiotic system, but also because it is not connected with visual range[4] or with light. In hunting, sound language must have been a prime necessity, as hunters could not see each other in the dark. It is not only in work, however, but in social contact as well – e.g. in public discussion – that the need for communication to be independent of vision makes itself felt. (I can make myself heard by everyone without being seen by everyone.) Other natural advantages of sound language which are only partially available to other semiotic systems, are, in comparison with this factor, of secondary importance. Thus, language enriches the perceptible world, it enables theoretical attitudes to be expressed, it is reproducible at will, is capable of infinite variation and can be freely combined with every variety of so-called meta-communication.

Other 'linguistic' systems (e.g. gesture language, which is the adequate communication system for deaf mutes, and writing) are secondary sign systems of the primary sign system: translations of sound language into secondary sign systems. Among these, gesture language has no social significance, while writing certainly has. Since language itself is the homogeneous medium, not sound (as in the case of music) 'translation' here does not mean transfer to another homogeneous medium. Writing has the same homogeneous medium as spoken language.

The specific nature of the semiotic system does, however, bring about changes in the use of language itself. In the case of spoken language, the situatedness of speech in interaction is clear and self-evident; but in the case of writing the situatedness must be linguistically expressed. (In spoken language I can say 'How are you?' without further specification, since the situation makes it clear whom I am addressing; in a letter, however, I have to specify the addressee: 'Dear Mummy! How are you?...') We need not stress the well-known fact that written language is less amenable to abbreviation than spoken language. In writing, we take whole sentences and descriptive passages, to express what can be expressed in personal contact by such meta-communicative means as gesture or voice inflection. With its potential distancing in time and space, the nature of the feed-back to an utterance changes, and the various functions of language are more sharply different-iated one from another. When we learn to write we are learning not only a new semiotic system but also – up to a certain point at least – a new way of using language.

Until comparatively recently written language played no part at all in everyday life. Only a tiny minority of people knew how to write or read and they used their skill in law, science and the arts, not in everyday life. It was not until the growth of bourgeois society that a written language became a factor in everyday life. The situation today is that ability to read and write is an essential pre-condition of viability in a cultured human milieu. Writing has replaced 'word-of-mouth' as the preferred way of storing and transmitting the accumulation of social experience over the whole wide range from instruction leaflets to cook-books. Writing has taken over certain signalling functions (instead of putting up a barber's pole, we now have the legend 'barber'); it plays a vital part in communication (letters, newspapers) and it is vital in more and more types of work-process. None of which alters the fact that today spoken language still remains the primary semiotic com-munication system in the business of carrying on everyday life.

CHAPTER 10

The general schemes of conduct and knowledge in everyday life

In what has gone before, we have been mainly concerned with the sphere of objectivation 'in itself'; we now turn to an analysis of the ways in which we appropriate this sphere. In turn, this analysis will throw new light on our previous topics: as we shall be talking about common attitudes towards species-essential objectivations 'in itself', attitudes which will help us the better to understand the proper nature of these objectivations.

The behavioural and cognitive modes which we shall be considering are those which are indispensable for appropriation of species-essential objectivations 'in itself'; but it must be stressed that in our analysis we shall not restrict ourselves to the circle of these objectivations, but shall seek to penetrate into the most generalized schemata characteristic of the appropriation of everyday life. After all, a main characteristic of everyday life is the fact that a relatively rigid sphere of species-essential objectivations 'in itself' governs and articulates an extremely wide spectrum of the most heterogeneous activities. Hence, we are necessarily obliged to appropriate the objectivations if we are to regulate and manage these heterogeneous activities. The various schemata of everyday behaviour and thinking are accordingly no more than modalities of subsumption (with the help of either repetitive or intuitive thinking). By means of these schemata, the person regulates and orders whatever he does or decides to do, whatever happens to him and whatever situations he finds himself in; and he does so in such a way as to bring these experiences, whether partially or totally, into line with what he is 'accustomed to'.

165

(a) Pragmatism

Our everyday thinking and everyday behaviour are primarily pragmatic. Following the principle of least effort, a person appropriates the signification (i.e. the function) of a species-essential objectivation 'in itself' in such a way as to react to the 'thusness' of the function, while disregarding its 'whence': its genesis does not interest him. In relation to species-essential objectivations 'in itself', questions concerning their genesis, their 'why', are in general childish questions; and when a child asks such a question, grown-ups will tend to answer, 'Because that's the way it is': in other words, they re-state the pragmatic propensity of 'thusness'. Why do we have to say 'thank you'? Because it's polite. Why do we use scissors like this? Because that's what they're for. Why do we say this? Because that's what people say.

The pragmatic relationship denotes the direct unity of theory and practice.[1] Since the signification of the norms-and-rules of species-essential objectivation 'in itself' is presented in their use, no purely theoretical component can be isolated in our relationship to them (within the framework of everyday life and thinking): nor indeed is such a component necessary for the correct use of these objectivations. Pragmatism is not a 'shortcoming' in everyday thinking. It is in principle impossible for us to adopt a purely theoretical attitude towards every objectivation designed to be used.

It is clear from this, however, that it is only as a general tendency that our pragmatic attitude towards species-essential objectivations 'in itself' can direct unity between theory and practice. There are instances (exceptional cases perhaps, but none the less real for that) where the pragmatic attitude itself demands that this direct unity yield to take-over by the theoretical attitude. The best example of this, in relation to the world of things, is provided by cases of failure, lack of success: when a method I have used over and over again fails to work, the pragmatic attitude itself, the desire for efficiency, makes me stop and ask 'Why'? 'What has gone wrong'? – and at once I am thinking along theoretical lines.

We find the same thing in language. We appropriate language in the same way as we appropriate objects. Again it is childish to ask 'Why'? or 'How has this come about?' (though some linguists have started to ask such questions). We use grammar and words as 'taken-for-granted'. But here again it happens (not infrequently) that pragmatism itself calls upon the theoretical attitude for help – for example, when the meanings of words have to be defined. Here, I am not referring to cases where we have to understand the meaning of a word as yet unknown to us, as this is only a question of presenting its pragmatic identity (the introduction of the scientific use of concepts into our linguistic currency always oversteps the limits of everyday thinking) but rather to 'meta-language'.

Jacobsen has shown[2] (to my mind very convincingly) that the elements of meta-language are already present in everyday language, to be called upon when necessary. We use certain words spontaneously in certain meanings, and perhaps only once in a given situation shall we be called upon to define the meaning of a word. (As otherwise we should not be able to react to it adequately.) If a man says to woman 'I love you', the woman could ask 'what do you mean by "love"?'; and if the man's answer is to be adequate to the problem raised by this question, that answer must be couched, in a sense, in the terms of and on the level of meta-language. But this does not necessarily mean a stage beyond the purely pragmatic: the reason for asking the question is, after all, so that the questioner may be in a position to react adequately to the original statement.

In the case of custom-systems, the problem is more complex. As far as the most primary norms of societal co-existence are concerned, we can assert that the pragmatic approach is just as unconditionally typical of these as it is of other constituents of species-essential objectivation 'in itself', and here again we find a direct unity of theory and practice. And as regards most particularistic customs we can say that the general tendency is the same. Here, however, motivation of a moral nature may intervene in observance of customs, assessment of their content, the ways in which they are observed, and in their possible infringement. In so far as this is so, if not a custom itself, at least the conviction with which, and the manner in which that custom is practised, may go beyond the purely pragmatic. Again, observance of one customary system may render another system questionable, not only ethically but pragmatically as well. A purely pragmatic relationship to such customary systems is characteristic of past-orientated societies rather than future-orientated societies; and it is characteristic of the state of subjective alienation rather than of the state of elimination of that subjective alienation in future-orientated societies.

(b) Probability

Whatever we do in relation to species-essential objectivation 'in itself' is always based on probability. Indeed, we can go further and say that everything we do on the level of everyday life is based on probability. Spinoza made the following distinction between everyday thinking and scientific thinking:

> In everyday life we look for the greatest degree of probability: in speculative thought we seek the truth. Man would die of hunger and thirst if he refused to eat or drink until it had been completely and irrefutably demonstrated to him that food and drink would be to his benefit. In cogitation, however, things are not like this. Here on the contrary we have to be on our guard that we never accept as 'true' what is only 'probable' ...[3]

Here, Spinoza is making the point that probable action is the direct result of the principle of economy of effort, of pragmatism and of repetitive praxis. We are called upon to do all sorts of things in the course of our daily lives, and probability has to play a very large part in our assessments if the ordinary business of living is not to grind to a halt. Assessment of likelihood – the probability of such and such an action succeeding – gives a maximum/minimum curve in the graph of daily activities. Action undertaken for no better reason than that it is *possible* is not a reliable guide in the business of everyday living: it lands us in too many catastrophes of everyday life. Let us recall Spinoza's example. If we are offered food at a party, we can take it as probable that it is not going to harm us, and we proceed to consume it without any *guarantee* that it is nutritious and not noxious. But if we found ourselves cast-away on a desert island, we should hardly eat the first strange berries we came across, without some experimentation. It is, of course, *possible* that the berries are edible rather than harmful: but in the great majority of cases we would not take the obvious risk of swallowing them – i.e. acting on possibility alone.

The objective basis of action based on probability is provided by habit and repetition. Since it is customary for a host to offer us something to eat, we can consume such food with confidence. Since we are accustomed to crossing the street in front of cars approaching us at customary pace, and have seen others do so, we accept and repeat this action as one 'likely to come off'. This last example raises a point to which we have already referred – the extent to which intuition necessarily reinforces repetition. For example, should one vehicle in the customary traffic flow suddenly

168

accelerate, our intuitive (reflex) action is to jump out of the way. Of course, the fact that an action is based on the probability factor is not in itself enough to preclude disaster. It is in situations, where for some reason or other we depart from a probability assessment consolidated in practice, that things are particularly liable to go wrong. Some types of activity are particularly prone to catastrophes of various kinds and here the unexpected has to be taken into account when we are making our probability evaluation. For example, when I am driving I hold to a safe braking-distance which allows for the unexpected – e.g. a blow-out on the car in front of me. But we cannot take every possibility into account and take equivalent precaution, if we are to continue to act on the probability principle: and we have really no option but to do so.

'Probable' action is probable in relation to a given situation or to a given type of activity. In the observance of the primary customs of societal life, for example, probability very largely guarantees success. Here, we can rely on simple repetition. Simple repetition is also successfully applied at a high probability level in the manipulation of articles of everyday use. In everyday life, however, we have to make choices and take decisions where more than one alternative is available, and here the probability factor is multi-valued. Here, acting on probability means acting on sufficient ground: and the basis for action regarded as 'sufficient' will be shot through with heterogeneous components and motivations. The less tradition has to do with it, the more multi-valued will the 'sufficiency ground' be. But however multi-valued it is, here too in the long run we have to take a decision based on probability values. If we tried to play absolutely safe, take into consideration every present and future factor, and make provision against every unknown, we would quite simply never make any decision at all about anything.

In the case of activity related to species-essential objectivations 'in itself', the sufficient ground (reason) for probability-guided action is found with the least effort. Here, observance of custom 'guides' us in the evaluation of probability factors. Where species-essential objectivation 'in itself', principally custom, fails totally or partially to point the way, or, if it does so in one respect only, it is mainly the personality which guides and leads in the identification of probability. The role of the personality here is, of course, not simply to come up with a sufficient ground for probability-guided action: personality also plays a part in setting the aim of the action – i.e. identifying what the action is supposed to realize. In the case of activity with a high moral content this is essential. In this case, the actual approach to evaluating the probability factor can take many different forms (depending on the person and on the specific case): it can extend from action based on nothing more than impulse, to action based on moral reflection or on calculation, or, for that matter, on combinations of impulse, moral reflection and calculation in varying proportion.

Another factor that plays an important part in the exploratory process of probability assessment associated with everyday action is *belief*. Belief is the effective concomitant of, and often the impetus behind, all our actions and all our choices. In this wide sense, belief is simply the feeling of affirmation which is inseparable from all decision, from the most primitive to the most lofty.

(c) Imitation

Three separate, though closely connected forms of imitation play an important part in the appropriation and conduct of everyday life: these are, imitation of action, imitation of behaviour and evocative imitation.[4]

Imitation of activity is found in the animal world as well. Imitation of action is the specifically human form of imitative activity: in action, as I have already pointed out, object and motivation are clearly distinguished from each other, and this is a specifically human property. We can teach a parrot to imitate the sound of a word if we repeat the word often enough; but no matter how many words are thus repeated, i.e. however large the parrot's 'vocabulary' becomes, this remains imitative activity. And indeed, a child's first repetition of a word it has heard may be no more than that; but when the word begins to act as a sign for the child – that is, when the child realizes that it can use this word in certain situations and not in others – the child has appropriated the meaning of the word, and we can speak of imitation of action. Imitation is, of course, only one component in the appropriation of language, as it is, for example in the process of learning a song.

In the case of language and the world of custom – that is, in those cognitive and conative types in which customs and languages are the 'road-signs' – imitation of action rarely appears in isolation; most frequently, it is a part or a phase of a behavioural complex, or imitation of a behavioural complex. At the same time, pure imitation of action plays an important part in our relations with the world of things – both in the use of things and in their production. A soldier does not learn to shoot well simply by

170

imitating standard military behaviour: here again, imitative acquisition of a skill is relatively independent of imitation of the behaviour associated with that skill.

Imitation of behaviour occupies a special place among the types of imitation found in everyday life. It is directed not towards individual customs but towards one or more behavioural patterns of greater complexity.

Of course, it is not *via* imitation pure and simple that appropriation of these behavioural patterns (stereotypes) takes place. Direction by speech acts (moral exhortation, words of command) plays a very big part in promoting the process of appropriation. Direction by speech act, however, is never detached from presentation of the 'example' which motivates the imitation. If I am telling a child how to behave in certain circumstances, I say, 'Watch what X or Y does, and you do the same'. However, imitation can function even where verbal direction of this sort is lacking. The need to be capable of 'movement' in a given environment is sufficient to generate it.

In contrast to imitation of action, imitation of behaviour entails the appropriation of socially specific value-contents, world-view and ideologies; and as part of this process, the person gears his behaviour to social stereotypes which incorporate certain specific values and certain specific ideological postures. When an African child unjustifiably scolded a black servant in imitation of his father, he was demonstrating that he had (whether consciously or unconsciously) appropriated a social prejudice. When another child treated a black servant as an equal – again imitating his father – he was showing that he had appropriated a socially significant attitude – rejection of social prejudice. When and where in life's stages the 'person' is confronted with only one type of behaviour with regard to some facet of life, the fact that he imitates this behaviour tells us nothing at all about his morals. To return to the example of the two children: let us suppose that apart from their father they had never seen any white person dealing with blacks – i.e. they had no other example to imitate. It is possible that later when they came up against other ways of behaving in the same circumstances, each would feel ashamed of his youthful behaviour: one would regret his callousness, the other his liberalism. The greater the variety of attitudes which the person comes up against in any respect, the greater is the choice available to him as to which attitude he should imitate, which attitude he should regard as normative: and hence the more does imitation of any one attitude and of its value content become a

171

moral issue. In the appropriation and practice of behaviour, imitation – whether selective or non-selective – is characteristic of all human beings, whatever their ages.

The amplitude and intensity of particularistic customs and the network of behavioural patterns are in direct proportion to each other. The nobleman's behaviour towards his king, his wife, his sons is homogenized as the 'behaviour of a nobleman'. With the growth of bourgeois society, it becomes typical for heterogeneous types of behaviour, behavioural stereotypes, to exist alongside each other, to lead relatively independent lives, instead of being synthesized: the behavioural stereotypes are rigidified into role-clichés.

Evocative imitation is that type of imitation which produces cognitive and/or emotional effect by conjuring up certain concrete deeds or feelings. Here, the imitation is mediated by a conceptual process. In modern everyday life, it usually takes the form of narration. When I tell others what sort of day I had at the office, my aim (whether overt or covert) in conjuring up these events is to induce some feeling or other in my audience – usually one of solidarity with me. I want them to agree that 'I was right'. In this act of mimesis, language is the guiding medium. At the same time, direct essays in imitation 'colour' the mimetic act of communication: I summon up a whole cast of characters whose voices, manners, gestures, etc. I imitate – even their syntax. Directly evocative – i.e. non-verbal – imitation also plays a part in everyday life: I imitate my teachers, my boss, and so on. But in comparison with the linguistically mediated evocative imitation of narration, this plays a very minor part.

In ancient societies, evocative mimesis was of fundamental importance in the process of appropriating species-essential objectivations 'in itself' (e.g. in cultures ruled by magic); in modern society, however, its role is continuously diminishing, apart from that of art as a factor in everyday life.

(d) Analogy

Analogy also has an imitative component, the only difference being that, whereas in imitation proper, an existent correlation, a form of behaviour, of action, serve to generate *identity,* in analogy the intention is to generate *similarity.* Analogy plays a key role in change within the sphere of species-essential objectivations 'in itself', so much so indeed, that here we can do no more than present a possibly random selection of its main aspects.

172

As regards the world of material objects for use – tools, implements etc. – here again analogy is of importance both in the production of new objects and in the manipulation of existing objects. Throughout the long (not primeval) period, during which humankind was gradually discovering how to make and use means of production, analogy with the functions of the human body (indeed of the animal body in general) played a big part. An effort was made to transfer to tools the various functions of the hand, the foot, etc. by using these organs as analogues in the manufacture of tools, that is, by introducing into their design traits that seemed functionally critical. Marx identified something similar in the construction of certain machines during the industrial revolution. Man's earliest ideas of a flying machine differed hardly if at all from the analogue of the bird in flight, and early attempts at experimental aircraft were also based on the analogous notion that such a machine should flap its wings. With the de-anthropomorphization of technology and the take-over of science as its guiding principle, this type of reasoning by analogy has tended to disappear. It is now only in art that machines can be elevated to a sort of analogous, anthropomorphically conceived existence.

The products we purposely design are often shaped in accordance with analogous antecedents, and social convention itself tends to work by analogy. (Cultured pearls began as imitations of natural pearls.) Only the modern consumer goods industry has the expansive potential to complete with this deep-seated desire for analogy.

In our use of things in everyday life it is functional pressures that generate analogous uses and give them a kind of permanence. If I haven't got the right sort of nail for the job, I look for one that 'will do instead'; if I haven't got a glass to drink out of, I make do with something similar – i.e. something analogous.

Linguists are well aware of the crucially important role played by analogy in language; and Saussure regards it as the means whereby random choice is eliminated from language. It is by analogy that foreign words are assimilated into languages: from the formation of tenses to vowel change in prefixes, analogy is everywhere at work. Lexicographically too, analogy plays a major part (cf. foothill, chair-leg etc.).

Analogy in language, as thus illustrated in metaphor, points to something wider – the analogical nature of everyday thinking in general. Recognition of novel relationships, concatenations, is bolstered up in our everyday thinking by appeal to older analogous

173

forms. Analogy is the prop we use to approach what is intellectually novel, even if it is a prop that will eventually be discarded. Controlled – i.e. methodologically controlled – analogy continues to play an important part in experimental models. Certain historians are still fond of substituting analogies for the understanding of the 'thusness' of a historical event or formation (cf. Trotsky, who never tired of comparing Stalin's political victory over his opponents to Bonapartism). The influence of everyday thought is particularly strong here.

Even in classical antiquity, social inquiry – particularly philosophy – had declared war on analogical thinking. The Aristotelean method of distinction which deepened into scientific analysis, boils down to the unravelling of everyday concepts, the partition of 'likes' on the basis of their differences: a process which was to turn everyday words into 'terminology' in the positive meaning of the word – terms, that is, invested with a precise and definite meaning, no longer blurred by analogy.

No socially binding custom (and hardly any socially conditional custom) owes its origin to anything but analogy. Customs which are generally binding for a given society simply cannot be 'invented'. Of course, once a custom has taken root, it may depart quite markedly from the objectivation in analogy with which it was established: the custom then proceeds under its own momentum and produces offspring in analogy with itself and for its own functional enrichment. For example, the Christian act of worship at the altar grew up in analogy with the Roman sacrificial rite (the ritual before the sacrificial altar). But the specific community in which the ritual was practised along with the new social conditions, had a far-reaching effect on the concrete forms of the ritual, transforming, deepening and enriching them out of all recognition. This is not to say that there is nothing new under the sun; all it means is that what is 'new' at any one time takes over by analogy from what is established custom, including ideology; and this under-current acts as a kind of bearer for the new output.

Much of our everyday activity is guided by analogy. Usually when I have to make a decision I do so in spontaneously analogical fashion – that is to say, I subsume my specific and personal case as a type case, and take the decision which is normal and customary in the type case.[5] The same thing happens when I have to express an opinion on some person or event: again, I subsume the person or event under the corresponding analogous type, and apply the relevant social-customary norm, assessment or opinion (assuming that it is one I share). In this sort of situation, intuitive and repetitive thinking (praxis) work together: *via* intuitive praxis I 'know' how to classify something and *via* repetitive praxis I take the requisite steps in implementation (i.e. deliver a verdict, express an opinion, etc.). Reasoning by analogy is therefore absolutely necessary if we are to act with due economy in our everyday lives (since expressing an opinion is also action).

Under the general heading of 'reasoning by analogy' we can include, however, a subsidiary type (customarily found in everyday life) whose economic *raison d'être* is not to save time or to speed up the process of making a decision, but rather to provide security, assurance. Here, reflection plays a much bigger part. The assurance sought is that provided by *precedent*. If I want to make a decision in some situation or other (whether with a view to taking action or expressing an opinion) I look for a *point d'appui* and find it in those cases which are on record as being similar to mine. Decisions arrived at in these cases serve me as precedents, and I can formulate my own decision accordingly.

'There's a precedent for this' we say, and this in itself is a form of disengagement, in as much as our feeling of being personally responsible diminishes as assurance based on precedent grows (illusory as this may be) and decision-taking becomes proportionately easier. I say 'illusory as this may be' and it is worth while stressing this. Since acting on precedent serves to facilitate not repetitive praxis but intuitive and inventive praxis, it is more open to gross error than any other form of analogy.

(e) Over-generalization

Both in imitation of behaviour and in analogical decision-taking we have to reckon with over-generalization. It is clear that if we subsume a particular case under an analogical type – i.e. type-cast it – we have, in fact, generalized it; we have imposed prescriptive norms and rules of a general nature on it, in order to reach a solution. In doing so, we can act (and very often this depends more on the particular case than on us) so as to 'settle things', i.e. do what everyday life and everyday thinking would expect us to do. In most cases this is precisely what happens. Sometimes, however, we have to do with singular cases, with a high degree of novelty and unfamiliarity, and here the normal generalization which we have been discussing leads to a rough treatment of the 'case'; generalization gives place (even when we take everyday demands as normative) to over-generalization, and the outcome is failure and the catastrophes of everyday life. Rough treatment of the singular case – something which follows from everyday thinking and everyday praxis – makes it unavoidable that from time to time over-generalization should arise in the process of repetitive praxis and thinking; which means in turn that the more or less serious catastrophes of everyday life are also unavoidable. (Intuitive thinking goes part of the way towards off-setting this.)

If we are to reach any understanding of the problematic nature of over-generalization, we have to ask ourselves the question: whence do we derive the judgments, typological classifications, behavioural norms, under which we so spontaneously subsume the singular case? Many of these are simply taken over, unquestioningly and on trust, from our environment: that is to say, they antedate personal experience. I shall call these 'pre-cast typologies', 'pre-cast norms' and 'pre-cast judgments'. By this, I do not mean to say that these are never associated with any sort of personal experience (though this is not impossible); I mean first and foremost that personal experience tends to be spontaneously subsumed under pre-cast schemata, which are themselves never open to modification, expansion or reconsideration. In fact, what we have here is a type of social thinking and acting which is intentional, but which is, as regards cognition and morals, passive. The employment of norms, types and judgments as pre-cast norms, etc. – i.e. the amalgamation of intentional activity with cognitive and moral passivity – provides over-generalization with one of its main bases.

Here, however, another question arises: in comparison with what, in relation to what, do we speak of '*over*-generalization'? It is, after all, possible that subsumption of something under a pre-cast type, judgment, behavioural mode, will in fact prove quite adequate in the practical business of everyday life, and will for a certain time (usually the person's lifetime) in no way detract from the person's ability to lead a correct and viable life in a given community. We must remember, however, that since such subsumption inhibits fresh perceptions and runs counter to the person's ability to take moral decisions (his *phronesis*) it prevents his development as a personality. And this can prove problematical, not only ethically but also from the standpoint of everyday life. The problems appear whenever the person is confronted with an unforeseen, unexpected situation, either as a result of social changes or as the result of a change in his own personal circumstances. In this sort of situation, action on the basis of pre-cast norms – even in the context of basic survival in everyday life – can prove disastrous for the agent.

Over-generalization in the shape of a decision taken or an opinion expressed on the basis of pre-conceived typologies or evaluations, has two functions in everyday life. On the one hand, it is necessary, indeed indispensable from the standpoint of economical prosecution of everyday life. Where personal experience is lacking, no other way is available to us on the level of everyday life (this is not true of science): the simple subsumption of experience within the framework of life as we are accustomed to it, more often than not 'hits the nail on the head'. At the same time, everyday life itself requires us to modify generalized types and evaluations – a process which may vary greatly in degree and in extent – and even suspend them altogether in practice. Were it otherwise, we could not accumulate new experience in everyday life. In as much as this is so, the surmounting of the over-generalization of pre-cast evaluations (depending on specific cases) is at least as much of a social necessity (i.e. not merely personal necessity) as subsumption as practised in the average.

If over-generalization on a basis of preconceived evaluations and types appears as a general social trait *vis-à-vis* the material world of objects, technical stagnation is the outcome. We find examples of this in various cultures based on the practice of magic, in which work was so strictly circumscribed by prescriptive and proscriptive norms and so weighted down by ritual that only simple subsumption was possible; and this in turn proved an ideological inhibition which hampered the development of production. Here, of course, over-generalization is not the cause but the modulus *via* which the ideological pressure is mediated. Social rigidity – particularly in the social division of labour – often ensures that simple repetitive praxis (on a basis of pre-cast norms) is so general with regard to production, distribution and exchange that any further development of the given society is impossible beyond a certain limit. But if we view this question from the standpoint of the person, we see that the result of over-generalization with regard to the world of material objects is, at most, personal failure.

Personal over-generalization with regard to social normatives, opinions and evaluations has, however, another specific property of ethical – in some cases also political – moment.[6] The fact is that what is from the standpoint of everyday life perfectly acceptable and successful action may well be, from the moral standpoint, unacceptable or, at least, questionable. If I accept the norms and evaluations of my society or my social class, if I regard its particularistic customs as an absolute normative structure and

177

spontaneously subsume all my experience thereunder, it becomes not only possible but probable that I shall be adept at knowing my way around my own community: from the standpoint of everyday life, I shall do all the right things, I shall support myself successfully and I shall not blunder into catastrophes. However, these customs and norms may contain moral contradictions or non-values; and what is a good solution from the standpoint of the moral content of the action may well be at variance with pure subsumption. In such circumstances, my pre-judgments turn into prejudices which my experience does nothing to correct or over-rule, since they are bound up with my interests: that is, I am affectively interested in retaining these prejudices (though not only affectively).

A pre-judgment becomes a prejudice only if there exists an objective possibility for the pre-judgment to be corrected: that is, if we have at our social disposal (or can at least work out) generalizations which can set experience in a more adequate framework, and if the pre-cast judgment runs counter to these more adequate generalizations. These may in turn be new social norms or customs, but they may also be scientific results.

It is not, of course, only in everyday life that we find pre-judgments and prejudices. In the sphere of species-essential objectivation 'for itself', however, action guided by prejudice hinders the actor in the proper appropriation of this sphere. A scientist or an artist who is guided by prejudice in his work forfeits his claim to be taken seriously, even if he or she scores high in everyday life and institutions (often precisely because of his/her prejudices). In bourgeois society, stubborn adherence to pre-judgments and prejudices can also prove disastrous in the economic sphere. This is one, though not the only source of the enthusiasm with which the nascent bourgeoisie attacks 'prejudices'.

(f) The rough treatment of the singular case

All aspects of the phenomenon we are now about to discuss belong to the sphere of species-essential objectivation 'in itself'. Wherever species-essential objectivation 'for itself' functions in everyday life, where a conscious relationship to such an objectivation can be formulated, in so far does what I describe as 'rough treatment of the singular case' either diminish or disappear altogether.

The problem as a whole can be divided in principle into two groups of problems, which are in themselves heterogeneous. In the first group, we are concerned with such questions as – how and to what degree can the 'person' be expressed in its own concreteness (ipseity), in its own qualitative quiddity, within the basic structure of everyday life; in the second, we shall ask the question: how can man lay hold on and grasp the qualitative 'thusness' of the cases, things and events of his world?

We have already seen that, as a result of its generalizing nature, language is incapable of expressing adequately the inner occurrences (perceptions, feelings, impressions) of the sentient subject. It is clear that a feeling for example, which we can express in terms of everyday concepts, cannot be expressed in its concrete 'thusness' in such terms. As everyone knows, we have as many kinds of degrees of friendly feelings as we have friends – but in each individual case, in relation to each of our friends, we can speak only of 'friendly feelings'.

This is not an isolated case; it is not evidence of any 'incognito' of our soul; it is simply one everyday example of the rough treatment of the singular case. The fact that the 'thus-ness', the ipseity, of the feelings cannot be expressed in everyday conceptual terms, does not necessarily mean that they are 'incognito'. Wittgenstein makes the very apt point that the 'inner' can be adequately expressed, if not simply *via* description (an everyday form of evocative mimesis), *via* behaviour – the concrete 'howness' of behaviour and attitude, of which words – as deeds – are simply moments: necessary elements but still episodes.

> The criteria for the truth of the confession that I thought such-and-such are not the criteria for a true description of a process. And the importance of the true confession does not reside in its being a correct and certain report of a process. It resides rather in the special consequences which can be drawn from a confession whose truth is guaranteed by the special criteria of truthfulness.[7]

The inadequacy of everyday language in the expression of private feelings and private thoughts is, therefore, not a fault to be eliminated. Language is only usable, is only 'language' *because* it is or can be inadequate in this respect. It is only in action other than speech or *via* the mediation of such actions or attitudes that language can adequately express the subjective state of the 'person': but adequacy can be thus achieved. Wittgenstein speaks of the mediating role of moral attitudes. In this case, it is the attitude and the morals overtly expressed in it, that confer veracity and trustworthiness upon a statement: that is, they vouch for its adequacy, the adequate nature of the words. The language of poetry (i.e. language as mediated through art) is capable of doing what everyday language cannot do – it can express the feelings and the thoughts of the person adequately in words.

As we know, the fact that a person observes the primary social norms tells us nothing about that person. And we recall that, in the case of particularistic customs, the degree of intensity with which the custom is observed – or, as may happen, rejected – does indeed tell us something about the 'person', in that it expresses his personal nature. But here again we have to do with a relationship which differs from that obtaining *vis-à-vis* the world of custom (as species-essential objectivation 'in itself') and morality, again, is this new component.

In the process of working I also generalize my capabilities. Furthermore, as a result of the division of labour, my specialized capabilities are made to 'absorb' other capabilities so that I may objectivize them. The 'person' producing the artefact 'disappears' in the production of the product. If 'disappearance' is not total, this indicates that we have to do with an activity which is intermediate between work and art. At the same time, the usage of things is typical, not personal. People of every sort and variety wear the same shoes; and use-objects can only be adapted within certain limits to personal requirement, or to suit certain traits in our personalities. But here again personality is not expressed in the way we use things. If personality *is* expressed, it is mediated through morals, through one's *Weltanschauung*, and, above all, in one's personal taste. Personal taste is that factor in the comparative ranking of use-objects in pursuit of a way of life, in which morals, word-view, culture and custom are synthesized.

To sum up, we can say that self-expression of the subject is indeed possible in everyday life, but not simply in conjunction with species-essential objectivations 'in itself' but in conjunction with other spheres and objectivations. The basic point of reference, however, remains the species-essential objectivation 'in itself'.

In similar fashion we can consider our possibilities of apprehending 'singularity'. As is well known, words do not express the ipseity of things. Neither do proper names, which are at most indicators. 'Mary Smith' tells us nothing at all about Mary Smith, unless we already know her. The words 'Smiths' table' refer to a particular object: but they conjure up the referent in our mind's eye only if we have already dined *chez* Smith, and therefore know what to expect. Language includes means which are designed to refer to the specific, the singularity: this is their precise function.

As Wittgenstein very pertinently says (*Philosophical Investigations*, p. 123): ' "I" is not the name of a person, nor "here" of a place and "this" is not a name. But they are connected with names. Names are explained by means of them. It is also true that it is characteristic of physics not to use these words.' The *intentio* directed towards apprehension of non-perceptible (or non-perceived) singular cases usually takes place *via* description (evocative mimesis, primitive art) or definition (pre-scientific thinking). In principle, singularity is, of course, inexhaustible. Its description or definition can at best be adequate with reference to a particular aim or situation. Customs, including moral customs, normative systems and stereotypes can be adequately applied to the singular case with the help of *phronesis*. But *phronesis*, as we have already seen, is again a moral propensity: and, indeed, a moral propensity which requires intuitive and inventive thinking and praxis if it is to be effective. In other words, here again we are going beyond the sphere of species-essential objectivation 'in itself'.

Every singular decision reached not simply by subsumption alone contains a moral element or the *intentio* towards knowledge of something new. It may – and often does – contain political intention as well. Subsumption by itself will not help us to pick the right moment to start a rebellion: what we need here is due analysis of the situation in the light of the possibilities, for the decision to be both morally and politically informed. When it is a question of choosing a path in life, subsumption by itself may be enough (for example, tradition prescribed that the second son of a noble family should become a priest). But this is where the singular case comes in for rough treatment: here we are still within the sphere of species-essential objectivation 'in itself'. But if tradition does not prescribe – or, at least, not inexorably – the course I am to follow, it then becomes at least possible for me to pay some attention to my particularity. I can pay attention to – that is, I can seek adequately to know – my character, my capabilities; I can take stock of my situation; and moral considerations will play a part in the decisions I come to. In all of this we are still on the plane of probable action: that is to say, we have not budged an inch from the sphere of everyday thinking and praxis. But we act in far-reaching awareness of our singular case because we are motivated not only by the norms of species-essential objectivation 'in itself' but also by other norms.

We have come to the end of our consideration of the ways in which man appropriates the basic patterns of everyday life.

Summing up, we can say that basically these patterns guide every man in so far as he is active on the plane of everyday life. The fixed boundaries of the appropriation process are delineated by the species-essential objectivations 'in itself'. But correction or emendation of the sphere of objectivation 'in itself' can and does take place within the framework of everyday life. In this respect, however, guidance is provided by objectivations which are heterogeneous with regard to the species-essential objectivations 'in itself'.

These heterogeneous objectivations can modify our relationship with the basic sphere of everyday life in two ways: firstly, by temporarily suspending pragmaticism and allowing the theoretical attitude a foothold on the everyday scene (pre-scientific thinking), and, concurrently, by analysis of 'type concepts' (analogical concepts) and their promotion to the status of scientific concepts; secondly, by apprehension of the singular case on a basis provided by species-essential objectivations and values – i.e., *via* the elaboration of artistic, and above all, moral attitudes, which again might take place within the sphere of everyday life. In an attempt to grasp everyday life and thinking in its totality, we shall now examine everyday life as the fundament of species-essential objectivations 'for itself'.

PART IV

The roots of the needs and objectivations making for species-essentiality 'for itself', as generated in everyday life

CHAPTER 11

Everyday knowledge

It will prove rewarding to undertake our analysis of everyday knowledge from more than one angle. So, after analysing the content of everyday knowledge we shall consider its anthropological properties; we shall then try to find out exactly what we mean, in everyday terms, when we claim to 'know' something, and finally we shall study the set forms of species-essential objectivations 'for itself' as manifested in everyday thinking.

(a) The content of everyday thought

By 'the content of everyday thought' we understand that totality of knowledge of which we make factual use in our everyday lives in all sorts of ways (e.g. as guidelines in action, subjects of conversation, etc.). The minimum requirement is that amount of everyday knowledge which every *subiectum* must internalize if he is to live and move successfully in his specific environment. This minimum requirement includes knowledge of the local language, knowledge of the primary customs, knowledge of these customs and collective images which are peculiar to the given habitat, ability to manipulate the means and implements of production etc. used therein, and so on. It must be stressed that not only the content of such knowledge varies according to time and social class, but also its force-field, its effective spread. The sum total of the knowledge necessary for the functioning of everyday life in any given age is never available *in its entirety* to any one *subiectum*; and indeed as the social division of labour intensifies we see a proportionate decrease in the amount of such knowledge specifically available.

Everyday knowledge – like the cognitive repertory as a whole – 'sheds' these items which are no longer of use to the person, at whatever stage of the social division of labour. At the same time, the central mental data-bank continues to amass those items of knowledge which no member of any social structure can do without if his or her everyday life is to proceed in adequate fashion. The sort of knowledge which foretells rain from the appearance of the clouds is obsolescent: nowadays, we listen (at least in Europe and America) to the weather forecast.

The mandatory component in everyday knowledge is also relative. As I have said, a minimum level of such knowledge is obligatory for everyone. Beyond this, however, the extent to which one or another kind of everyday knowledge is mandatory varies from one position to another in the social division of labour. Until very recently, the everyday knowledge which women were expected to appropriate was quite different from that incumbent upon men. However, mandatory and possible knowledge are distinguished from each other in every position in the division of labour.

Knowing 'what' and knowing 'how' play equal parts in the content of everyday knowledge; usually, indeed, they are indissolubly linked. The one conditions the other. In what follows, we shall be concerned with detailed analysis of the pragmatism of everyday life; for the present, we need only point out that this coincidence of 'what' and 'how' is purely tendential. The fact is that everyday life contains – also as an integral structural component of everyday thinking – knowledge of the 'what' type which has no 'how' correlative. Yet 'knowing what' remains pragmatic if it is knowledge which is mandatory if the person is to orientate him/herself in society. Thus, from the knowledge that 'God created the world' no sort of *practical* action is likely to follow directly. But it is knowledge without which, in a Christian community, men could hardly function on the social plane: indirectly, then, there is a dispositive relationship between this knowledge and certain social practices, though these practices are not implementations of the item of knowledge.

Who and what are the bearers – and the relayers – of the cognitive content of everyday life, i.e. of our everyday knowledge? And what decides exactly how much of this content we can appropriate?

The content of everyday life – a content which often differs according to stratum or class – is carried and spread by the generations of adult human beings whose life it is. The everyday knowledge of one generation provides the foundation for the everyday knowledge of following generations. The ratio between traditional and acquired knowledge will vary depending on whether the society is future- or past-oriented. In past-oriented societies, the content of everyday knowledge is taken over very largely from that of preceding generations: while the striking thing about the content of everyday thought in future-oriented societies is the rapidity with which it changes. Not only do young people in such a society look more and more to other sources for part of their knowledge, but older people too are called upon to 're-learn' and to appropriate new kinds of knowledge for use in everyday life. But none of this alters the basic fact that the fundamental corpus of everyday knowledge is transmitted from each generation to its successor.

Though it is true to say that, in one way or another, all of us participate in the transmission of everyday knowledge, all societies contain certain representative personalities or institutions which are more intimately connected with this process than others. First and foremost, it is the function of parents to impart everyday knowledge to their children. In certain societies this role falls to the aged who are by definition those with most social experience. In both cases, though the exact extent varies from one historical period to another, the ways and means used in the transmission process can be more or less institutionalized. In strictly religious communities priests play a major role in the transmission of knowledge; the school is an institutionalized relay station for the transmission of knowledge, whose social importance is growing. With the emergence of bourgeois public space and the appearance of a mass literate audience, the press too has come to play an important auxiliary role. Today, all forms of mass communication are brought in: from radio and television we learn what we should eat, how to keep fit, how long we should sleep, how to be a success at parties, etc. etc. – all of which would once upon a time have been transmitted personally by a member of the older generation. This new way of securing the transmission of everyday knowledge is highly ambiguous. In principle, it enables a whole society to acquire the everyday knowledge of a relatively cultured segment of that society (a possibility which our mass means of communication are far from exploiting to the full). But it is never addressed to the 'person'. In the old days, when father told his son how to do something, his advice may well have been couched in terms of general experience but through the personal relationship it was 'made to measure' for the particular case. Radio and television address their audiences of hundreds of thousands – and, what is more, impersonal hundreds of thousands – so that there is no way in which the instruction transmitted can be made to measure for the particular listener, either in form or in content. The obfuscation of strata and class differences in the way knowledge is presented in mass communication prevents certain strata (principally the underprivileged classes) from expressing their own 'knowledge' as generated by their needs; in place of which, the knowledge expressing the needs and interests of other classes is thrust upon them. All of which makes mass communication methods a more or less successful instrument for manipulation.

I said above that it is mainly the adult section of a generation which acts as the bearer medium in the transmission of everyday knowledge. But it goes without saying that the everyday knowledge of a successor generation – even in a past-oriented society – is not reducible to what that generation has taken over as its inheritance from earlier generations. The core stock of inherited knowledge shrinks or expands according to need, as one generation follows another. We have already dealt with shrinkage in this context: shrinkage ensues when one sort of knowledge becomes superfluous to the everyday requirements of a successor generation. Expansion may be due to either of two factors. On the one hand, new social conjunctures, new social demands generate new social experience, which takes root in the form of everyday knowledge. This new intake is then transmitted to the successor generation as part of the ancestral estate. In the second place, knowledge may infiltrate or may be consciously induced into the realm of the everyday from the sphere of species-essential objectivation 'for itself'.

As an example of knowledge consciously induced into everyday life, which is not directly derivable from everyday experience, we may specify certain kinds of religious knowledge, especially the 'knowledge' prescribed by dogmatic religion. Structurally, religious thinking is akin to everyday thinking. But that is not to say that the corpus of knowledge associated with this or that religion is derivable from everyday experience by simple application of *intentio recta*. Where a corpus of religious knowledge has already crystallized, such elements of it as are indispensable for efficient everyday knowledge are propagated in the everyday knowledge of the adult segment in any one generation, thence to be transmitted to the successor generation. However, the institutionalized representatives of the religion in question (priests, soothsayers, the theocratic establishment, etc.) keep on 'chipping in' and preventing the transmission of this knowledge from following its natural path: otherwise, as a result of the infusion of local idiom and particularistic knowledge, the corpus of knowledge as transmitted would gradually drift further and further from the original dogmatic system. This constant process of intervention and rectification aimed at 'restoration' of the original doctrinal body, is particularly striking in the case of the great world religions.

In the same way, scientific knowledge also infiltrates everyday knowledge; but this is a modern phenomenon which bears little resemblance to the traditional induction of religious knowledge. The *conscious* introduction of scientific results into the content of everyday thought is an even more recent development, which has run in parallel with modern methods of mass communication.

Traditional as the method of transmission was, the 'thus-ness' of religious thought could very well be assimilated into everyday thinking: for one thing, the two types of thought are akin, though, of course, religious concepts had to be translated into the language of everyday concepts. But this is not the case with scientific infiltration: here, everyday thinking can or does take over certain scientific facts, *but it cannot take over scientific knowledge per se.* When a scientific fact percolates into everyday thought, it is assimilated into the matrix of everyday knowledge in itemized form, i.e. detached from its own matrix. Snippets of scientific information appear in such isolated form in everyday knowledge, detached from their own homogeneous medium, victims of the pragmatism of everyday thinking. Partly they serve as springboards for everyday action of some kind, partly they provide heterogeneous information; finally, they may contribute to the de-fetishization of everyday life (this is particularly true of such philosophical knowledge as infiltrates everyday thinking).

It will help if we take examples of each of the three ways in which scientific fact is utilized in everyday thinking. We tell the children to eat oranges because they are rich in vitamin C. The statement contains scientific information. But what if we ask the mother who utters this statement – what is vitamin C? What is its chemical composition? How can it be shown that oranges contain it? The enthusiastic champion of vitamin C will not know what to answer. Nor does she need to, for, as far as she is concerned, 'vitamin C' is not the object of scientific research but shorthand for something she has come to regard as usefully connected with her children's diet. The vitamin C content of oranges is not to be proved or disproved: it is simply taken for granted, like the local customs and the household utensils; 'scientific facts' are applied in everyday thinking, much as old wives' tales about what you should and shouldn't eat.

Scientific facts 'handed down' to everyday knowledge are not always used as springboards for practice. They may simply serve to satisfy man's curiosity. Curiosity about what things really are – what makes them 'tick' – is the everyday version of the scientific spirit of abstract theory. Human curiosity was a necessary precursor of this scientific and theoretical attitude. But, scientifically true *information* garnered from curiosity about how the world works is very far from being scientific *knowledge*. The way in which such information is appropriated into everyday knowledge is essentially no different from the way in which non-scientific knowledge was once gathered from a rigmarole of myths and superstitions. Everyday knowledge will accommodate the statement that the earth is an oblate spheroid just as readily as the statement that it is supported by a giant tortoise. Neither statement can be verified or refuted in this sphere; each can be accepted as hearsay. It can, of course, happen (and not infrequently does) that someone or other is sufficiently interested and inquisitive to refuse simply to accept a ready-made piece of scientific information as a datum, and tries to go a bit further into its background – i.e. penetrates a medium proper to some branch of science. When this happens we are no longer dealing with everyday knowledge but with upward transfer thereof to scientific thinking (though the 'person' concerned may not himself be aware of this).

The search for scientific information and the subsequent montage of such information into the corpus of everyday thought need not necessarily be the result of interest and curiosity. In some social circles, the acquisition of such knowledge counts as a desirable component of general culture. It may indeed contribute to preferment in a given society: which means that, in an indirect sense, it may be acquired for pragmatic reasons. In secondary schools, pupils are taught specialist subjects on a (admittedly low) scientific level, they are introduced to the homogeneous medium of a given science, much of which they will retain in later life, even if they are not specifically concerned with science; but essentially this is no more than that degree of scientific information which one can or must use in a given social milieu.

Yet another function attaches to scientific (mainly philosophical) knowledge in the formulation of the everyday conduct of life. Knowledge of Epicurean principles guided followers of this philosophy for centuries; and knowledge of Marxism has transformed the life-style of hundreds of thousands. Even here, however, reception is not total, nor is there any good reason why it should be. Anatole France's Abbé Coignard knew very well how to live according to Epicurean principles, though he would hardly have been able to refute anti-Epicurean arguments on a purely philosophical level.

In the enjoyment of a work of art, in catharsis (and, naturally, in proportion to the intensity of that catharsis) the everyday 'person' is lifted out of his everyday-ness and elevated, *via* the homogeneous medium of art, to a sphere of objectivation 'for itself' which thereby becomes 'for him'. But if we approach the question from another standpoint, and ask whether a work of art enhances our everyday knowledge in any way, or how it fits into the structure of that everyday knowledge, we reach conclusions which are similar to, if not identical with, those we arrived at in the case of philosophy and science. Every work of art provides some information about, knowledge of, the world and ourselves, and at the same time it presents its own hierarchy of values corresponding to the hierarchy proper to the species-essential values. Not infrequently, the knowledge content (i.e. of the work of art) begins to lead an independent life of its own as an after-growth of the artistic experience: that is, the 'person' experiencing the work of art internalizes it as 'information' in the exact sense of the word. And in this sense we can learn from a work of art knowledge of a sort which will serve as a guideline in the practical guidance of everyday life. Ideals are born when we decide to match up to fictional heroes. The work of art may be the object of, and satisfy, interest and curiosity, just as scientific information does. From fiction we can learn how people we have never met behave in places we have never visited. The composition of a work of art, based as it is on its hierarchy of values, can have great influence on the shaping of one's life as a whole. Let us recall Rilke's 'Du musst dein Leben ändern' – the message which, according to Rilke, every work of art imparts. Inasmuch as this is so, the work of art acts as a mediating agent for moral content and moral judgments which can, precisely because of their *moral* properties, exercise a transforming and articulating influence on our lives (thus performing in the aftermath of the aesthetic experience a practical and high-grade function).

I have indicated how the content of everyday knowledge can be transformed or modified in two different ways: how this can happen 'from below', i.e. from the nexus of social needs and personal experiences, and how this transformation is affected by the infiltration, the mediation of species-essential objectivations 'for itself'. We must now say a few words about the way in which knowledge from these two sources 'meets' on the level of everyday knowledge. The meeting-point or juncture can be considered from the structural point of view, and from that of content.

As regards the structure, it follows from what we have just said that in the case of juncture the structure of everyday thought puts its stamp on knowledge as a whole. But in so far as the role of non-everyday knowledge in everyday life is to transform the way (or conduct) of life, even if the structure of everyday knowledge does not itself change, the relationship between the subject of everyday life and this structure does change. Ultimately, this can lead to gravitational shift within the given structure. This is a point to which we shall return.

As regards content: species-essential objectivations 'for itself' arise from the intention of satisfying needs felt by members of a given society (whether those who create them are aware of this or not). In everyday experience, people living everyday lives feel and react to (even if only partially) the same social needs, and build them into everyday knowledge as well, whether on the particular-istic plane or on the generic plane 'in itself'. One-sided and partial as this everyday experience may be, as a result of the social division of labour, in its direct unity with practice, it remains in a certain sense the same experience as that embodied and general-ized in objectivations 'for itself'. For this reason, the meeting with species-essential objectivations 'for itself' where this has infiltrated everyday knowledge means or can mean 'awakening' or 'illumina-tion'. The (social) sciences, philosophy, art, can bring experience into conscious focus, can prompt us to see our own person in a new light; and in this way they can influence everyday perception itself. For example, Impressionist painting taught us to perceive colours in our everyday experience of nature of which we had been previously unaware. And the other way round: everyday experi-ence can invalidate, confute objectivations 'for itself' and unmask them as inauthentic. The penchant displayed by the Enlighten-ment and by German Classicism alike for folk poetry shows that both saw something normative in it – the possibility that once men were released, if only partially, from the social division of labour, they could achieve a more organic unity between everyday know-ledge coming from 'above' and from 'below'.

All knowledge comes naturally from personal experience; but not all personal experience is likewise socially relevant, not all personal experience is equally general, equally extendible, equally meaningful for the members of a given stratum or integration. It is clear that the experience of 'persons' is built into the general content of everyday thought and generalized for transmission to future generations, in so far as these experiences relate to relatively general social needs and/or to their satisfaction: i.e. in so far as they derive from typical situations. Everyday knowledge may therefore be purely personal, i.e. applicable to a singular case, or it may be generally relevant: and between these two poles there is a wide range of possibility. If I discover that X has been making a practice of swindling me, this is no doubt an important item of knowledge as far as I am concerned, but not one which is, in this form, capable of more general extension (at most, it could only be of interest to others who do business with X – though even here it does not follow that X has been swindling them too). Personal knowledge is of crucial importance in the everyday life of the 'person' – as long as he recognizes it as nothing more than 'personal' knowledge. Such knowledge ceases to be relevant only when we over-generalize it and lend it an appearance of general validity: to use the example just given, if I say 'everyone is swindling me' or 'everyone is a swindler'. Mistaking the particular for the general is a fertile source of prejudice.

Knowledge can be particularistic in two ways – by reason of its character, and by reason of social pressure (from prescriptive norms, custom, etc.). Knowledge is particularistic in character when it really does apply to no more than a very narrow circle. A research scientist has to know who else in the world apart from him is engaged on similar work. This is not scientific knowledge, but the everyday knowledge of the scientist, and therefore as such, particularistic like a merchant's knowledge of the demands of his customers. Of considerable historical importance, however, is the second category – everyday knowledge which has to remain particularistic because of social prescription. 'Secrets' come under this heading: a secret represents privilege applied to an item or items of everyday knowledge, 'initiation' into some area of everyday knowledge which is not simply handed down from generation to generation, but which is only vouchsafed to certain persons, adepts, selected according to some principle or rule of admission. These secrets may, of course, have an economic function (as was the case with the handicraft guilds in the Middle Ages) or an ideological function (initiation into various mystic cults and practices); but they can also be simply of a separative nature or due to a desire to be 'secretive' (some kinds of family secrets). Knowledge generated in anticipatory thought (i.e. thought concerned with something likely to happen in the future) often takes on particularistic form. This can have great social significance if the anticipatory knowledge concerns an action which would be inhibited if knowledge concerning it were more widely spread. In these circumstances, preservation of the particularistic nature of the knowledge is held to be so important that it is always tied to ceremonial. The recipient of the knowledge is required to swear that it will go no further, plans will not be revealed, etc. etc. Divulgation of such particularistic information to non-authorized circles always rates as an offence, irrespective of whether the breach of secrecy is attended by damaging consequences or not.

'Privileged' status in everyday knowledge is surrounded by an aura of irresistible attractiveness. It is enough to mention the enormous role played by secrecy in children's games. It is also very attractive to be able to boast of privileged status. Secrets are inadvertently disclosed at least as often as they are guarded, but this is due less to evil intent or desire for gain than to the exhibitionism which attaches to the privileged status. Very often this is what happens in the disclosure of purely personal confidences.

The knowledge conveyed by species-essential objectivations 'for itself' is in principle public and general: which means that none of it can be secret. Morals have never been secretive – there are no such things as secret virtues! A main step forwards in the emergence of science was taken when the right of the guilds to keep certain processes secret was challenged: that is, when the principle that knowledge should be publicly and generally available to all was successfully defended. On the technical side of art, there could be – and were – secrets: how to mix certain colours or adhesives, how to carry out certain processes. But the creation of the work of art itself neither was nor could be 'secret'. If nowadays a species-essential objectivation 'for itself' contains secret areas, this is due not to the objectivation in question but to its relationship with everyday life or to institutional constraints. Secrecy as observed in medicine is not with regard to scientific results: these are published just as are those of any other scientific discipline. Secrecy in medicine is empirical in that it refers to 'persons': which patient has which disease is a confidential matter. But this is part of everyday knowledge, and is, scientifically speaking, a matter of complete indifference. Here the word 'secret' means what it means in general: it refers to particularistic knowledge which should only be released to certain initiates (in this case, other doctors) and the disclosure of which counts, for this very reason, as a breach of ethics.

(b) The anthropological properties of everyday knowledge

As a starting point here, we can assert that if we are to internalize the knowledge of adult generations and acquire new knowledge we must first of all learn to perceive, to feel and to think. These three components are only in theory separable; in practice – i.e. in everyday life – they form an indissoluble unity which is from our point of view of decisive importance. In everyday life there is no such thing as 'pure' perception, 'pure' emotion, 'pure' cognition: though the first – 'pure' perception – may occur in certain extreme cases of no great significance (Gehlen gives as an example the perception of a sudden strong light). When I make a good job of something, when I make friends with someone, when I gaze at the night sky, declare my love or look at my watch and jump out of bed – in such everyday events who is to draw boundaries between perception, feeling and cognition?

We are oriented towards types of perception – objects, forms, colours – which means that our perception is ordered by conceptual schemata: our way of perceiving is socially performed. Primarily, the knowledge we have taken over from previous generations guides our perceptions – a process in which language plays the leading role. The child perceives not 'roundness' but 'a ball': the naming of the object, the identification of its functions, turns perception into human perception. We begin by perceiving not 'red' but 'red objects': that is to say, objects which are distinguished from other objects by possession of a differentiating property – in this case, the colour red (in the case of colours, function does not play a primary role). But if we do succeed in perceiving 'redness' or 'roundness' this is not a retrograde step, but, on the contrary, the product of a higher level of conceptual generalization.

The fact that it is impossible to conceptualize the 'thus-ness' of the secondary qualities (and the human feelings) does not alter the former connection. In principle, we can only become aware of the difficulty of conceptualizing 'thus-ness' by applying the socially consensual types of perception to it. When I say 'you can't imagine what I'm suffering' I am making the assumption that the person I am addressing knows what is meant by 'suffering': in other words, I assume a consensus. In such a situation, deliberate deception is, of course, possible, but this has nothing to do with the specificity of

195

perception: deception may also consist in the false reportage of mental occurrences.

It is into the knowledge taken over from previous generations that we 'mount' or 'assemble' our new perceptions. Analogical subsumption has a part to play here. Our reaction, explicit or tacit, to any completely novel or unexpected perception is to say: 'What's this?' The question itself expresses the desire to integrate the new experience, the new sensation into the category of everyday knowledge. The concept of 'wonder' plays, accordingly, a very big part in everyday thinking: being simply the means whereby we subsume whatever we may have experienced (or heard others claim that they have experienced) though we have not yet been able to fit it into the structure of everyday knowledge. A child fails to perceive lots of things simply because it does not know they exist. But it pays closer attention to certain things it *does* perceive than an adult does, because these things are of greater primary importance to it. The actual field of perception varies modally from one social class or status-group to another. A high-class window display will simply look expensive and glittering to a poor man; a rich man, however, will look for what distinguishes one article from another, and his perceptual differentiation will extend even to fine detail. The work we do, the position we occupy in the social division of labour, our particular need, our particular interest – all of this has a guiding hand in the delineation of our field of perception and the selection of its content.

Window-shopping in a street of brightly lit, expensive shops can be accompanied by joy, sorrow, anger, desire, indignation, envy, admiration, pride – by any or all of them in the most inextricable confusion. It is clear that the emotive content of a perception will depend very much on the social and personal significance of the object perceived, the associations and memories it recalls, the extent to which it satisfies or fails to satisfy our needs, etc.

Emotion may play the leading part in the generation of personal perceptions, just as cognition does. The lover sees more in the face of his beloved than the casual onlooker, and antipathy can help us to see many things we might not otherwise have noticed. Anger, they say, 'makes us blind', that is, inhibits our perceptual capacities with regard to a person, an object or a situation. Conceit makes us incapable of seeing ourselves as we really (i.e. by social consensus) are.

It is not rare for perception and feeling to be indistinguishably united in one and the same event or experience. Can we possibly separate perception from feeling when we sink into a warm bath,

196

or see a beautiful colour? These are relatively simple instances; let us take the more complex example of familiarity. Is this a feeling? Or is it the perception that everything is 'in its right place', everything is 'what we're used to'?

Everyday thought is thought aimed at the solution of everyday problems, and this explains its pragmatic character. Its pragmatism means not only that everyday cognition is the preparatory step towards the realization of some practical purpose, but also that this thought process does not become detached from the work to be performed, it does not organize itself to form its own sphere or homogeneous medium: it is meaningful in relation to the proposed aim and to nothing else. Hence, everyday knowledge *qua* knowledge does not constitute a specific sphere of its own but remains at all times a heterogeneous amalgam embedded in everyday life.

First and foremost, everyday thinking is thinking concerned with solving the problems of the 'person' in his environment. Everyday knowledge – the knowledge which the 'person' uses as a basis for his thinking – is, as we have seen, primarily not personal but general: it is a generalized distillation from the everyday experience repertory of previous generations. But the purpose for which the 'person' uses this knowledge is more often than not, personal; it is to find and secure his personal position in the given world. Mentally the 'person' appropriates just as much everyday knowledge from accumulated experience, as he needs for his sustenance and his advancement in a given place at a given time. That is to say, what we have here is not pragmatism in general, but personal pragmatism in particular: a personal pragmatism which uses ready-made everyday knowledge as its raw material, along with an admixture of personal experience gained on that basis.

This personal pragmatism often includes activity pursued in and for a broader integration. When this happens the activity directed towards the integration is carried out with everyday or slightly more than everyday knowledge. Little more than everyday knowledge was required to participate in the public sphere of the ancient city-state or the dealings of the medieval nobility. Everyday knowledge simply comprised the experience which 'persons' in these situations required if they were to take adequately informed decisions in practical matters affecting the given integration and its prospects. With the emergence of bourgeois society, activities aimed at self-preservation began to diverge from activities directed towards the preservation of the integration (the schism between '*homme*' and '*citoyen*') and it comes as no surprise to find everyday thought turning more and more into the cognitive foundation for purely personal action, while, at the same time, it becomes more and more difficult for decisions concerning the integration to be taken on the basis of everyday knowledge alone.

It is a specific property of the pragmatism of everyday thinking that cogitation is either in preparation for some activity or a reflection of concrete action already carried out. Mental preparation and retrospective reflection may, of course, yield very different spectra. When thinking is purely repetitive, it is separated neither in time nor in space from praxis. But thinking can be a process of prolonged deliberation, and this is not simply repetitive thinking even when the outcome of such deliberation is no more than subsumption of action based on analogy or precedent. Prolonged deliberation such as is involved in sizing up a situation or in painstaking examination of the possible means to adopt, differs from simple repetitive thought in another respect also – namely that the cognitive process may become a relatively independent phase. I say 'relative' because, though the thought still focuses on the activity, a certain independence is generated in that the cognitive process within the whole nexus demands a somewhat different – a theoretical – attitude. In such cases, the cognitive process is detached from praxis in time and occasionally also in space. And this holds good, whether the cognitive process precedes action or is a reflection thereon.

Preparatory thinking – i.e. thinking which is distinguished from action in time, or in time and space – is what Ernst Bloch calls 'anticipatory thinking'. Anticipatory thinking is always directed towards a future object and towards action likely to bring this object about, and is relatively theoretical in mode; intentionality assumes the form of theoretical attitude of a kind.

The fact that anticipatory thinking (like all everyday thinking) is directed towards the practical aims of the 'person' and towards ways of attaining these, does not mean that all anticipatory thinking is followed by action. We often think about how this or that is to be done, without ever really getting down to doing it. We have words like 'day-dreaming', 'pipe-dreams' to describe that brand of anticipatory thinking which lacks even the resolution of putting thought into action. Here too there is a distinction: non-everyday day-dreaming can be distinguished from purely everyday day-dreaming, in which the castles in Spain are purely 'personal': i.e. the day-dreamer is concerned with his own prospects alone. We cannot use this as evidence to decide whether the 'person' is particularistic or an individual (in our sense). It is one thing to 'dream' of taking over my neighbour's business, and quite another to 'dream' of helping my friends in need; but each is an everyday dream concerning the life of the 'person'.

The basic significance of anticipatory thinking in everyday life is again pragmatic or, eventually, ethical-practical; day-dreaming in which resolution to act plays no part is something we all know from our own experience. The type of day-dreaming we indulge in is a pointer to our character and potentialities, and can therefore help us to know ourselves as we really are. At the same time, it is a sort of 'free', uncommitted play of the human spirit: and I stress the word 'play' as synonymous with 'uncommitted' and in this sense it appertains to the wholeness of our everyday life. Day-dreaming only becomes problematic when it takes over the whole sphere of anticipatory thinking, if the majority of our mental plans turn into day-dreams. In the extreme case, this leads to non-viability of the day-dreamer, such as Goncharov describes so well in the figure of Oblomov. It is worth pointing out that, as a variant of anticipatory thinking, day-dreaming also serves as the anthropological basis of a species-essential objectivation 'for itself' in everyday life – art. Indeed I can go further and say that no objectivation 'for itself' could exist without an everyday base in the shape of day-dreaming. Bloch makes this point when discussing certain forms of day-dreaming which are transformed into species-essentiality – e.g. in Utopias.[1]

Action is often followed by review of that action: a reflection or recapitulation of the action, and distanced from it in time or in time and space. (Whether I approve in retrospect of what I have done or not – I think about it.) We all know what it feels like to realize after the event what we ought to have said or done in the first place – in other words, to have hindsight. But inadequacy of preparatory thought is not necessarily to blame here: often, action itself produces the feeling that we ought to have acted or spoken quite differently.

An important aspect of everyday thinking is summed up for us in the saying: 'It's a wise man who learns from the misfortunes of others'. Subsequent reflection is not confined to my own actions; in exactly the same way, I can reflect on those of others as well, and observe the results. Indeed, this is one of the main channels whereby we acquire experience in everyday life. In the final resort, however, this kind of thinking (acquisition of experience) is directed towards my own praxis. The words 'I learn from the misfortunes of others' simply mean that my thinking prior to leading up to some action, will take into account what has befallen others.

The total inseparability of everyday thinking from everyday practice means that in everyday life 'true' and 'right' coincide; and the same goes for their negatives 'false' and 'wrong'. If I know enough about an implement to use it properly (i.e. in accordance with its purpose), then I can say that my information is 'true'. Again, if I know enough about the society I live in to lead my life therein adequately, I can say that my information is 'true'. If I know a man well enough, I can treat him in a certain way and predict his reactions; again I can say that I have true information about that man. Everyday knowledge, cumulated in the sphere of objectivation 'in itself' provides us with 'true' information on an overall scale, though not for the whole manifold of its field of application: for it is thanks to this knowledge that we can sustain overselves in the framework of a particular everyday life.

Thus it is not by chance that 'true' in the everyday use of the word, comprises both informational and ethical components. True knowledge is knowledge which corresponds to the facts. What facts? Our knowledge of facts – including rules and norms – as handed down to us from previous generations, plus the results of our own personal experience. The former category – that of knowledge taken for granted – predisposes the way in which persons acquire experience, and the way in which this experience is evaluated. A 'right' deed is one that corresponds to 'true' norms. Again, this is no more than the application of inherited knowledge (in the shape of norms, knowledge of customs) and of personal experience (i.e. the knowledge of which norm applies to a given experience, and how). There is accordingly one single unit criterion of what is 'true' – what is 'right' (i.e. right knowledge, right action).

The converse of 'right' behaviour is 'wrong' behaviour. Possibly, I am the only one to suffer when I behave 'wrongly': in this case, 'wrong' behaviour still attracts moral disapproval, though such disapproval will be intensified when others also are harmed.

The opposite of true (or right) everyday knowledge is 'wrong' knowledge. Three sources of wrong knowledge can be identified. First, we may be ignorant of certain facts or norms. In this case, wrong knowledge is the result of inadequacy of information. This is, of course, not something that can be measured in an absolute sense: inadequacy here is a function of the available possibilities, and of the extent to which, and the manner in which, a kind of knowledge is imposed on a given community. A second source of wrong knowledge is 'error', which we may define as incorrect deduction from experience which is itself adequate: incorrect filing resulting from a weak analogy or inadequate subsumption. The latter is a frequent source of error in our knowledge of human character. The third source of wrong knowledge is principally different from the previous two – lying. In this case, correct information is available but is deliberately withheld. That is to say, this is a moral, not an epistemological category.

Discussions about the rightness and truth of knowledge and action are not infrequent in everyday life, particularly when they concern the correct interpretation of concrete cases: that is to say, how is such and such an experience to be evaluated from the standpoint of received (inherited) true and right knowledge. Often, however, those ways of acting and those items of knowledge which are accepted as traditionally 'right' turn out to be questionable. When social needs generate new social experience, or when knowledge of certain species-essential objectivations 'for itself' percolates into the everyday (and, as we have seen, these two processes reinforce each other and usually join forces), 'What is true?' will be a decisive question in certain social groups. In the Enlightenment, for example, speculation on whether the claims of religion were true or not, was a daily and self-authenticating topic of conversation.

Everyday thinking is imbued with perception, it is immediate to 'perception'; at the same time it is shot through with feeling. Our everyday concepts are, as we saw above, extraordinarily graphic and highly imaginative. When I utter the word 'table', am I thinking or imagining? Clearly, it is science alone that works with concepts which are totally stripped of visual imagination. Here, it is pointless to raise the question of priority. Perception, even *human* perception has no priority *vis-à-vis* conceptual thinking; nor has the latter priority *vis-à-vis* perception. It is only when I already possess the concept 'table' that I can perceive 'a table'; and it is only by perceiving 'tables' that I can arrive at the concept 'table'. The two components are inseparably intertwined in one unified cognitive process.

It is, of course, not only concepts that are saturated with perception but everyday thinking in general. Let us recall what we said about anticipatory thinking. When I think something out in advance, when I anticipate what I am going to do, say, etc. I always imagine the outcome on the basis of previous perceptions. It appears before me; I run through the whole scenario of ensuing events. True, pure conceptual thinking may put in an appearance on the everyday plane, but only as an importation, as a result of the infiltration of scientific knowledge into everyday: for example, when I add up how much I have spent in a shop. But everyday counting (in so far as it has become purely conceptual) has also become a knack of repetitive praxis. Where it is inventive, as in the case of a child learning to count, it is hardly separable from associated images: the two peaches, the figure '2' as written.

We turn now to an important corollary of the fact that everyday thinking is shot through and through with feeling: belief. Anticipatory thinking is usually accompanied by feelings of fear or hope, depending upon whether I am anticipating success or failure. But even my most matter-of-fact statements can also have an emotional content, in so far as they relate to my life. When my son comes home from school and says, 'I came top today' or 'I was bottom of the class today' these statements will fill me with pride or with shame (possibly anger). When I am considering whether I shall go out visiting tonight, my cogitation is deeply influenced by my feelings: do I like the person, shall I be bored in the company of so-and-so, etc. – and this will affect my decision. Wittgenstein points out how many different feelings pertain to conditional sentences, how many different feelings can be expressed by the word 'if'.

Everyday perception, everyday thinking and everyday feeling are anthropologically primary; in no way can they be abstracted from the human being as a whole. It is for this reason that none of them appears in isolation. Simultaneously and in conjunction they characterize man's cognition and man's action, virtually indissoluble the one from the other. Husserl called the everyday attitude to things the 'natural' one. This is not to say that the scientific or the artistic attitude are 'unnatural'; but it means that these attitudes are, anthropologically and ontologically, secondary. As such, they can suspend pragmatism, they can make independent use of those components (perception, thinking, feeling) which are inseparable in everyday attitudes; they can abstract from the totality of the anthropological 'thus-ness', and, what is more, they can surpass the anthropologically given frontiers of human understanding (e.g. the limits of sense perception).

It is not the content of everyday knowledge alone that provides the basis for knowledge 'for itself' in so far as it propounds the questions which the species-essential objectivations 'for itself' answer, and collates the experience which these objectivations raise to a higher level of conceptuality or transform into

202

expressions of human species-essentiality in general. Our everyday anthropological-ontological attitudes (our 'natural attitudes') are also the fundament for attitudes appertaining to all other objectivations 'for itself'. These latter grow from the former and even when everyday attitudes are confronted by them (in *intentio obliqua*), either of two things can happen: either they can be fed back into everyday life and thinking (as in the case of *intentio obliqua*[1]) or at least they have recourse to certain aspects of anthropological 'thus-ness' as it has emerged in everyday life. The correlation is reinforced by the fact that, for example, a scientific truth becomes a scientific truth only if it is able to impugn everyday knowledge concerning the same subject (assuming that the two are at variance) and, at the same time, explain how this everyday knowledge came about. (In art, this function is performed by the value-hierarchy inherent in a given work, acting as a 'measure' of the authenticity of a particular way of life.) From all of this, it should be clear that everyday knowledge as the basis of all non-everyday knowledge, and our everyday natural attitude as the foundation of all other possible attitudes, are but two aspects of one and the same complex.

(c) What do we mean when we say we 'know something'?

Everyday knowledge is always opinion (*doxa*), never philosophical or scientific knowledge (*epistémé*). This distinction has nothing to do with the problem of whether truth is absolute or relative, temporary or eternal. Certain items in our everyday knowledge can be much firmer, less subject to change, more 'eternal' than our stock of scientific information. Men have always – and correctly – known that when an object is dropped it falls to the ground; but our scientific explanations of free fall have undergone radical change more than once. We have known that we can buy things for money for several hundred years; monetary theory has changed several times in the same period. Everyday knowledge remains '*doxa*' even if it is invariably proved to be true: scientific knowledge remains '*epistémé*' even if it is impugned and discarded.

As we know, *doxa* is inseparable from practical activity: it is in practical activity and nowhere else that *doxa* is verified. But this does not refer to praxis as a whole or even to a major segment of it; it is always in certain types of particular concrete and successful action that *doxa* is verified. Thus, different opinions are not related to each other in any other way (or only very loosely so): they all refer to different types of action. We recognize bird song or the sound of thunder and we know how to react to each, but of sound itself we know nothing, nor is there any reason why we should wish to know more. A common factor shared by various phenomena is of interest only if and when this common factor has become of crucial importance in one or another everyday activity. *Epistémé*, on the other hand, is not simply knowledge of or about phenomena, but knowledge of a phenomenon in its relationship with other phenomena (i.e. with a complex). Knowing something on the *epistémé* level, therefore, does not simply mean that we are thereby enabled to react to it (or even produce it); it means that we can recognize what links this phenomenon or event to other phenomena or events, and that we can offer a satisfactory explanation of this relationship. The truths of species-essential objectivations 'for itself' have therefore a dual referential system: they must prove valid in practice, and they must be capable of insertion in a given cognitive system (or of acting as organic components of a work of art).

Doxa is knowledge for which the information and values contained in the world of everyday knowledge and everyday norms are obvious or 'self-evident' (as a general rule, of course, and not in every single case). The sun rises, things fall to the ground, all men die, there is a God, there are masters and slaves, alcohol is intoxicating – all such items of information are taken for granted. On the level of everyday knowledge, they cannot be questioned; and if they are, one is straight away confronted with knowledge pointing to species-essential objectivation 'for itself' in embryonic form (e.g. why should there be masters and slaves?). *Epistémé* begins where the 'taken-for-grantedness' of knowledge itself becomes questionable. Against the evidence presented by 'given' truths, the man who is thinking on the level of *epistémé* will adduce counter-evidence and counter-arguments. It is possible that the recalcitrant thinker along *epistémé* lines will end up by accepting the knowledge he sought to impugn. But in this case the previous knowledge he now accepts has already been tested by counter-arguments and has been proved true on a higher level.

Causality also comes under the heading of self-evident truth in everyday thinking. As we saw, this is built into the work process, even in its most primitive forms. But here it always refers to the concrete causes of concrete results (whether causality is real or imagined). The generalized concept of causality – the concept that everything has a cause – is however, the product of the theoretical attitude, although it can make its appearance in everyday life as a step towards *epistémé*.

Proof and disproof do not mean the same thing in *doxa* as they do in *epistémé*. In the first place, the perceptual and emotional aspects of *doxa* are principially not open to either verification or refutation. I cannot prove that a certain item of knowledge makes me feel sad, any more than anyone else can prove me wrong if I claim to have had a vision of my late grandmother. Proof here is replaced by a probability weighting, disproof by calling in question. Wittgenstein stresses the crucial role played by 'casting doubt' in this connection. If I am sufficiently well acquainted with someone I shall know that what he says in a given situation expresses grief or sorrow, and I shall be in a position to doubt his word if he claims to be unaffected. If he claims to feel one thing while his actions indicate something else, I shall be entitled to cast doubt on his claims. On the *epistémé* level, however, there is no such thing as an undemonstrable or incontrovertible statement. Thinking on the scientific level is tantamount to exposing statements to refutation.

Of course, this does not mean that everyday thinking knows nothing of refutation or of verification. Proof and disproof in everyday life are usually connected with the facts of a case. If X says that Y was at school, when I know perfectly well that Y was playing truant, I can refute X: what I am refuting is a statement about a particular fact. Verification and refutation of this sort of factual content are the forerunners of legal thinking on the plane of everyday *doxa*: with the difference, however, that law always construes the constatation of fact within the terms of its own homogeneous medium.

Doxa is that knowledge which provides me with a basis enabling me to lead a successful everyday life guided by probability. As we shall see, particularistic attitudes require nothing more than *doxa*. But if most of an individual's everyday knowledge is also derived from *doxa*, it remains true that *epistémé* has a part to play in the way he organizes his life. We shall go into this in more detail later. For the moment suffice it to point out that while it is by and large mistaken to contrast the 'eternal' knowledge of *epistémé* with the 'ephemeral' knowledge of *doxa*, the distinction is not entirely irrational. The 'eternal certainties' of *epistémé* do not derive from any 'certainties' in our factual knowledge; rather, *epistémé* represents the degree attained, at any given time, of species-essential (generic) knowledge: and by virtue of this, it is always the bearer of the possible maximum of the truth-content of human cognition.

What is the meaning of 'to know' in everyday life? It means that we have appropriated the available public experience, we have built into this our own personal experience, and thus we have become capable of carrying out the heterogeneous types of action required in everyday life. Wittgenstein has rightly pointed out the 'family connections' of 'I know', 'I understand' and 'I'm able to do it'. 'I understand' means that I have appropriated an item of knowledge and 'become competent' to apply that knowledge. The levels of 'understanding', 'knowledge' and 'competence' are usually parallel: they may be superficial or they may be profound. If I take someone on as a typist, it's enough for me to know that she can type. If I am making friends with someone, I want to know something about his or her character, how he or she is motivated: only thus can I 'know' (i.e. I can reckon on the probability) that the friendship will be rewarding. Levels of understanding, knowledge and competence vary, then, according to the given aim or function. Failure to take level variation into account, or simply to ignore it, can land us in the catastrophes of everyday life.

It is in everyday thinking that we first encounter the problem of belief. I should like first of all to contrast my own conception of 'belief' with two other conceptions which are in some respects contradictory but which agree on one point. One of these two conceptions dates from the Enlightenment: it sets up an opposition between 'belief' on the one hand and 'knowledge' on the other. 'Believe' according to this viewpoint means 'not yet know', for knowledge makes belief superfluous and replaces it. This conception derives from two sources: firstly, from anti-religious polemic: religious belief was to be replaced by the firm and certain knowledge which, in Newton's day, it was 'believed' science could supply; secondly, it derives from the everyday use of the word: in everyday language 'I believe so' and 'I know' are functionally different. The second conception of 'belief' arises from the modern crisis in science: it denies the *epistémé* status of scientific knowledge. As I said, the two conceptions agree on one thing – they both regard belief as an epistemological category. But belief is not an epistemological category but a feeling which accompanies the most heterogeneous human behaviour and human attitudes *including* cognition.

Russell regarded belief as a 'feeling of affirmation' accompanying cognition. Belief is a specific variety of the 'feeling of affirmation' – the feeling of certainty. Like all our everyday feelings, the feeling of certainty too is always related to cognition. I can 'believe' that something exists, that a thought is accurate, that a cause will win, that people are decent, that a friend is loyal. In all such cases, belief is simply the registration of subjective certainty (a feeling of certainty). 'I believe' is not equivalent to 'I do not know': the co-ordinate system has changed. The statement 'I know I'm going to win' is not necessarily different from the statement 'I believe I'm going to win': but the former is a cognitive statement, the latter is an emotional report (naturally with cognitive connections).

All knowledge is accompanied by a kind of 'feeling of certainty': i.e. by belief. Hence, belief cannot act as a criterion in deciding whether the content of an item of information is true or false. That is, belief does not mean absence of knowledge, nor does it vouch for the truth of knowledge either; and this is what we mean when we use such expressions as 'I believe so' and 'I believe that's right' in everyday life.

Quantitatively, belief plays a bigger part in everyday life than anywhere else. As we have seen, people normally take over the forms of everyday life, the species-essential objectivations 'in itself', everyday knowledge, in ready-made form, and the feeling of belief is a component in the acceptance of these in their ipseity as taken for granted. Most people take their customary system, the prevailing moral norms, everyday ideologies and ideas as certainties and internalize them accordingly. In all situations involving a decision, situations in which the 'person' has to perform the subsumption as quickly as possible under the schemata of species-essential objectivations 'in itself' – in other words, fit them into a stereotype – 'belief', the feeling of 'certainty' plays a big part in that decision. The fact that belief is almost invariably present, however, tells us nothing about its intensity. Everyday beliefs proliferate, but few of them become passionate. It is mainly in the case of direct personal relationship with species-essential objectivations 'for itself' that belief turns into passionate belief: in crucial situations, for example, arising from such a conscious relationship with species-essentiality, and in the acceptance of such situations. Examples of this will be found mainly in the field of political action, in morals and in religion; but they also occur in science and art. It was Goethe who said that great historical periods are richly endowed with beliefs passionately held.

Belief – the feeling of certainty – can multiply our capabilities, give us wings, imbue our activities with new and greater energy: it can 'move mountains' though by the same token, it can breed the criminal and occasion the disaster. This is especially the case when our feeling of certainty leads us to discount knowledge, reasoning, even material evidence: that is to say, when we invest the feeling of certainty itself with cognitive value as the proof of truth.

The same thing happens – though to a lesser degree – in everyday life as well; and for this reason belief is accompanied in everyday life by that suspension of belief which we call scepsis. Scepsis is not the same thing as scepticism. Scepsis is always what we might call a 'local' suspension of belief in relation to a certain event, an item of information, a person, a solution, an expectation. In contrast, scepticism is a way of life, a mode of behaviour which sets out principally to suspend not a specific area of belief but belief, the 'feeling of certainty' in general. In other words, scepticism is not an everyday attitude, but a philosophical attitude coupled to a *Weltanschauung*. As such, it lies outside the scope of our present inquiry. We may note, however, that the so-called 'systematic scepsis' which makes its appearance with Descartes, does not turn scepsis into a behavioural principle; it merely seeks to question pre-cast knowledge and pre-cast information in so far as this falls short of the *point d'appui*, the evidence of the '*ego cogito*', in which basis the feeling of certainty is re-established, the firm ground underlying the acquisition of any new certainty. For our purposes, it is sufficient to note that, just as everyday belief provides the basis for the intensive beliefs which appear in certain species-essential objectivations 'for itself' and relate thereto, so does everyday scepsis provide the foundation for scepsis as raised to the status of a principle, a way of behaviour and a philosophical attitude.

The importance of the part played by scepsis, by the suspension of the feeling of certainty, in our daily lives, should be clear to everyone. I believe in someone – as a friend, as a partner, etc. – until a piece of evidence comes my way, suggesting that my belief is not well-founded: I then suspend my belief and try to find certainty, that is, to reinforce my knowledge either way. I am told conflicting stories about life in a foreign country – so I suspend belief in my sources till one or another is proved right, etc. Scepsis can indeed be generalized in everyday life, if on a less than philosophical basis. Here it takes the form of accepting only what is customary, ready-made, as worthy of belief, as giving a 'feeling of certainty', and reacting in principle with scepsis to whatever is unusual, unfamiliar, a singleton; in a word, showing 'suspicion'. It is found also in 'distrust', which is an excessive suspension of the 'feeling of certainty' with regard to people, especially people we don't know. Given their common origins, it is not surprising to find suspicion often coupled with distrust in one and the same person.

208

I said above that scepsis can be elevated to the status of a philosophical attitude, a principle. But this is exceptional. Both philosophy and science regard the assumptions and premises of everyday knowledge with scepsis; and religion turns belief into a principle, in that it excludes the possibility of suspending the feeling of certainty – scepsis – in relation to religious tenets.

As we have seen, both in everyday life and in species-essential objectivation 'for itself', belief can be the cause of tragedies and disasters and we can say the same about suspicion, distrust and scepticism. Many a man has missed out on life, has failed to take the chances life offered him, because he was distrustful of his fellows and suspicious of novelty, of new ways of doing things and of new experience. If we are to find the right mixture of belief and scepsis in each concrete case we need the Aristotelian *phronesis*: and we have to be on our guard against over-generalization. This is worth stressing. By and large, we tend as persons to be biased in this respect – that is, to be over-trusting (endowed with too strong a feeling of certainty) or over-suspicious; and this tendency can easily harden into a generalized attitude as a result of over-generalization with regard to experience. Abandoned by her lover, a woman tends to over-generalize and denounce all men as faithless, she will never believe one of them ever again, etc.; if I try to do something and it doesn't come off, I may over-generalize and say, 'It's no good trying, I may as well give up, I'm just not up to it', etc. Over-generalization of scepsis is on a level with over-generalization of belief as a source of prejudice.

So far, we have dealt with 'belief', the feeling of certainty, in abstract terms. The content of belief, however, can vary quite extensively, depending on why (i.e. cause and motivation), how and in what we believe; or, why, how and when we suspend our feeling of certainty *vis-à-vis* someone or something. Ethically, this is, in the vast majority of cases, very far from being a matter of indifference. Accordingly, I divide the 'feeling of certainty' into two main types which differ significantly on the ethical plane: 'blind faith' and 'trust'.

'Blind faith' is the belief of the particularistic 'person'; 'trust' is the belief of the individualistic 'person'. The particularistic 'person' armed with 'blind faith' clings unquestioningly to what- ever information, knowledge, idea or event appears to reaffirm his particularity; and he only withdraws his belief from something (i.e. he turns 'sceptical' regarding an item of information, knowledge, etc.) if it appears to threaten his particularity. The individualistic 'person' armed with 'trust' clings unquestioningly to any information, knowledge, idea or event which he sees as wholly or partially invested with sublime values: and adopts a sceptical attitude towards them when they appear to him to violate or at least run counter to species-essential values.

As we might expect, it is not only in everyday life that the contrast between blind faith and trust plays a part: we find it active as well in the sciences, in the arts, in politics and in morals. Even religious behaviour can give rise to not insignificant divergencies between blind faith and trust.

It has to be pointed out here that suspicion and distrust as behavioural forms tending towards generalization, express particularistic reactions. This kind of reaction will arise as a rule in cases where blind faith has suffered a disappointment – particularly if the disappointment is conclusive. I do not mean to suggest that one may not act particularistically to disappointed trust (for the individual may also have particularistic reactions): and shock suffered thus may well lead to the generation of suspicion and distrust. But since the trust characteristic of the individual 'person' is bonded to the species-essential values which provide him with his feeling of certainty, a loss of trust usually remains partial (trust can be reallocated): if this is not possible, i.e. if no suitably generic (species-essential) values can be found as replacement, and seem unlikely ever to be found again, the result can be despair. The way back from despair to trust is theoretically open, but not for all in all cases: it depends on a new and worthy object being found for trust to attach itself to. I may add here that blind faith and trust are not always sharply distinguished from each other. In many cases they are indistinguishable from each other; in other cases, disappointment leads through the intermediary stage of despair to total separation (incomparably portrayed by Shakespeare in the figures of Lear, Othello and Edmund).

The feeling of certainty is closely connected with the acceptance of the responsibility we bear in everyday life for our knowledge. We are responsible for whatever knowledge we transmit or use as a basis for action by word or by deed. We are responsible to ourselves and to others. If I feel myself competent to mend a fuse, I take the responsibility (if the fuse blows I am responsible because, clearly, I didn't know enough). If I say to someone, 'Come and see me tomorrow evening' I make myself responsible for being at home tomorrow and for trusting my visitor as a suitable person to invite to my home, etc. etc. Responsibility varies in degree, of course, proportionately to the results of my deeds or words: are these results far-reaching or restricted, serious or trivial, etc. People are spontaneously aware of this kind of everyday responsibility. Restriction, concessive modification of information-bearing statements tends to reduce the responsibility component. If instead of saying, 'Peter is a bad character' I say, 'I have the impression that Peter is a bad character' I am reducing my responsibility for the judgment. Similarly, if instead of saying 'That's enough' I say 'I think that's enough'. Of course, it is not so easy to apply this way of reducing responsibility to non-verbal acts, even though it can occasionally be done (an indistinct gesture which may or may not be a greeting, a cautious overture which can always be nipped in the bud, etc.).

Fear of responsibility can encourage us to stick to proven stereotypes, to lead our everyday lives on the 'average' principle, to use repetitive praxis even in situations which cry out for inventive thinking. And the reason why the average man is conventional in his belief – which readily turns into 'blind faith' – that he is deeply distrustful not to say suspicious of innovation, is very often fear of responsibility. And yet, fear of responsibility is by no means a purely negative category. We know only too well what men are capable of, once they place themselves, whether by virtue of their position or out of despotic caprice, beyond the reach of this fear. Nero burned Rome down so that he could write a poem about it. The individual who acts on a basis of norms informed by positive values may also be afraid of taking responsibility; but here, given that real values are at stake, what results is not a flight from responsibility but a decision to shoulder it, with fear as an undercurrent. 'The time is out of joint,' says Hamlet, 'O cursed spite, That ever I was born to set it right.' For Hamlet, overcoming his fear of responsibility is equivalent to testing his knowledge, to convincing himself that what he is about to do will prove an adequate answer to the situation, and neither a capricious nor a purely conventional action.

(d) Types of theoretical attitude in everyday thinking

So far, we have had much to say about the foundations of those mental attitudes which are peculiar to species-essential objectivations 'for itself' (i.e. peculiar in that they are not 'natural') in everyday thinking. We have spoken of the elementary forms in which the theoretical attitude appears within the pragmatic structure (spatial and temporal distancing from praxis), including anticipatory thinking; we have mentioned the 'fact of the case' and discussed belief, blind faith and trust as a 'feeling of certainty' relating to knowledge; and we have tried to show that everyday knowledge – both in its anthropological specificity and by virtue of its cognitive content – is the basis for the higher-ranking species-essential objectivations. In what now follows, we shall try to approach this group of problems from a new angle. We shall analyse certain cognitive types which, as such, have no relationship with everyday pragmatism; though this does not prevent them from taking root within the field of everyday experience, and even becoming typical faculties. These then are pure non-everyday attitudes which are nevertheless organic components of everyday life and thinking, and which, as such, become in turn the basis for species-essential objectivations 'for itself'.

Since the very earliest times, man has indulged in contemplation. The contemplative mood is generated in any relationship with nature which is not purely pragmatic: i.e. when we do not use or subdue nature, but neither do we fear her. Its primeval character is, of course, no more than relative. And indeed the emergence of contemplation as an independent mental attitude depends on man's having attained a state of existence beyond the struggle for mere survival. As we have already said, the world in which he lives and moves, awakens man's interest and curiosity. And wherever there is neither need for, nor possibility of a pragmatic attitude, man's interest and curiosity become ends in themselves. Anything which is of pragmatic interest in one co-ordinate system can become an object of contemplation in another. The shepherd raised his eyes to the starry heavens: what were those brilliant objects, variously grouped and clustered, which lay so far beyond his reach? He marvelled at them and was awed by them. He gave them names, and sought to impose images on their various constellations. He learned to look at something he did not use; he learned to take pleasure in something he did not consume. From such contemplation it is still a long way to discovery of the 'beauty of nature'. This could, in fact, only be mediated through art. But once the discovery was made, the beauty of nature became an inexhaustible source of daily pleasure: the fine traits of a face, the harmony in a landscape, the concord of sound – all of this adds up to a modal complex which has no parallel in the satisfaction of our vital needs. Contemplation becomes the basis for both science and art in our everyday perceptions.

Closely allied to contemplation is the description of qualities. Primarily, of course, the description of qualities is pragmatic in intention. I describe the qualities of something so that I may know how and when to use it (that is, how I should react to it).

But one can assume that at a very early stage in man's history description of qualities seems to have taken off on its own, and separated off from its purely pragmatic function: while continuing to describe what is pragmatically essential, it begins to take notice of and portray other qualities which have no pragmatic significance whatever. These qualities are also constituents of knowledge and passed on to future generations. The drawings of bison in the Altamira caves are very good examples of the independence of observation as intention. The drawings not only notate qualities which are of concern in the chase and in the utilization (cooking, consumption) of the bison, but also show amazingly keen, almost naturalistic observation of the bison, a precise inventory of properties which could not have been of the slightest interest to anyone engaged in hunting, butchering or cooking the bison.

A kind of homogenization is associated with classification. Primarily, the act of classification arises from a pragmatic need. For example, men had to be able to distinguish edible plants and fruits from poisonous ones; and, within this classification, the first category – that of edible items – had to be further subdivided. So, appropriate forms of classification were needed. Once man had developed the practice of classifying things, however, he did not restrict it to the purely pragmatic sphere. As Lévi-Strauss shows, the 'edible/poisonous' taxonomy is soon followed by classifications distinguishing certain poisonous plants from others – not on the pragmatic basis of their toxicity but by all sorts of non-pragmatic criteria. These subdivisions have no pragmatic significance at all. A way of arranging objects in homogeneous fashion had been worked out: a capability which tended to become independent of its pragmatic origins in that its practice was found to be *interesting*, satisfying man's curiosity. Man had found a way of pinning down reality not only for action but in theory as well.

Everyday preparation for something, the collection of the requisite data, the attempt to ensure that action when taken will be accompanied by a feeling of certainty, all of this can be seen as a cognitively informed pre-praxis, a form of experimentation which is particularly common in everyday life. This is a specific practical activity which is, whether I can carry it out on my own or in conjunction with others, neither an end in itself nor simply the preparation for the performance of some purpose or other (e.g. for a game). Its aim is to provide sufficient information for a decision to be taken: to ensure that that action will be taken which has the highest probability value rating; amounting in the optimal case to certainty. For example, we try a new paint on a bit of wood to see what it looks like before starting to use it: that is, we acquire preparatory knowedge of this particular paint. (Increase of information here is designed to reduce responsibility.) There can be little doubt that in such everyday processes we see the germs of certain forms of scientific practice. (Experimentation with human beings is morally ambiguous and therefore problematical; but this is not the place for discussion of this theme.[2])

As we have seen, everyday knowledge (*doxa*) is not connected with a homogeneous *Weltanschauung,* but nevertheless a unified world-view does emerge on the level of everyday thinking: the need for a synthesis makes itself felt here too. Such a need is based partially on teleological questions regarding the 'person' such as 'Why am I in this world? For what reason? To do what? Why should this happen to me!?' But there is more to it than that. Teleological questions concerning 'us' are also bound to arise: questions deriving from 'we-consciousness' suggest themselves, such as how did the tribe originate, etc., questions posed by the work process but detached from it (pseudo-pragmatic magic, especially its analogical form which Frazer called 'transfer magic'). Initially the needs and thought-forms which arise from these multifarious sources form partial syntheses in the shape of myths, which are religious and artistic modalities as yet undifferentiated from everyday thinking. These myths explain the 'thus-it-is' of man's world. But only religion welds such partial syntheses together to make a global synthesis. The Greeks were the first to construct a philosophical synthesis; a synthesis which from its very inception had to fight against the synthesizing procedures and the content of myths arising from the anthropomorphic cast of everyday thought.

The great syntheses of religion and philosophy do not, however, prevent everyday thought from continuing to form its own partial syntheses. In character these are partly mythopoetic, partly synthetic generalizations from everyday experience – 'folk wisdom' so-called. For long historical periods neither religion nor philosophy (nor, latterly, science) could afford to relax in their struggle for man's soul – in their struggle to bring everyday life and thinking under the control of their own synthetic world-views. Developments over the last hundred years (their causes need not be discussed here) go to show that these claims are obsolescent if not actually in part at least obsolete; and that the species-essential objectivations 'for itself' are relinquishing their pretensions as the sole providers of holistic world-views and their entitlement to implant these in everyday thinking. It is equally true that fewer and fewer partial syntheses are spontaneously formed: those that do appear are organized and manipulated, and turned into ready-made consumer goods.

CHAPTER 12

Everyday contact

I must first of all make it clear that the phenomena of everyday life cannot be 'parcelled up' according to whether they relate to knowledge, to contact or to personality. If I utter the words 'dispute' or 'game' I am referring to two phenomena which have to do with knowledge and which are of no small importance in the development of the personality. It might look arbitrary to analyse them in a chapter on everyday contacts. But some degree of arbitrariness is unavoidable if we want to apprehend theoretically a sphere which is essentially heterogeneous, in which every phenomenon is a part of a heterogeneous complex. Of course, this arbitrariness is only relative. In the following pages we shall discuss those phenomena which have primarily and decisively to do with contact (though they may well have other aspects as well) or which it is desirable to approach from the angle of contact.

(a) Everyday contact as the basis and mirror of social relations: equality and inequality

'Everyday contact' does not mean that 'man' is in communication, in contact with another 'man': what it means is that the occupier of one place in the social division of labour communicates with, is in contact with the occupier of another place: the lord of the manor communicates with his vassal or his serf, the managing director with his departmental head or section chief, the conductor with the passenger, the small-holder with the labourer, etc. Even where blood relationships are concerned, the form, content, customary and normative aspects of contact are determined by relative position in the division of labour (father-son and brother-brother relationships have often changed throughout history); to say nothing of contact forms between men and women, which depend on prescriptive and proscriptive custom and which are infinitely variable. When someone says to someone else, 'I'm going to talk to you, man to man', what this means is that in this particular contact both parties are going to be abstracted from the positions they hold in the social division of labour, and from observance of the prescriptive customs which delineate their contacts on the social average.

Of course, when I say that contact between people is a function of the positions they occupy in the social division of labour and of the prescriptive (and proscriptive) norms governing these positions, I do not mean that contact is between pure embodiments of social roles: contact is still between 'persons'. The character of the 'person' as a unified whole makes itself manifest in contact types of every kind, remaining 'identical' with, a facsimile of itself in every kind of relationship with all sorts of people.

Depending on allocated site in the division of labour, the contact relations which take shape in everyday life can be divided into two fundamental categories: relations based on equality, and relations based on inequality. The latter comprise (a) relations of dependency, and (b) hierarchical relations between superordinates and subordinates. Relations of dependency are always personal relationships, in the sense that one man depends on another. Hierarchical relations, on the other hand, reflect relative position in the social division of labour, and are not necessarily based on personal dependence. Between a landowner and his own serf there was, in addition to the hierarchical relationship, a dependent relationship as well; but this was not the case between the same landowner and a serf belonging to someone else. There is a dependent relationship between teacher and pupil, but certainly not a hierarchical one. Potentially, the pupil may very well end up in a higher social slot than his teacher. Personal relations of dependency may terminate without change of place occupied in the social division of labour (a child grows up, a woman is divorced, a worker changes his job), but hierarchical relations change only when the position of the 'person' within the system of division of labour changes, or when the social division of labour is itself transformed.

It should be pointed out here that personal dependency relations (especially when they are simultaneously hierarchical) do not necessarily include personal contact. It is in principle impossible for a king to have personal contact with all his vassals, to say nothing of his lowlier subjects, or for an entrepreneur to have personal contact with each of his administrative and financial personnel, workers, etc.

Since, as we have seen, the hierarchical relationships reflect relative position within the social division of labour, these relationships are necessarily those of inequality. As such, they are principially alienated relationships. Mankind's age-old desire for equality is fuelled by hatred of and protest against social inequality as embodied in the hierarchical relationships. In stratified societies as a whole, the relationships of dependence are the manifest forms of the hierarchical relationships. But the personal relationships of dependence are not necessarily hierarchical. If they have been freely chosen, if they are founded on differences in skill or ability, if they have been called into being by the need to direct or integrate action or a series of actions, then the inequality they are undoubtedly based on is not social inequality but personal inequality. For example, parents and children, teachers and pupils, are linked by a relationship which is essentially one of inequality, because one side has far more knowledge and experience than the other. But this sort of non-alienated inequality might be temporary in duration and limited to one or another aspect of human contact which it does not touch as a whole.

Contacts formed on a basis of equality are the correlatives in a class society of hierarchically ordered contacts, i.e. those ordered on a basis of inequality. Landowner meets with landowner, departmental head with departmental head, housewife with housewife, as equals. Personal equality is alienated since it is a function of social inequality. More, it turns into an equalizing factor of what is unequal, since it designates as 'equal' sets of 'persons' who vary in human quality. Here, I am speaking not merely of the outward enhancement of personal capabilities (money will make you beautiful, witty and clever): the key point is that only priviliged position in the social division of labour enables certain human capabilities to be developed (certain kinds of knowledge, taste etc.). Whereupon this fact becomes an argument against equality in the mouths of those who defend the class system. (E.g. 'Women cannot really expect equality with men, for clearly they have never produced great works of any kind and even today they are less cultured, they always take a reactionary point of view', etc.) We can speak of non-alienated personal equality only where personal relations of dependency based on real differences in capability take the place of superimposed hierarchical relationships. The real antithesis of 'inequality' is then not 'equality' but 'free equality', 'unconstrained equality' in which contact between men becomes genuinely 'man to man' contact: i.e. contact between 'this man' and 'that man'.

The anthropological fact that human beings differ from each other is the indispensable basis for human contact. It is a point we hardly need to develop. Were it not for the fact that human beings differ from each other, the fact that each 'person' has some sort of 'personality', most types of contact would be superfluous. If you react to something in exactly the same way as I do, then there is no need for me to advise you, persuade you, explain something to you, and so on. But this has really nothing to do with the equality/inequality problem.

Everyday contact is the basis and the reflection of general social contact. Let us first consider the question of the base.

Everyday contact is always personal contact, contact between two or more persons. I use the words 'personal contact' in the widest sense. Personal contact does not necessarily involve cohabitation: ringing someone up or writing someone a letter is also personal contact. Then again, contact can be transmitted *via* things: selling shoes involves personal contact with the customers. The concept 'personal contact' is not, of course, synonymous with the concept 'relations between people'. Every social relation is a relation between people, but as complexes these are not relations of personal contact: these latter, however, provide their basis. Again, the fact that everyday contact relations are always relations between persons does not mean that they are always non-alienated relations. As I said above, hierarchical graduation as a fact of everyday contact is the way in which alienation expresses itself. But the extent to which a society is alienated is also expressed in personal contacts.

The extent to which the contact relations of everyday life reflect general social relations was discussed in some detail in the first part of this book. It is clear that the personal contact relations of one man or of a group of men do not, cannot, even when summed up, adequately reflect social relations as a whole. At the same time, every personal contact relation expresses something appertaining to the essence of the social aggregate. When the master boxed the servant's ears and the servant put up no resistance – when a man bullies a woman whenever he feels like it – or when, to take an example on the positive side, I make a lot of friends on a basis of equality – all of this exposes some important trait of the given world as a whole. The greater the number of personal relationships (human relationships) that arise on a basis of free, unconstrained equality in a given society, the more humane is the society.

(b) Modalities of everyday contact

Before we analyse the modalities of everyday contact, a few words on its main types are called for. These are (a) chance or random contact (b) customary contact (c) attachment, and finally (d) organized contact. Naturally, these are not necessarily isolated from each other; they often amalgamate. In themselves, these types tell us little or nothing about the intensity of contact involved. If two men, strangers to each other, meet at the scene of a fire and work together to put it out, this is chance contact in the sense that they had never seen each other before and will never see each other again; but the intensity factor in this chance encounter is very high, far higher than that found in customary contact between neighbours. From the social point of view, the most intensive of the four types is organized contact as found in the family, trade union, religious order, political party, i.e. in forms which are necessary for the self-reproduction of society. Taking emotional intensity as a criterion, however, we find that attachment takes pride of place. The essence of attachment consists in two or more people being in continuous and emotionally charged contact: the contact is based on mutual participation in an emotional bond. On the positive side, we have love and friendship; on the negative side quarrelsomeness (rancour) and hate.

We have already dealt (in Part I) with the socially most important types of social contact (i.e. such organized forms as groups and communities) and attachment will be considered at a later stage. For the present, then, we confine ourselves to analysis of the ways in which contact takes place. Essentially, there are two such ways – direct action and speech act.[1]

Direct action is, of course, not independent of speech act; that is to say, it is not 'mute' action, though mute action occurs (e.g. we may shake hands without speaking). But direct action is distinct from speech act in that it comprises a deed or deeds, and expresses itself directly without intermediary. Direct action takes place in the great majority of our everyday contactual relationships, the role of speech act being mainly to prepare for direct action or to reflect on it.

The number of forms expressed in direct action in everyday

contact is so great that we cannot even attempt to list them. A few examples may be given: doing something together (a walk, for example), doing something to another (I give someone something), reciprocal action (we play football). A taxonomy of direct action types could be attempted from all sorts of points of view. We shall concentrate on the one which interests us here – other people considered as ends or means in everyday contact.

In everyday contact of whatever type one party is being 'used' to some degree by the other: a contact situation in which neither party is being 'used' in any respect whatsoever, is an impossibility, indeed a contradiction in terms. When I engage an accountant I am using him as a means of ensuring good business management. When I invite people for the evening the thought that they may help me to pass the time agreeably is, if not uppermost, at least not absent from my mind. Marriage is, *inter alia*, a means for bringing offspring into the world. In a sense I can even regard my children as a means: a means of enhancing my own enjoyment of life, a means of support in my old age, or simply a means towards added prestige. It is in fact part and parcel of everyday life that, in certain types of contact, the other party participates solely as a means towards some end of mine: the conductor is there to give me a ticket, the electrician to fix my wiring. The alienation of everyday (personal) contacts does not, therefore, derive from the fact that other parties function, *inter alia*, as a means with regard to me, and that in certain (usually random) functional contacts one party serves exclusively as a means. Everyday life becomes alienated when and to the extent that, all my *human* contacts are for me contacts with means: that is to say, when, in what is the most important form of contact, I do not relate to the other person as to an end in itself. To put this another way: I said that in everyday contacts it is often unavoidable that a second party should serve in some respects as a means, but that does not mean that this second party should not also be an end in our relationship. Of course, not every contactual type is equally conducive to my regarding the second party as an end: this is most likely to ensue in attachments, least likely in random contacts. As a general tendency, however, we can assert that the more we are involved in contacts in which the second party is regarded as an end rather than a means (which means that the contact itself will be purposive) the more humane our everyday life will be.

Contact in which a second party is treated as, or virtually as, a means and nothing more is typically found in the hierarchical relationships based on super- and subordination. For the capitalist, the worker is a means in the business of making money; for the master, the servant is there solely to serve him personally. In so far as a second party *does* figure as an end rather than a means in such relationships, even this revised attitude is governed by utilitarian considerations: the reasoning being along the lines of 'If I treat my servant well, he will serve me more efficiently.' Only with the abolition of hierarchical relations of super- and subordination will it become socially unacceptable for anyone to be treated primarily as 'means' in everyday life.

The relationship in which a 'person' can be treated as 'means-to-an-end' and nothing more, becomes questionable *via* and is finally vetoed by morality. On the basis of the abstract moral norms (not the concrete norms) I have to treat this other being – in whom I recognize someone like myself – from the standpoint of what he needs and what he desires. What is 'good' is now not simply 'what is good for me': 'good' becomes a general value, and includes 'what is good for him' too. At the same time, if morality constitutes the substantive aim, the 'person' can still find himself being used as no more than a means to an end. The problem of the relationship between the end and the means arises in every objectivation 'for itself'. 'The end justifies the means' is an accepted attitude in politics; and we might also mention the use of a model in art, and experiments on animals and human beings in science.

It is not easy to separate the speech act in its primary manifestation as a category of activity in its own right, from the linguistic aspects of direct action. These primary forms are: information (report), discussion and persuasion.[2] All three can be directly related to action, and in the great majority of cases are so related. If I inform you that your train goes at 8.30, my information is concerned with your catching your train. Work on any major project is normally preceded by discussion: who does what, where and when. Someone persuades me to wear grey instead of black. Examples could be multiplied. Each of the three primary forms, however, has its own specific function as detached from direct action. Let us begin with information. We impart some information without calling for direct action. The more complex the society the more knowledge (not directly related to action of the 'person') is required, if the 'person' is to be fully competent in his social environment, and the greater the significance of items of information which are not thereupon realized or reacted to in action. If I am told that Thomas Mann has died, that there has been a *coup d'état* in Uganda, that the hundred and tenth heart transplant has been carried out, there is really nothing I can do about any of this, nor is your purpose in imparting this information to me to make me do something. The statements are 'for information only': and the more such information I hear, the 'better informed' I am – but not 'the more able to act'. It is a mistake to believe that the impartation of news as a form of verbal activity is anything 'modern'. What has happened is that the scope and time of news dissemination has altered, largely as a result of changes in the means employed. Thanks to press, radio and television, news reaches all points of a target area quickly and simultaneously: the catchment area is much wider than it used to be, and we have access to far more 'news' than ever before. But news has always been passed on, imparted, in one way or another, and has always played a more or less important part in our everyday life – starting with gossip, the oldest form of newscasting in everyday contexts. Then there were travellers who brought tales from far places, strangers with something to relate, bards and minstrels who told stories in song. The ratio of information which is merely to be stored, to information which has to be acted upon, always tells us something about the cultural and social standards at a given time; and a swing towards the former can no doubt be seen as an index of an increase in 'knowledge'. But C. Wright Mills is probably right when he condemns the all-too-prevalent desire to be 'well-informed'. If the desire to be well-informed completely ousts the urge to act on the basis of information received, human knowledge tends to be passive rather than active, and ceases to play a significant role in the structuring of life (which is what everyday knowledge is really supposed to do). And this in turn leads to a trivialization of human personality which *quantity* of information can in itself do nothing to offset.

As a relatively independent form of speech act, 'discussion' is a collective form of anticipatory or 'stepped' thinking. It may concern imminent or distant action: preparation for a job in hand or plans for something which might not even happen. In fact, the only difference between 'discussion' and 'conversation' is that the former is normally undertaken in order to reach a decision of some sort. Take, for example, family discussion on a child's future: differing viewpoints are put forward and comparatively assessed, and a decision may be reached. Again, some past event may be discussed and agreement reached on how to evaluate it. And it is probably not necessary to stress the importance of discussion in a species-essential activity which transcends everyday life – politics, science.

Here too, as in so many categories of everyday life and thinking, we have to underline the ambiguity of the social and ethical value-content of 'discussion'. It serves to safeguard the 'person' from taking wrong decisions, from getting the wrong idea, from unilateral decisions, etc. In a way, it is an antidote to particularity in that the opinion of 'others' is taken into account alongside one's own (based on one's own particularity). At the same time, however, it is an *Entlastungsprinzip*, a disengagement device, in that it absorbs some of the responsibility for taking a decision. This is precisely the point at which the Aristotelian 'mean' should be observed. If discussion proliferates to the point where anything and everything is left to collective decision, this can so inhibit personal responsibility that what is achieved by discussion is actually the opposite of what should be achieved: instead of reducing or eliding the chances of a decision being taken on particularistic attitudes alone, 'discussion' turns into a hot-bed for one of the basic affects of particularity – cowardice.

Persuasion and its correlative, discussion, are no more than relatively independent forms of advising or counselling. The function of persuasion (dissuasion) however, is not merely to give positive or negative advice in connection with a given action: its effectiveness resides not in the nature of the advice but rather in the form in which it is given. It is a question of continuous verbal activity – deliberately continuous to ensure the maximum effect. When and to the extent that the statement is not 'for information only' but also aims at convincing the listener, of getting him on our side, – in so far, the statement is 'persuasive'. It may be directed by one 'person' or more at one person or more. In purely informative statements both parties are relatively passive: the source merely passes on information; in discussion both parties are active, while in persuasion one party is active and the other passive, i.e. we have to distinguish the one doing the persuading from the one being persuaded.

Skill in persuasion has much to do with the successful prosecution of everyday life, and it requires special capabilities. We often say of someone: 'He's very persuasive', and this is not a matter of technique but always of personal charm. It is a quality which has a very special part to play in political activity, especially in rhetoric. Indeed, rhetoric is nothing more than an attempt to persuade people to believe this or do that. In classical antiquity, rhetoric was regarded as a special art or indeed a science whose rules were taught and in which every good citizen was expected to be adept. Rhetoric is, of course, neither an art nor a science, merely an everyday capability with extra polish, aided by various technical tricks of the trade and effects calculated to impress the impressionable. It is not a science; science suspends 'personality' but if rhetoric were reduced to working with general rules it would be empty and ineffective. For rhetoric to be successful, it must, as we said, carry the impact of personality, the individual turn of speech, ability to seize upon and turn the situation to one's advantage: it needs personal charm. But neither is rhetoric an art, for the evocative property, though present, is very subordinate. The aim of rhetoric is not to achieve an indirect or mediated effect through evocation – rhetoric aims at making a direct effect. And as dramatic verbal activity, persuasion is a fundamental weapon in the dramatist's armoury.

Disclosure (confession) is another very ancient fact of everyday life as a special case of information. Malinowski describes how in the evenings tribesmen would gather and take turns at 'disclosing'. A lot of prestige attached to this action, and tribesmen could hardly wait their turn, so eager were they to 'disclose'. I am sure no words of mine are needed to show that in this respect we have hardly changed, if at all, from Malinowski's islanders. The main difference is that instead of doing it in public we prefer more intimate private forms: we do it in private with a friend, a lover, a priest or a psychiatrist. The more complicated a 'person's' individuality becomes, the more intensely do two claims make themselves felt which culminate in 'disclosure'. One of these is the desire to reveal my ego to another or others: a need which arises perpetually from the fact of man's existence as a social being. The other, much more ambiguous, is the feeling that my responsibility is somehow lessened if I talk about it, the feeling that thereby I rid myself totally or partially of the moral responsibility or guilt I have incurred. This claim is positive in so far as the sharing of responsibility (a shared load is half the load) is a step towards better self-knowledge, not towards self-exoneration. It is a negative claim if it represents a flight from responsibility in that once the 'person' has unburdened himself he tends to regard that as the end of the matter. For this reason, the actual forms taken by 'disclosure' are ethically significant. We need not belabour the point that as a fact of everyday life, 'disclosure' becomes the basis for species-essential objectivations 'for itself': we have already stressed its ethical significance. But it is worth mentioning that, as an art-form, subjective lyricism can be seen as the 'disclosure' of a 'person' who has thus achieved upward transfer to the generic level.

225

Conversation, as a special case of discussion, is another basic component in everyday life. We can define it as a speech act, the sole purpose of which is to exchange ideas. It arises, therefore, when persons elaborate ideas which they want to pass on to others: an 'exchange of ideas' takes place. In certain historical periods and in certain social classes, thoughts worthy of exchange are the exception rather than the rule; and here conversation is not a stable factor in everyday life but a rare, we might almost say a ceremonial exercise. In one of her novels, Anna Lesznai tells of a peasant woman who was forty years old when she had her first conversation (with her lover). For the citizen of the greek *polis,* on the other hand, conversation was as much a part of everyday life as physical exercise.

Conversation as a normal, stable element in everyday life bespeaks a relatively high standard of culture. But where it is stabilized on a given cultural level it at once engenders its own alienated reflex. Where people meet for a chat, failure to 'converse' stamps one as an outsider: so people 'converse' when they have no ideas to exchange and nothing worth saying. Conversation continues, however, as silence amounts to rudeness. This sort of alienated conversation reduces to chit-chat. There are a few standard topics – the weather, dire happenings, local gossip – and, for the rest, we talk for the sake of talking. This sort of alienated chit-chat is portrayed in grotesque close-up by Ionesco.

In social settings, where conversation is not practised, being together in silence is normal; and by the same token, in circles accustomed to conversation (or chit-chat), silence acquires an aura of confidentiality and intimacy. Only those people can be silent together who are in complete harmony with each other, who trust each other, and in whose contact, speech is no longer (or not always) needed.

The ratio between conversation proper and chit-chat, between alienated and non-alienated verbal contact, in any given stratum, community or group, cannot be read off from a single conversation (though a single example may be sufficient in a work of art where the semelfactive can be typical). Even the most subtle individuals do not always converse to exchange ideas: like their less subtle fellows they too can enjoy 'chatting'. (The intimacy of silence is likely to be associated with couples or very small groups.) It is only as general tendencies take shape over a series of conversations that we can assess the depth and content of the contact established.

At this point we must say something about silence. Existentialists have made a myth out of silence, though there is really no such thing as 'silence': there are only concrete 'silences' with concrete meaning. To return to Malinowski: he points out that anyone who keeps silent during a 'disclosure' session is regarded as dangerous: his refusal to 'disclose' suggests that he has something to hide and is therefore a threat to others. However, if a teacher's question to a pupil is met with silence, the concrete content of this silence is usually, and simply, that the pupil doesn't know the answer. Again, situations occur in which silence implies concurrence or approval. As we have seen, silence in the case of those who are unaccustomed to engaging in conversation, is something quite different from silence maintained in a society devoted to conversation (which can be taken to mean boredom, rudeness or deep intimacy). The moral evaluation of silence varies according to historical period and position in the social division of labour. It is not so long since children were supposed to speak only when summoned to do so by adults; and in many cultures women have been expected to hold their tongues. 'Speech is silver, silence is golden', says the well-known proverb.

The mythicization of silence follows from the view of everyday life as necessarily alienated – the alienation extending to all forms of everyday contact and everyday speech. It is assumed that in being silent one 'withdraws' from everyday contact: i.e. from an alienated state of being into authenticity. But silence can be just as much alienated as the speech act: there is a silence of submission, there is a silence of complicity – and both derive from an acceptance of alienation as something inevitable. The silence of refusal can be authentic; but so can speech acts of doubt, challenge and indignation – and these are more effective.

All the actions we have been considering so far (including speech acts) have one feature in common: they appertain to, and are founded on social reproduction, they are objectified therein. For these actions, and for the knowledge made manifest in them, man takes responsibility. There is, however, a form of activity (including speech acts) with its concomitant awareness which never enters the social bloodstream directly, and for which we are therefore not responsible. This is 'play'. The essence of play lies in its deployment of human capabilities and propensities without incurring their real-life consequences and reserving the right to opt out when you feel like it. When you play the part of the king who slays his sons, you have no consequences to bear: for the sons do not really die. When you beat someone at chess there are no consequences, for no harm is done. When and wherever this formula no longer applies – that is, when consequences do follow, though the framework is still that of play, a game – it means that components other than 'play' have entered the content: that more than 'play' is at stake. This is the case in all professional sport. Of course, play often arouses passions as well as other human capabilities. The absence of consequences, however, means that on the average these passions can be mastered. It is *de rigueur* in sport to be 'a good loser' and anyone who fails in this respect is regarded as a spoilsport.

Because of the lack of consequences, the morals of play are quite different from those of real life. There is only one moral prescription in play – to go by the rules: though this only applies to games which have rules. Within this framework, all things are possible, anything goes. A player is not called upon to 'consider' his opponent: no one plays badly so that the other will win. Again, should such a thing happen, it would be a case of extraneous influence, of importations from real life, which should have no place in the proper sphere of play.

The moment that moral responsibility affects play, its frontiers have been crossed. Some children are quick to spot when this happens – when the limits of make-believe have been passed and 'it's no longer a game'.

All human capabilities can be utilized in play, and games are *inter alia* distinguished from each other according to which capability they make their main demands on. One human capability, however, plays a leading part in all games: fantasy. In games, reality is replaced by a world of fantasy: when we play we enter this world which has its own ways and rules, and it is because of this that games satisfy our fantasy. Gehlen has been perceptive enough to identify this need for fantasy-satisfaction, even in those games which are very decidedly directed towards real life, and which therefore have significance going far beyond the proper sphere of play – e.g. erotic play, or games conducted for speculative gain.

Play can be divided into three main types. The first of these comprises pure fantasy-play. According to Leontiev, most of the games played by small children come under this heading, and a majority of these assist in the process of social interiorization. When a little girl dresses her doll and fondles it, when a little boy builds a castle with his bricks, the essence of the play lies in the fact that for the girl the doll is a real baby, and what the boy builds is a real castle. Nor, we need hardly add, does fantasizing end with childhood: it merely takes on new forms. Most hobbies satisfy our need to fantasize. The same is true of that form of anticipatory thought which has become an end in itself, of day-dreaming, and of erotic games.

The second type comprises mimetic games. The need to fantasize is here satisfied in 'play-acting'. The theatre is obviously the mimetic game brought to its highest potential. Indeed, mimetic play is, in a sense, a starting-point, a basis, for all art. Which is not to say (as many, e.g. Schiller, have asserted) that art *is* play. As a species-essential objectivation 'for itself', art is not simply evocative mimesis, but its objectification raised to the species-essential (or generic) level. In contrast, play is typically an everyday phenomenon, and never oversteps the parameters of the everyday. It is not, of course, to be denied that there are very many transitional forms between pure everyday mimetic play and the work of art or its interpretative evocation.

Mimetic play requires a cast as well. In children's games, 'role transfer' on a temporary basis is common (e.g. in cops and robbers – 'It's my turn to be cop'). Some games of this type are transitional stages, half-way to being rule-games. Here Leontiev sees evolution typically at work: as he puts it, 'play evolves from what used to be *overt play-acting,* imagined situations and covert rules, towards *overt rules ....* imaginary situations and roles'.[3]

The third type comprises rule-games, i.e. games in which play is governed by a precise set of rules. The significance of 'role' is here greatly diminished (if it ever existed); 'role' being replaced by 'function' within the given set of rules. Rule-games have two characteristic properties. First of all, they are group or team games. The team aspect may be expressed in simultaneous action (e.g. football) or in consecutive action (cricket). In either case, performance of the game requires a certain number of players. This number varies from one game to another: the minimum is two, the maximum varies but cannot be very large (ten thousand people cannot 'play' with each other: the role of such a number is to 'root for' the players, i.e. cheer them on). Secondly, rule-games are competitive: there is a winner and a loser. We can say, indeed, that much of the attraction of rule-games lies in their competitive nature. This provides a breeding-ground for fantasizing (i.e. the role of the unexpected in rule-games) but, more, it generates its own tensions which affect not only the players but the spectators as well. Fantasy-games proper generate hardly any tension: they are relatively private, there are no cheer-leaders. Mimetic games do generate some tension, but this arises primarily not from the game situation itself but from the content of the action or the problem to be solved. By their very nature, rule-games tend to form groups and attract participation (active or passive). Of course, skill and quality play a part here: top seeds attract more attention than third-rate players. But all contests attract an audience: the spectacle of someone beating someone else, the tension generated in expectation, will always draw the crowds.

What is the function of play in everyday life?

The activity which we call 'play' is one in which a wide range of human capabilities can be used and expanded under the general direction of fantasy, as it has no vital consequences: 'playing' is never mandatory, it cannot be and never is induced. On the one hand, the fact that human capabilities can be deployed without any social consequences and on the other hand, its non-mandatory character create a specific sphere of freedom plus concomitant awareness thereof. In other words, the activity is a fusion of positive and negative freedom: negative in that the activity cannot be induced, positive in that it offers free rein and wide scope to the development of human capabilities. It cannot be over-emphasized, however, that whether the positive side or the negative side is uppermost, the freedom involved in play is always subjective. Performance in play does not go to indicate whether one could develop equivalent abilities in 'real' life, and if so how.

In as much as children have not yet reached the stage of full consequentiality in everyday life, subjective freedom necessarily plays a larger part in their world than in the adult one. For them, play is a 'natural' life-form, an unconscious preparation for life. Not so in the world of adults. Here, the content of play, the function it discharges in adult life, is very largely dependent on the extent to which we have become really free. Where chances of the free deployment of capabilities are relatively high, and where the degree of alienation, in work and in social relations alike, is low, the capability to exercise subjective freedom in play, to find therein a child-like gratification of fantasy, is retained unimpaired. In these circumstances play is not preparation for life, but rather the exercise of capabilities acquired in, conferred by life, with an attendant suspension of responsibility. Those thinkers, like Fourier and Rousseau, who looked forward to an alienation-free future, laid great emphasis on the role allotted to play of this kind in their non-alienated world. Conversely, the greater the degree of alienation in social relations and in the work process, i.e. in the 'real world', the more decisively, the more unmistakably does play become a flight from that reality to a small island of freedom. More and more, adults play games in order to forget the real world, to create another world in its place; and to substitute another *persona* for the one they have to live with. This latter reason is the main one underlying the rash of 'hobbies' which spread like the plague. As we have seen, however, the freedom that opens up in a game is only a subjective freedom, and play-acting instead of living can never provide true gratification. Play as escape from reality tends to become obsessive, and we end as slaves to a game which we took up precisely because it offered subjective freedom (cf. Dostoievsky, *The Gambler*). And this is so not only in the case of games which are far from being consequence-free (e.g. roulette) but also in the case of those which are consequence-free. The man who is absorbed by day-dreaming, or who compensates for his own failures and disappointments by identifying with a top football team, is just as much a slave to play as the most incurable gambler.

So far we have dealt with only one of the ways in which 'real life' and play influence each other. We now come to mention a more general and more serious interconnection between the two. As social relations become more and more alienated, and as stereotype clichés or 'roles' are formed, our awareness of moral responsibility for our actions tends to diminish. Once a cliché-attitude has been appropriated, we rarely stop to consider the moral implications of what we are doing, we rarely feel personal responsibility, and we rarely extrapolate to the likely consequences of our actions: and if we ever do give a thought to these issues, it is likely to be a very superficial one. The world of 'that's what everyone does' takes shape, and we relate to social norms as if they were the rules of a game.

(c) Orientative feelings in everyday contact (love and hate; attachments)

Everyday contact arouses many different emotions and feelings, some of which stand out in that their primary function is to orientate us precisely in our everyday contacts. Such are the feelings of affirmation which I may enumerate here in order of intensity: sympathy, inclination, love, and likewise the feelings of negation: antipathy, aversion, hate. Between these series, we have, as a 'neutral' centre, indifference. This is not the place to attempt an exhaustive treatment of these feelings, so we shall limit ourselves to a consideration of the extremes, the poles of each series, and of the central 'mean'. The feeling of love connects us with someone – someone with whom contact is deemed by us to be important, to 'matter' for our personality. We are connected by hate to someone, contact with whom we deem – again for reasons connected with our personality – is to be shunned at all costs. We are indifferent to people, contact with whom affects us in neither one way nor the other.

Let me stress the proviso 'for our personality'. Contact can be important for us for reasons unconnected with personality: e.g. if we are deriving some sort of material benefit from it, and this is true of many types of contact. We may make every effort to avoid contact by which we are bound even to someone we love (i.e. contact with whom is satisfying for our personality) for reasons belonging to a different order – e.g. we are trying not to disturb him/her, etc. Similarly, we may for all sorts of reasons deem it desirable or undesirable to have contact with someone to whom we are really indifferent.

There can be no doubt that the affects listed above are primarily derived from human contact, i.e. from that kind of contact to which they primarily refer; but from the very earliest times they have been analogically applied to animals, objects, institutions, etc. Analogical extension does nothing, however, to alter the basic affective structure, as set out above. If I am fond of a dog, it means that I like to have it as a companion, if I hate something (because it awakens bad memories) I try to avoid it, if possible, to blot it out altogether.

I call love, hate and indifference 'orientative feelings' because their primary function is to help us to find our way about, to orientate ourselves in everyday life. They act as signposts to satisfactory and unsatisfactory relationships. Here, I should like to stress that these feelings are by no means as subjective, as closely bound to the personality, as might at first sight appear to be the case. We are all born into the web of love and hate relationships, though the extent to which we are immediately caught up in it may vary from one historical age to another. Children are born into a situation in which they 'love' their parents: not simply because they are dependent on them (without parents they could not survive) but also because this filial love forms part of the accepted order of social requirements. Equally, it is a social requirement that parents should love their children. Here again love derives from the fact that the child is important for the parent: in his child, the parent 'lives on', and to his child he bequeaths name, qualities, property, aims in life, etc. – in addition to the attraction felt for the weak and defenceless, and the biological grounds for loving one's offspring. Above and beyond this, however, love as a social norm is so powerful that children who have long ceased to feel anything at all for their parents and parents who are equally indifferent towards their children, keep up the pretence – even to themselves – that they love each other. Only where aversion intervenes, or, in extreme cases, hate, does either party pluck up the courage to admit that they no longer love what they 'ought' to.

Many of our hates are socially prescribed in the same way. Children are brought up in the knowledge that they have to hate those who are hostile, inimical to their motherland or their own family. Contact with such enemies is possible on one venue only – the battlefield. 'Anti-feeling' of a very high order is necessary for someone to abrogate personal allegiance to a ready-made conventional 'hatred' – i.e. a feud or vendetta: Romeo has to be *in love* with Juliet, before he can contemplate a liaison with a Capulet.

We see, then, that up to a point the question of who and what is to matter to me, whom and what I am to love or repudiate, is socially prefabricated. Of course, within the prefabricated cast, personal initiative can always be brought to bear, and personal viewpoint can be validated. Even a small child may discover, perhaps to his shame, that he prefers one parent to the other. Nor is parental love distributed to each child in equal measure (personal preference is selective). But the social norm is so powerful that in such cases 'injustice' may be detected: the rest of Jacob's children found the patriarch unjust because he preferred Joseph to them.

Since the emergence of the bourgeois individual, the social prefabrication of the contactual affects has gone into decline, or has, at least, tended to do so; and even in the most insignificant areas of human contact freedom of choice in the selection and establishment of love and hate relationships has gained ground. Whether this does no more than increase the opportunities for arbitrary selection, or whether it represents a genuine step forwards in the quest for freedom, depends, as we shall see, on *the reason why* someone becomes important or unimportant for someone else.

Attraction and aversion (the less intense forms of love and hate) never motivate anything more than pursuit or avoidance of contact. Love and hate, however, increase in intensity to a point which may far exceed these boundaries. The existence of the love-object, the non-existence of the hate-object can become ends in themselves. Man will give his own life for someone he loves, and he will take the life of someone he hates.

Any attempt at evaluating the intensive forms of the orientating feelings must be based on analysis of their content (first and foremost their moral content) and their motivation (primarily their moral motivation).

It is true that their very existence confers *some* value on them: in themselves they are not neutral. The contrastive pairs: sympathy/ antipathy, attraction/aversion in so far as they are tendencies, have no value-content; but we connect the set love/hate with certain values. Love is deemed to be an abstract value: hate is deemed to be a non-value (*Unwert*). Of course, this is not to say that all love is positive in content, and all hate negative. All it means is that in the general run of human contacts love plays a positive, hate a negative role; and that, while either may accompany a particularistic attitude, the general tendency is for hate to be rather more associated with particularity than love.

If we are to assess a given concrete case of love or hate in terms of its value-content, we must first ask ourselves who is loved (or hated), why and in what manner. As a basic guide line we may first ask: to what extent is the loved (hated) person, object, institution objectively *worthy of* love (or hate): i.e. what degree of species-essential value-content, or what degree of non-value (*Unwert*) does it incorporate. The greater the importance for us of persons, institutions etc. which are in themselves worthy of love, and the more our feelings are guided by this worthiness, the more rational is the feeling of love. And conversely, the greater the extent to which a feeling of hate is motivated by the hate-worthiness of the object, the more exclusively this factor is the determining one, – the more the content of the hate can be identified as rational. It is common knowledge that what is worthy of love may be loved in worthy or unworthy fashion (and conversely, what is worthy of hate may be hated in worthy or unworthy fashion): that is to say, our feelings may call forth adequate or inadequate reactions (possibly expressed in action).

Although it is in everyday life that the orientative feelings play their most decisive part, two of them – love and hate – are also active in species-essential objectivations and contacts 'for itself'. The history of the development of morals, politics, the arts and sciences, is one of great loves and great hatreds. Here, however, adequate or inadequate identification of what is worthy of love (or hatred) is expressed in success or failure in the given sphere. Mistaken love and mistaken hate turn out to be dead-ends and nothing more, in objectivations based on them. Often, to take a well-known example, it is in spite of his everyday liking for certain types that the great artist can create a hierarchy of values in his work.

Indifference is that everyday feeling (the feeling of absence of feeling) which plays no part whatsoever in species-essential objectivations 'for itself', although it is a general concomitant in all of our everyday contents. Its value-content is, in general, neutral. However, if it hardens into a stereotyped attitude, if it engulfs the other orientative feelings – that is to say, if it turns into general apathy – it acquires a negative value-content. Once apathy is generalized, the person concerned can never hope to rise in any way to species-essential spheres 'for itself', and can never formulate a conscious relationship with species-essentiality.

The orientative feelings have a major role to play in our personal relationships. We have already described the category of personal relationships as that continuous series of contacts which are, whether primarily or secondarily – but always intensively – characterized by the orientative feelings. Every personal relationship carries a charge of love or hate, though, of course, the presence of love or hatred does not by itself indicate the presence of a personal relationship. For one thing, I can only have a personal relationship with another human being, whereas my love or hatred can extend to things and institutions; for another thing, I may love someone in secret (which means that there is no relationship), my love may not be returned (again there is no relationship); and in the same way, hatred may be secret or unilateral, and hence not a factor in a relationship.

The essential factor in emotional personal relationships is their reciprocity. Where there is as yet no reciprocity, relationship is no more than a possibility; where reciprocity has ceased to exist we can speak of a relationship which has failed. I may be in love with someone, but only if my love is reciprocated can I speak of a relationship. The presence of reciprocity does not necessarily mean that feelings on both sides of the relationship are of equal intensity, or even that they have the same content. It is certain, for example, that there was a personal relationship between the feudal lord and his faithful squire; but the relationship was based on inequality, so that the nature and the content of the affections aroused could not be the same. A relationship based on inequality, can still be established, even if the reciprocal affections differ in content. In such circumstances, however, personal relationships based on equality remain unfulfilled (this is not necessarily true if the affections differ in intensity).

Broadly speaking, personal relationships can be divided into two types – those which are freely chosen and those which are not. Ignoring the content of relationships and intensity of feeling for the moment, we may say that freely chosen relationships have the more significant value-content. There is, of course, no hard and fast dividing line between the two. Essentially, the relationship between parents and children is biological and fortuitous, not freely chosen. But even here and in the most patriarchal of settings, we find evidence of free choice – e.g. the celebrated example of Jacob and Joseph. Here again we can say that the more higher-order relationships within the family are motivated by 'worthiness to be loved', the higher the value-content of these relationships will be. At the same time, we can hardly conceive of a freely chosen relationship in which fortuitous, random factors play absolutely no part. It is after all fortuitous that any two people should meet in the first place. It can rarely be said that the person with whom a relationship is established is the 'only possible partner'; but where such a relationship is formed, its very intensity confers upon it an air of uniqueness, of fatefulness, of high destiny.

From the standpoint of our development as human beings, these personal relationships are the most essential, the most fertile contacts we experience in everyday life. In so far as they are intensive, based on equality, freely chosen, and in so far as our lives are guided by relationships freely chosen *because of* their intrinsic worth – in so far are our lives humanized and rich in content. Such relationships encompass the highest values of everyday life.

(d) Everyday space

Everyday contact takes place in its own space. This space is anthropocentric. At its centre there is always a human being living an everyday life. It is his everyday life that articulates his space, in which experience of space and perception of space are indissolubly fused together. We have to distinguish between this joint experience and perception of space and the *concept* of space which has percolated from the sphere of science into everyday parlance, where it now figures as an image of space, without in any way affecting our everyday experience of space-orientation.

We shall consider first of all the categories of experience and perception of space before taking up the problem of the concept of space; finally we shall try to analyse the problem of position.

Man has aspectually segmented his spatial domain by super-imposing thereon the localizing and orientating categories 'right' and 'left'. There is very little objective basis for this spatial experience and orientation, apart from human biological propensities (e.g. right and left hand vary in skilfulness, position of vital organs, etc.). The differing value-content attached to these words is also anthropocentric in that it is traceable to the physiological fact that our two hands and feet are unequal in skill and capacity, an inequality which has been carried over into derived meanings of the two words (meanings which have nothing to do with space).

Primarily, 'up' and 'down' are also categories of space perception and experience but they have an objective basis which 'right' and 'left' do not have. The natural locus of all everyday life and thinking is the earth, and 'up' and 'down' can be defined in real terms in relation to the earth. That is to say, the value-content of these categories has an objective basis and is not reducible to man's physiological make-up. What has most value for man is often 'up', above all most gods. The sun shines and the rain falls from 'above'; 'up' is visible, 'down' (what is below the ground) is invisible. However, several valuable things, from *Rheingold* to potatoes, are to be found 'down below' to make the contrast relative. (Metaphoric usage of these categories preserves their value-content, as in the case of 'right' and 'left'.) The objective reality of 'up' and 'down' and the importance of this for our perception of spatial relations, can be easily demonstrated. In a mirror image, 'right' and 'left' are reversed, but we do not see the world as 'reversed'. But if we see ourselves upside down, we at once recognize an 'unnatural' posture.

The distinction between 'near' and 'far' serves mainly to calibrate our radius of effective action. Action we take is more likely to be effective at close quarters, and the further away something is from us the less does it fall within our sphere of effective action: very distant objects lie totally outside that sphere. The distinction also points to the effort involved in reaching a place. The 'near/far' contrast is also used as a criterion in discriminating between similarity (or identity) of custom and dissimilarity. Places where people behave the way we do are described as 'near' or 'close': in 'remote' places, people behave differently. As Simmel has pointed out[4] it is not by chance that relations between people are described as 'close' or 'remote': in natural communities it is precisely the degree of spatial separation that determines the intensity of a relationship. A 'close relative' was originally one with whom we dwelt under one roof: a 'distant relative' was one who dwelt some distance away. In a village, your 'neighbour' is the man 'near-by'; the 'stranger' comes from further away, and therefore has customs and habits which differ from yours.

Our everyday life has a frontier which is the limit of our effective radius of action and movement. For the villager who never sets a foot outside his village all his life, the village is his frontier. And this in two senses: for one thing, whatever he does is necessarily motivated by what he has experienced in this domain and nowhere else; secondly, the effective radius of his activities does not extend beyond this frontier. In the first sense of the word, the 'frontier' is very fluid. Over long historical periods, the everyday knowledge of the average person was contained within a relatively narrow circle. Today, the whole wide world is there for us to know, and in this respect our 'domain' has been greatly extended. In addition, we can travel: that is to say, what is 'far' becomes 'near for us' and forms part of our own personal experience. Even in these circumstances, however, the frontiers remain, and even today no mortal could claim to know the whole world from his own experience. But this is not the essential aspect of the spatial frontier: what is essential is the question of the effective radius of our actions. However his spatial domain is articulated, the effective radius of action of the person living his/her everyday life is and remains limited, circumscribed. Only upward transfer to the sphere of species-essential objectivations 'for itself' can, at least in principle, transcend earthly frontiers.

I said above that the *concept* of space is an importation from scientific thought into everyday thinking. Today, every civilized person has a fairly exact idea of the distribution of continents, countries, cities, etc. and their relative distances one from another. Thanks to the jet aircraft, we now feel ourselves 'nearer' to London than we did previously (i.e. our personal experience of the 'near/far' contrast has been modified); but we still know, of course, that London is further from Budapest than, say, Lake Balaton. Again, every civilized person has today some idea of the infinity of the universe. And, exceptionally, this abstract awareness may affect personal everyday awareness, in that we may 'feel' that the earth is infinitely small in comparison with the universe. But the scientific concept of space has no effect on our everyday activities. At least for the present, the planet we live on is the maximum field of action at our disposal and the co-ordinate system we have to live by. We know that 'up' and 'down' are anthropocentric categories, or at least 'earth-centred'; but the physicist too has perforce to use 'up' and 'down', 'right' and 'left' when he seeks to orientate himself in his everyday life.

Let us once more recall the crucial role of familiarity, of 'being accustomed' in our everyday lives. Familiarity provides the basis for our everyday activities, and at the same time it is an everyday need. Integral to the average everyday life is awareness of a fixed point in space, a firm position from which we 'proceed' (whether every day or over longer periods of time) and to which we return in due course. This firm position is what we call 'home'. 'Home' is not simply house, roof, family. There are people who have houses and families but no 'homes'. For this reason, familiarity is not in itself equivalent to 'feeling at home' though familiarity is, of course, an indispensable ingredient in any definition of 'home'. Over and above this, we need the feeling of confidence: 'home' protects us. We also need the intensity and density of human relationships – the 'warmth' of the home. 'Going home' should mean: returning to that firm position which we know, to which we are accustomed, where we feel safe, and where our emotional relationships are at their most intense.

(e) Everyday time

The time in which everyday life proceeds is anthropocentric like the space in which it takes place. Just as everyday life is always related to the 'here' of a person, so is it related to that person's 'now'. The present is the referential system in which everyday life takes place. Indeed, not only everyday life: the present is also the referential system of many species-essential objectivations 'for itself' – e.g. of politics, and, with certain reservations, of historiography. In the case of politics and historiography, however, the 'present' is an integration: it is the 'present' of a people or of mankind, while in the case of everyday life it is the present of a person and of his/her environment. The present 'separates' past and future. For the purposes of everyday knowledge, the time dimensions are connected with the practical business of orientation. In this sense, a separation is effected between the 'bygone' (i.e. that which no longer affects the present), the 'past' (which may still affect the present), the present itself, the 'uncertain' (the object of our intentions), and finally the unforeseeable.[5]

We saw that science, as it develops, can influence our everyday notions of space only in so far as it is reflected in the field of activity potentially available to us; and the same goes for our notions of time. In their everyday lives, specialists in the theory of relativity have to live according to the same experience of time as anyone else; and, in the sense of everyday knowledge, everyday time divisions lose none of their 'truth'. We have seen how scientific knowledge percolates through to everyday knowledge: the everyday notion of time is 'special' in that the reverse process has also been at work – an attempt was made to elevate a kind of experiencing of time, 'durée' (of great importance in everyday life) to the status of a philosophic concept. Reduced to a philosophical concept, time is nothing more than the irreversibility of events. As a concept, irreversibility plays no part in everyday thinking: but the fact of irreversibility is an organic part of everyday knowledge. It is enough to think of how we feel over a missed opportunity. Who has not reflected over and over again in the course of everyday life: 'Well, that's that, and it'll never happen again' or 'what has happened has happened, there's nothing to be done about it', etc. At the same time, although in our everyday lives we have no option but to accept the fact of irreversibility, we cannot always resign ourselves to it. We cannot help ruminating over the irretrievable past and playing with possibilities: 'if only I had ... ', 'what would have happened if ... ' The gloomier a person's life is, the less does that person seem able consciously to accept the fact that what has happened is irreversible. Here we can detect one of the roots of the need for religion. For religion seeks to present the hard facts as 'the will of God': repentance for our sins can wipe them out, and we shall be requited in the world to come where 'eternal life' is offered as 'eternal compensation'. The freer a man's relationship is with his own fate (having regard to both objective and subjective factors) the more consciously will he be able to accept the fact of irreversibility and the less need will he have of religious comfort.

In part, man's unwillingness to reconcile himself with the fact of irreversibility is a reaction against the unappealable fact that our life is limited: it has a set term. This limit is death – our own death and that of others – and it permeates the whole field of our doing and thinking. Spinoza said that the wise man thinks not of death, but of life. But most people are not so wise, and cannot bracket off the thought of death from their everyday activities. If it were not for the term set by death the great majority of people would be honest, since dishonesty is very often reducible to 'pressure of time', 'shortness of time' – the awareness that if you fail to get what you want today, you will very probably not get it tomorrow either. I am not suggesting that people are always thinking about death – on the contrary, instead of brooding on death most people are preoccupied with anticipating, living through and reflecting on everyday life, their hopes and fears, their work, plans for the future, their interests, their joys and sorrows. The existentialist awareness of 'being towards death' is characteristic of certain modern intellectuals only, which says little for the alleged 'superiority' or 'transcendence' of these insights. Still, it only takes a severe illness, the funeral of someone close, a bad dream, for the spectre of death to arise on the horizon of life as the power motivating our actions. Reaction to the awareness of death varies very widely from one culture to another, and from one social stratum to another; and even within strata it can be a very personal attitude. Ignoring historical differences, we may limit our analysis to three types of attitude. The first we may describe as 'obtuse-ness': 'obtuse' people are aware of death as 'only natural', and do not let it bother them. Neither the demise of others nor even the prospect of their own death affects them deeply, since they have failed to develop as individuals, and are unaware of the uniqueness of individual human beings. The second type is characterized by a fear of death. People belonging to this second type are not obtuse: they have made the discovery that personality (their own and that of others) is unique, and for this reason their imagination tends to linger on death, either habitually or at times of crisis. Here we find differing attitudes: there is the man who refuses to give in, the rebel who cannot accept the fact that *he* should have to die, and there is the man who not only acquiesces in the prospect of death but may actually look forward to it. Our third type comprises those who regard death as natural (especially their own deaths), but only if it really is natural, and who are loud in their condemnation of all modes of dying which are the work of man. Those belonging to this type are individuals, and it is individuality that they value in others, the uniqueness of another's personality – however insignificant the other may be. While not meekly acquiescing in death, they accept it as an organic part of life; and they try to live rationally as befits human beings, so that in due course their death also may be fitting. They are not 'wise men' in Spinoza's sense: engaged in constructing rational lives, they give due thought to death, but what they do is never motivated by thoughts of their own deaths.

Historical junctures establish the framework of development and the subsequent fate of social integrations. The incidence of such junctures, their 'density', is not a matter of indifference for everyday life. The higher the rate of incidence, the less durable is their content in relation to the life of the 'person', and the more intensive is the 'interference' of history in the life-style of that 'person'. I agree with Ernst Fischer[6] when he says that the 'generation' – as a fact of our everyday lives which has now acquired considerable significance – is linked to the density factor of historical junctures: a factor which moreover has increased dramatically since the eighteenth century. When we say that people 'belong to a generation' we do not mean simply that they belong to the same age-group; we mean rather that they were roughly of the same age when they lived through and reacted to a juncture in history. That is to say, the generation is the discrete movement in the continuous process of human propagation, which is generated from the mutual effect upon each other of historical juncture and content of personal life.

The natural division of time (i.e. its division arising from its everyday character) allows us to make far more complex and elastic (though less precise) use of it than we do of space. We can measure a field in paces, a piece of cloth in handspans; but it is rather more difficult to measure the distance between two villages in such simple natural units. The day, from sunrise to sunset, and the year are natural divisions of time which we can use, if not too accurately, for both time and space. Before acquiring a system of numeration, certain tribes used to indicate the distance to the next village, for example, by indicating in sign language the number of sunrises and sunsets the journey would take. Even today, when both space and time are divided up into agreed units and sub-units, we tend in everyday usage to indicate distance in terms of time. One doesn't say the station is two kilometres away: it is 'half-an-hour's walk' or 'fifteen minutes in the bus'.

The division of the day/night unit into twenty-four hours is principially different from the division of time into years and days: it is similar to all forms of spatial division, in that it is a quantitative homogenization of qualitative disparates. An hour is an hour, whether it is the hour after sunrise, the midday hour or the middle of the night. Here we have to do with a quasi-scientific factor in our everyday knowledge.

The role of space in our everyday life is less significant than the role of time. It is mainly in man's relationship with nature that partition of space becomes important, e.g. in construction or other kinds of building work. In everyday life we can make do with simple concepts based on everyday experience such as 'big', 'big enough', 'very big' and so on. This is the situation even today. In contrast, the social significance – and hence the significance for

242

our daily lives – of partition of time is actually increasing. The calibration and ordered partition of time becomes necessary because of two factors – the finitude of our earthly existence, and the (increasing) economization of our everyday lives which I have already dealt with. The daily round becomes more and more demanding and we have to get through it more and more quickly under pressure from both internal and external causes: rational partition of our time becomes mandatory. This is why 'punctuality' has come to be associated in everyday thinking with time alone, though in its basic meaning (= accuracy) it refers equally to both time and space. It is only in connection with the performance of work that the concept is applied in a non-temporal sense (one should work precisely, properly ...). The rational partition of time is equivalent to the organization of time: simultaneous activity depends on synchronization of skills. The importance in everyday life of partition of time in comparison with partition of space can be gauged if we compare the number of people who wear a watch with the number who carry a foot-rule or a metre-stick about with them.

The fact is that the partition of time is today of far greater importance and significance than at any time in the past. What this means in terms of human values is not something we can go into here. But it is worthwhile asking ourselves why we tend to find ourselves with more and more 'time on our hands'. 'Shortage of time' has always been a familiar experience, but in the past it was mainly the leisured classes, those who did no work, who found themselves with too much time on their hands: today, however, it is a characteristic of the working classes as well. 'Time to spare' is a consequence of the growth in the amount of time which is not taken up with work or similar activity. Its subjective concomitant is boredom. The popular cure for boredom is work: the bored king learns how to chop wood and is no longer bored. But Kierkegaard was right when he diagnosed boredom as the product not simply of inactivity alone but also of the monotonous nature of the feverish 'clock-bound' round of daily activity. And indeed, the antithesis of boredom is not activity in general, not even mandatory activity, but purposeful, reasoned activity which allows man's capabilities to expand and develop. The more generally such activity is available to the members of a society, and the more it is made use of (and here both objective and subjective factors are of equal importance, though the former are socially fundamental), the less will the members of that society suffer from boredom. Conversation and the enjoyment of intensive human relations on a basis of

243

equality are not lowest in the scale of such reasoned and purposeful activities.

Time never 'goes' more quickly or more slowly; and all events are equally irreversible. But the rhythm, the pace of life does vary very greatly from one historical period to another. In certain historical periods, the structure of society hardly changed at all over hundreds of years; in others, a decade was enough to bring violent and fundamental change. But we can say that since the onset of capitalism, the general historical tendency has been for the pace of life to quicken.

Any change in the rhythm of life is bound to affect everyday life, but not everyone's everyday life in equal measure; and not every area of everyday life is affected to the same degree. Acceleration of the rhythm is primarily a formative influence on the lives of those social classes and strata who are active participants in socially (politically) relevant action, and, secondarily, on those who are deeply affected by a certain historical change. Lukács has shown, for example, how Balzac's novels are bound to fixed historical points; only at certain precise historical junctures, at a specific historical 'moment' could the lives – the everyday lives – of the protagonists turn out as they do. But even here there is a distinction to be made between active participants in, and those passive strata whose lives are merely affected by, history.

The effect of acceleration in the rhythm of historical change is primarily expressed in the fact that within a generation human life is transformed (often more than once): that within a man's lifetime he finds himself called upon to cope with a series of new and unheard-of situations. (Here we have one root source of the 'future-oriented society' we have already discussed.) Accordingly, life has to be 'reorganized' repeatedly. This realignment is mainly concerned with the content of life, but very often it has an effect on the tempo of life as well. For example, when capitalism began to oust older methods of working, people had to get used not only to a new system of needs and requirements, but also to an acceleration in the tempo of life.

Both in content and in tempo, therefore, everyday life may be restructured and modified by any acceleration in the rhythm of historical events, but even within this framework a relatively stable and continuous rhythm must prevail. The very nature of work makes rhythmic stability desirable (we work so many hours a day, and the rest of the day has to be 'arranged' round this central factor) but so does the economization of everyday life. There is a measure of 'disengagement' (*Entlastung*) in rhythmic reiteration of daily patterns, whereas a disorderly life-style which is constantly changing in rhythmic pattern wears us out physically and nervously and renders us incapable of doing what we have to do, let alone of diversifying it. A stable rhythmic pattern will include equally regular breaks in tempo (Sundays off) which are not to be regarded as merely cessation of activity but as the patterned adoption of a different rhythm belonging to what we call 'relaxation' or 'recreation'. The contrast between the normal tempo of life and that of recreation is not synonymous with the contrast between 'tension' and 'relaxation'. The latter pair is connected with the obligatory nature of alienated work and the sensation of joy felt at release from it. Construed as 'relaxation', therefore, recreation is the antithesis of the obligatory rhythm set in alienated labour, and is itself a manifestation of alienation. Schiller was right when he said that in so far as man has to live in the duality dictated by tension of work and the relaxation therefrom, he is not a fit subject for activities on a species-essential level (he was, of course, speaking primarily of art).

As we go about our business in everyday life we very soon realize that there is a 'right time' to do things. In fact, success or failure in work very largely depends on picking the right moment, whether it is a question of breeding animals, harvesting the crops or whatever. Picking the right moment is no less important in the area of everyday contacts. 'Time to act' we say, and that means that action at a given point of time will yield optimum results: action earlier or later would not have the desired effect. A declaration of love, a friendly gesture, a punishment – such things will be all the more effective if we hit on the right moment for them. So patience in awaiting this right moment is of cardinal importance. Often, the realization that events are irreversible only hits us when the crucial moment has passed, and nothing can be done about it.

Important as it is in everyday life, it is only in activity on the level of species-essential objectivation 'for itself' that the art of picking the right moment becomes of absolutely crucial import-ance – and this is particularly true of political activity. Here, ability to pick the right moment can affect the lives and the fate of whole peoples. In fact, not the least of political skills is this ability to do things at the right time. The quicker the historical rhythm, the more important does it become for statesmen to recognise 'the right moment'. It was this *inter alia,* that Machiavelli recognized and analysed as the *sine qua non* for successful politicians.[7] In everyday life we are concerned not only with specifying time (e.g.

for a meeting) but also with the correlative of that specification – adhering to it. Social existence would soon become impossible if people made a habit of ignoring 'appointments'; if no one turned up at the appointed time for a meeting, the word 'meeting' would soon lose its meaning altogether. The exact meaning of 'punctuality' varies, of course, from one historical age to another, and also depends on the nature of the work or activity concerned. What we, thanks to the general speeding-up of living tempo, would regard as a 'late' arrival would simply have passed unnoticed in the Middle Ages. Being late for work is not at all the same thing as being late for a party. But in all cases and in all societies there is some way of measuring failure to adhere to a set point in time.

The time categories we have been considering so far are anthropomorphous and, at the same time, objective; time-as-experienced, however, is not only anthropomorphous but subjective as well. There is no way of measuring time-as-experienced, or of correlating it with time elapsed. We all know what we mean when we say that 'time drags' or 'time flies'; and equally we know that there is no correlation between 'dragging' and 'flying' and the time-span which a consensus would show had actually elapsed.

Time-as-experienced is in fact dependent on its subjective content: its plenitude or its vacuity. In the course of an hour we may live through experiences which are crucial for our whole lives. But the same hour can elicit two opposite kinds of time-experience. Some will say 'it seemed like ages' because 'so much happened': others will say 'the time simply flew', 'it only took a moment'. As I said, subjective content plays a very big part here: it all depends on what sort of experience we are talking about. Five minutes of torture will seem like years; several hours of love-making will seem like five minutes. The same considerations apply to our empty hours as well. If I am expecting something pleasant to happen, the minutes of waiting can seem like days. 'Time drags' if it is empty: but if I look back over an uneventful existence, I have the feeling that 'time has flown' and the decades shrink to wasted moments.

A very particular role in our experiencing of time is played by day-dreaming, recollection and imagination. Proust has shown very convincingly how one's whole life can be relived in a moment of recollection. But of all the ways of experiencing time available to us, time-as-recalled is the most subjective. The life I lead is indeed irreversible, and recollection is merely one moment in that irreversibility. Time as experienced by me is subjective because it is *my* time; time as experienced by others is *their* time. Which is

246

not to suggest that social contact has no influence on time as experienced by any ego. On the contrary, the number of significant events shared in, the richness of human contacts, the extent to which a person has been challenged by his environment to show initiative, independence of action and reaction – all of this will determine the 'density' of his time-as-experience (at least in the average case) and the 'more' time will be experienced in a given time-span. For the most convincing examples of this we turn to the arts. Novelists cover several years in a couple of pages, and then devote whole chapters to the events – admittedly crucial events – of a day or an evening. This only goes to show that the 'content-rich moments' which are more inexhaustible than years, are never, either in their content or in their frequency and density, completely independent of society as a whole.

(f) The collisions of everyday life

Friction in everyday life contacts usually takes the form of the quarrel. This can be defined as the collision of two or more sets of particularistic interests. The more particularistic a man's interests are, and the more this is true of those with whom he comes into daily contact, the more likely is it that such contact will be marked by friction, i.e. by quarrels. And since (a) not even individuals (in our sense) are entirely without particularistic motivation, and (b) there is no environment in which particularistic motivation does not play some part, it follows that none of us are exempt: we all quarrel. But quarrelsomeness can only become an established deformation in those who have let particularistic motivation take over to the point at which it becomes an organic part of their make-up.

As I said, it is particularistic interests that give rise to quarrels: but 'suspension' of quarrelsomeness does not mean the cessation of particularity. In the first place, we cannot quarrel with just anybody. In social relationships based on inequality, the person in a dependent position cannot quarrel with the person on whom he is dependent. Master can quarrel with servant, but not vice versa. Thus, suppression of quarrelsomeness in a subordinate means nothing more than acceptance of the *status quo,* possibly with an eye to one's own interests, but certainly with no hint of 'virtue' about it. Indeed, virtue would often be better served if the subordinate *did* quarrel with the master. For this would express (though admittedly in somewhat banal form) a demand for equality in conditions of inequality; a demand for one set of particularistic interests to be treated as equal to a factitiously 'superior' set of equally particularistic interests.

Quarrels are usually conducted verbally, though in exceptional cases they may escalate into exchange of blows. But a verbal quarrel is not at all the same thing as an argument. An argument is bound to arise, and therefore in everyday life as well, whenever we pay attention to other people's opinions, that is, take them seriously as worth discussion. In a quarrel, on the other hand, each participant is speaking *at* not *to* the other, and giving voice to his own particularistic interests and affects.

Everyday conflicts may also take the form of altercation (clash of opinions). Here again particularistic interests and affects may well play a part, but the altercation is motivated not by these but by generic values, particularly moral values. In altercation we often come up against our own particularity: for example, we may engage in altercation with someone we love or with someone to whom we are bound by common interests, and thus the very acceptance of, the readiness to engage in altercation, may have a positive value-content. At the same time, the deliberate stirring up of altercation cannot be said to have positive value-content unless it concerns moral issues of crucial importance: otherwise, it tends to be merely an expression of intolerance.

Like a quarrel, an altercation is normally conducted by means of a clash of opinions. Unlike a quarrel, however, an altercation involves genuine discussion: there is a clash of moral values, of ideologies, and each party has to take stock of the other's views (whether profoundly or superficially does not really matter), in the light of which the discussion can be continued.

Quarrelsomeness belongs to a life-style based on particularity, which means that it can never generate a change in life-style. After a quarrel or a series of quarrels, everything remains essentially the same. Even the quarrels themselves do not rise to a higher level: indeed they cannot. The level remains unchanged, whether the provocation is novel or not. In contrast, altercations can induce change in lifestyle, or can be reiterated on a higher level. One typical way for change to be thus induced is through a change of heart in one or other of the parties (possibly even in both) so that the dispute is settled or at least cooled. Equally typical is progressive exacerbation of the clash until breaking-point is reached. By definition, a clash cannot be reiterated except on a higher level, and few of us would be prepared to go on 'clashing' ad infinitum.

Where conflict takes the form of altercation, the parties have to reckon with the consequences, which, in extreme cases, may be tragic. In Ibsen's *A Doll's House* Nora accepts all the social and personal consequences entailed in clashing with her husband – a total break, that is, not only with her husband but with her whole way of life.

I said that we can have any number of quarrels, even with one and the same person,[8] while this is not true of altercations. Even in a run of quarrels, however, there can be a point of no return: a final rupture, or what is popularly known as a 'bust-up'. This may be, and in the vast majority of cases is, temporary. But it may also be permanent, in which case it simply means that the two or more parties involved have finally decided that they cannot stand each other any longer, and that mutual toleration would be more harmful to their particularistic interests than final rupture. If there is a point of no return in altercation it does not come in the form of a 'bust-up' but rather as a formal separation, arrived at because two sets of moral and ideological principles are, in the end, incompatible.

The dominant affect in all stages of quarrel up to final rupture is animosity; and this remains true even if in periods of appeasement following a quarrel animosity is bottled up, and all appears well on the surface. It only takes a fresh quarrel to bring out the old hatred. (People of blameless character experience sudden aversions rather than sudden hatred.) In altercations (in other words: clashes of opinion) however, it is not unusual for love to remain the dominant affect throughout. It is possible for me to love someone even when his/her views on a given subject are totally incompatible with mine.

From all of this it should now be obvious that, in practice, quarrel and altercation (clash of opinions) are often closely intertwined, however clearly they may differ under analytical scrutiny. Quarrels may rise to the level of altercations (clashes of opinions) and altercations may degenerate into quarrels. Attempts at moral self-justification may lead us to 'stylize' quarrels into altercations (clashes of opinion); and altercations turning on a genuine difference of opinion may end in compromise. Only the morally developed individual is capable of 'standing his ground' in an argument – avoiding a slide into a succession of particularistic quarrels on the one hand, and lame compromise on the other.

When I spoke of 'bust-up' or 'rupture' as the closing scene of both quarrel and altercation, I was speaking of personal contact relations. It is worth while noticing that the two types of collision arise in other relationships as well. For example, a man quarrels with the police if he thinks he should not have to pay a fine for an alleged traffic offence; but he comes into altercation or clash of opinion with the police at a political rally. In the first case, the solution of the conflict is personal but not private (since it also involves the court); in the second, the solution is both non-private and collective.

Feud – which may also be typical of everyday life – can be defined as the stabilization, the perpetuation of an everyday conflict, which does not however presuppose everyday personal contact (as quarrels and altercations do). Continuation and/or exacerbation of the conflict tends to become an end in itself. A feud may originate in either a personal or a social conflict. As it gathers force, however, it becomes detached from the original cause of conflict and becomes an end in itself. There have been feuding families and feuding villagers, as well as feuding barons and feuding poets.

The feud does not turn on the assertion of an interest or the validation of a viewpoint: it is rather a form of competition. One party in a feud is not concerned with persuading or convincing the other party but with outdoing it or defeating it. Competition here is not the competition we find in play, but something that takes on the appearance of war and is indeed not often pursued by peaceful means. The end-game in a feud is the defeat of one of the parties, or reconciliation (but not appeasement).

Feuds between integrations are transitional forms between everyday conflict and political conflict. Such feuds may take the shape of political struggle where the relevant integrations are indeed bound to specific political interests. Where they are merely carried onwards by their own impetus as ends in themselves, however, they are never lifted above the plane of everyday contact.

Everyday life untroubled by conflicts or collisions of any kind could be described as 'idyllic'. As life in society has never been – and never will be – untroubled by conflict, the 'idyll' is imaginable only in connection with the everyday existence of people who live very far indeed from the world of social struggle. For this reason, the concept of the 'idyllic' is always associated with the concept of isolation, of insulation from society. At the same time, confrontation with the great species-essential objectivations is also conflict-ridden; and it is for this reason that the 'idyllic' life is imagined as innocent of science and the arts (at least in their advanced forms) just as it knows nothing of political or moral friction. But even assuming that everyday life could be lived

250

in total isolation from the species-essential objectivations 'for itself', it would still only be possible to describe it as 'free of conflict' if those living it did not come into confrontation with each other in a daily struggle for existence. So, the 'idyllic' existence is also imagined as one of plenty: there is no scarcity, no selfish interests, but noble simplicity. It was thus that pastoral life was pictured, a sort of 'golden age', in which everyone drew a livelihood ready-made from nature, or the closed family circle which was 'sufficient unto itself' and so on.

In a sense, this concept of the 'idyllic' is a narrow-minded one (in the Marxian sense of the word). A life which repudiates limitation, which is directed towards the species-essential objectivations, which is never self-satisfied or complacent – such a life never shirks conflict of any kind, least of all clashes. It is not satisfied with the 'stable warmth' (Thomas Mann's expression) enjoyed by a simple and complacent community, but strives towards enlarging its sphere both in knowing and doing. If we cannot extol the idyll as a desirable way of life in the long term, it can yet be seen as a beautiful phase therein, a kind of charming intermezzo in life's drama. It is thus that Shakespeare portrays it so lovingly. We recall the idyll in the Forest of Arden: an idyll born of necessity which ceases to exist as soon as the Duke returns from exile to face once again the challenges of life in society. At its given moment, 'before' and 'after' the turbulence of social activity, the idyll represents a beautiful and noble interlude; its function is to give man a moral breathing space worthy of him.

(g) Everyday 'contentment': its components

Satisfaction in everyday life is an amalgam of two main components – pleasure and usefulness. The degree of intensity and the continuity factor present in these two components determine the extent to which a person can describe himself as 'contented' or 'satisfied' with his everyday life.

Of the two, it is pleasure which is exclusively relevant to everyday life. It might be defined as that feeling of affirmation which accompanies and permeates our physical and mental state at a given time: induced perhaps by a warm bath, a good dinner party, a comfortable home, music – or simply *dolce far niente*. In some way, the feeling of pleasure may be connected with the feeling of joy: but neither of these necessarily involves the other. 'Joy' is rather the feeling of affirmation generated by certain happenings or achievements. We may experience pleasure in looking forward to a meeting on which we place high hopes ('pleasurable excitement') but what we feel when the meeting takes place and goes right for us is 'joy'. Standing our ground in a moral trial can elicit joy, even if our physical and/or mental state is not 'pleasurable'. A good match-up of colours will give me pleasure, but not necessarily joy. However, it remains true that in most cases a feeling of joy or happiness will contain a feeling of pleasure; and pleasure is often imbued with remembrance of happiness experienced or anticipation of joy to come.

I said that the feeling of pleasure, 'taking pleasure' in something, is really relevant to everyday life alone. The emotion felt in major achievement, the successful conclusion of a non-everyday enterprise, is either not pleasure or more than pleasure. The spiritual trepidation accompanying the birth of an artistic masterpiece, the successful thinking through of a scientific problem, taking part in decisive political action – none of these can be described in terms of 'pleasure'. Nor is study pleasant, even if joy is to be found therein. When I say that these things are not pleasant, I do not mean that they are 'unpleasant': both the positive adjective and its negative are simply inadequate to deal with the emotions and feelings involved in these activities. We cannot say that we take pleasure in the catharsis induced by a great work of art: indeed, if the enjoyment of such a work can be described in terms of 'pleasure', what this means is that the beholder or listener has failed to rise to a level of species-essential comprehension and remains firmly rooted in the everyday. After all, the whole function of the catharsis is to shake us out of complacency with ourselves and our world, and to adumbrate ways of changing both. In contrast, the contrastive pair of 'joy' and 'grief' *is* adequate to express the relationship established between the emotions generated in a catharsis and my personality: I feel grief and pain that the world is so and that man must suffer, and I feel joy in insights gained, in decisions taken, in accomplishment.

If pleasure and joy are closely associated in a person's life, or even coalesce, this goes to show that that person hardly ever steps out of the world in which particularity and species-essentiality 'in itself' 'co-exist'. The richer a person's life is in joys and sorrows that do not stem from what is pleasant or unpleasant, the more that person is in touch with species-essential objectivations 'for itself'.

Since the 'pleasant' and the 'unpleasant' (i.e. the positive and negative reactions accompanying our psychosomatic or mental state) can never originate from a conscious relationship with the species-essential, it follows that these feelings are principally particularistic. Which is not to say that certain types of pleasure (but only certain types) could not be in intermediate relationship with a person's particularity or individuality. Of course, a warm bath, a good rest are things that everybody finds pleasant, just as having a tooth out or getting soaked in the rain are things that no one likes: but these are data from which we can make no inference of any kind as to the moral development of the person, or his status as a human being. Certain types of pleasure exist which can act as pointers to the degree of cultural development reached – but they still tell us nothing about personality. For example, one kind of 'good taste' is a way of distinguishing 'pleasant' from 'unpleasant'. Preferences in cooking or in colours depend largely on general cultural environment and tell us nothing about the individual personality. But a liking for dirty stories and rude practical jokes does tell us something about the personality, as does a penchant for friendly and informative conversation. Then again, pleasure can be coupled with a kind of joy which has not originated in pleasure.

So then, if someone can be said to be 'satisfied', 'contented' with life simply because it gives him a continuous and intensive feeling of pleasure, that person's life is centred round particularity; and this kind of contentment has a negative value-content. Conversely, permanent absence of a feeling of pleasure, its total subtraction from everyday life, may beget a feeling of dissatisfaction even in people who lead individual lives, and who are primarily or at least partially guided in all that they do by a conscious relationship with species-essentiality. As I said at the outset: even for the most highly developed individuals certain particularistic needs are vital needs.

The category of usefulness or serviceableness has acquired two meanings, a dichotomy which varies in practice from one society to another. Someone, something can be 'useful to me' or 'useful to others'. (This dichotomy does not arise in the case of pleasure which is by definition a particularistic feeling: what is pleasant is always 'pleasant for me' even if it is at the same time 'pleasant for others'.)

The dichotomy with regard to usefulness is a mark of alienation, and its degree depends on the extent to which others are or can be obstacles to my activity and my self-assertion. Where the person is so completely an organic member of a community that he can assert himself only through the mediation of that community, the discrepancy remains covert. With the final disappearance of 'natural' communities under capitalism, it becomes glaringly obvious, however, and it underlies the bourgeois concept of usefulness according to which the common interest is best served if we all of us look after our private interests (see Mandeville, *The Fable of the Bees*).

'Looking after one's own interests' can be understood in various ways. In the widest sense, it simply means 'self-preservation'; in everyday usage, it means the pursuit of success, if necessary, at the cost of others. This is not limited to what is called 'material use', but extends also to the wielding of power, the gratification of whims, etc.

No class society has ever been so alienated that attention to self-interest has totally ousted awareness of the need to be 'useful to others'. The belief that his existence is not 'without use', that 'others have need of him' has been and still is a vital component in man's everyday contentment. Nor have people ever doubted that they need others, that others are 'useful' to them: not simply as means to an end (as in the daily struggle for subsistence) but as ends in themselves. 'Nothing is more useful to a man,' said Spinoza, 'than another man', where 'man' is construed not as a means but as an end.

But the more alienated a society is, the greater the abyss and the conflict between the dual versions of usefulness: 'useful to me' and 'useful to others'. What we are accustomed to describe as the possible 'unity of public and private interests' is no more than a socially established compromise between conflicting practical interpretations.

I said that in so far as contentment stems from nothing more than pleasure it is a particularistic property. The same can be said of personal satisfaction in attending to one's own interest. While the feeling of pleasure is in itself passive, 'stative', however, the quest for 'use to oneself' is active. Thus, even within their common field of particularity, there is a difference between the two as regards their value-content. Quest for a pleasurable life need not necessarily conflict with the interests and claims of other people: in this sense, others are not essentially 'obstacles'; and from this point of view, the negative value-content in the quest for a pleasurable life is less than than in the quest for 'use to self'. At the same time, by virtue of its activity, the personal quest for 'use to self' can serve in various ways as a driving force – admittedly, an alienated driving force – making for progress. The two principles often come into conflict with each other. Thus, while feudalism in its period of decline made pleasure its principle, the advancing bourgeoisie raised the banner of usefulness.

As we have seen, 'being useful to others' is in itself invested with positive value-content. We also know that its motivation often derives from loftier species-essential spheres and percolates into everyday life. Thus, the feeling of satisfaction which derives from being useful to others, is the only kind of everyday contentment which has an unambiguously positive value-content.

CHAPTER 13

The personality in everyday life

Here we shall discuss personality only in its general relations with everyday life; and here we return, albeit from a different point of view, to the questions which gave us our take-off point. Our first question is: in the light of what we have learned about the structure of everyday life, can we say that human personalities relate in *uniform* fashion to that structure? We shall then turn our attention to the individual as 'personality for itself', and lastly I offer a concluding analysis of everyday life as a domain in which 'being for us' *par excellence* becomes possible.

(a) The relationship of personality to the structure of everyday life

It is a fact that every man is born into the structure of species-essential objectivations 'in itself'. It is also a fact that every man must appropriate a particular objectivation 'in itself' and that this happens *via* repetitive praxis and thinking as well. Pragmatism, over-generalization, economization – to mention only a few examples – are accordingly irreversible action patterns of our everyday lives. No one can survive in everyday life except by appropriating these structures in the ways we have described. But does it follow from this that every man relates in uniform fashion to the ready-made structure into which he is born? Does it follow from this that always and for everybody the world of everyday life is that domain in which a purely adaptive process of appropriation of heterogeneous activities ensues?

Heidegger's answer to these questions is in the affirmative.[1] For him, the world of the objectivations 'in itself' is the world of

'Readiness-to-hand', in which objects are 'to hand' for my use: all I have to do is use, make use of the object, custom or mental process which lies ready 'to hand'. It follows that everyday life cannot be the arena in which the human personality can act as such. Authenticity is born in the resolve to renounce being-in-the-world. But since no one can factually withdraw from everyday life, man has perforce to become a dual being: he combines an 'inauthentic existence' of activities, like 'others', like 'anyone', with the authentic existence as 'Being-unto-death' (*Sein-zum-Tode*).[2]

My answer to the above questions is in the negative. I do not question Heidegger's penetrating analysis of alienated everyday life. I deny however that everyday life must necessarily be alienated. In the final analysis, the reason for the alienation of the everyday world is not its structure, but those social relationships by virtue of which an alienated relationship with everyday life becomes the typical relationship. I do not deny that there is an affinity between everyday life and alienation: by which I mean that the structure of everyday life is such that we can successfully lead life therein, even without any conscious relationship with the species-essential. And if we relate to our world, our environment, as to something 'to hand', this is because in fact we can sustain ourselves therein, even without any special resourcefulness of query and reflection, on a basis of simple alignment with others (doing what 'anybody else' does). For this reason, in so far as social relations are alienated, everyday life inclines towards alienation.

But this is still not to say that everyday life must *necessarily* be alienated. It can be said straight away that where there is a decrease in the degree of alienation present in social relations, there is an equivalent decrease in the degree of alienation in everyday life. It becomes possible for the person to achieve a degree of species-essentiality even within the confines of the everyday. The content of this development, however, and the rank of individuality attained, are not simple functions of the presence or absence of alienation. In certain historical periods, the degree of alienation is slight enough for generic development to culminate in a given order: beyond this – in the given order – there is 'nothing further' and we can speak of its representative achievement in everyday life as 'limited achievement'. The person in such conditions can lead an everyday life worthy of human beings; but expansion of the given parameters, feedback to wider generic development, creativity, – these become impossible for him in principle. Those historical interludes characterized by 'limited achievement' are, in a sense, exemplars for the humanized conduct of everyday life, precisely in that they afford a measure of achievement. They cannot serve as absolute exemplars, since they are limited: they are the products of a world in which the successive transcendence of limitations is, by definition, impossible.

Even within the framework of social alienation, subjective rebellion against alienation is always a possibility. In such circumstances, the origination of a subjectively non-alienated everyday life is a declaration of war on alienation. *Subjective* rebellion against alienation with the aim of creating an everyday life worthy of man is, in itself, a necessary precondition if man is to succeed one day in overcoming alienation socially, so that a subjectively non-alienated relationship with everyday life will finally become *typical*.

A purely particularistic attitude towards the objectivations of everyday life is always alienated. The subjective transcendence of alienation can therefore only take the form of a conscious relationship with species-essentiality (species-essential values or objectivations): this relationship presupposes the existence of objectivations 'for itself'. It further presupposes that, over and over again in everyday life, needs arise which induce transcendence of the purely particularistic attitude. Whence do these needs arise? How is it that, to judge from history to date, at least, they appear to be ineradicable? Wherein is what we may figuratively call the invincibility of the human substance rooted? We can find terminology for these facts and we can formulate the questions: but we cannot answer them. The need to become individual exists, and so does the need for objectivations 'for itself' – the need for some way of transferring the conflict on to the generic plane and fighting it out. But 'why' should this be so? To this question, there is, at present, no answer.

I said that all contemporaries in a given time and space find themselves confronted by the same everyday structure. How then does it come about that we relate to this structure partly in particularistic fashion and partly in individual fashion, while retaining the structure of everyday life intact.

Let me stress anew that it is not possible to relate in uniformly individual fashion to every aspect of everyday life. Since much of man's time is taken up with work (I use the word in its wide sense) the type of work which any one man is called upon to do, very largely determines the extent to which that man can individualize himself: i.e. the work fixes the boundaries beyond which the process of individualization is in his case unlikely to go. For example, the craftsman was idealized by the Romantic anti-capitalists because his craft allowed him to expand and develop all his potentialities and skills in the work-process itself. If every man is to have the chance of becoming an individual, two things must happen: the alienation of the work process must be overcome, mechanical means must replace human labour in all types of work which give little or no scope for the development of personal talents.

Of course, we can relate in more or less individual fashion to the *same* work. This is primarily because alienation ensues even in those types of work which, taken by themselves, offer some scope for development and enrichment of the personality. Teaching for example (a type of work which occupies an extremely important place in the social division of labour) can easily turn into a stereotyped, cliché-ridden, mechanical occupation: but it can also claim the whole personality, man's inventive and innovative powers, etc. Thus, whether the man called upon to teach children to read and write, does his job in particularistic or in individual fashion, depends not so much on the nature of the work itself as on the relation between it and the man who has chosen it as his calling.

As we have seen, if everyday life is to be successfully carried on, it is obsolutely imperative that in certain types of activity our praxis and our thinking should become repetitive. It is also essential that we appropriate the forms of this repetitive praxis 'ready-made' from the species-essential objectivations 'for itself'. Even in the life of the individual (in our sense of the word) there are numberless examples of such repetition. The individual uses the same language as the particularistic 'person'; and both communicate, wash, eat and handle the ready-made objects which satisfy their needs, in the same way. The difference between the two – and it is a difference which puts them worlds apart – is that the individual *knows* where to abandon repetition in favour of an innovatory approach to a problem – be it invention, reflection. He knows when the customary has to be questioned, and when a value taken for granted needs to be devalued.

Again, it is in general true that the individual, like the particularistic 'person' acts pragmatically and takes decisions on a basis of probability. Again, however, he *knows* when, where and why it is time to drop the pragmatic approach and adopt a theoretical attitude: he can recognize situations calling for action or decision, in which the probability factor is not enough and in which absolute certainty must be sought.

In everyday life, the mind of the individual is, like that of the 'person', riddled with over-generalizations. Again, the difference is that the individual *knows* when an over-generalization turns into a prejudice. The individual's actions are also accompanied by 'trust' or 'belief' – but not by 'blind faith'. The individual internalizes the ready-made customary order: but he knows when and why to act *contrary to* a generally accepted particularistic norm.

What all of this amounts to is the assertion that the individual relates in a relatively free fashion to the species-essential objectivations 'in itself', and to the customary system of requirements and norms as a whole which he receives as a datum in everyday life.

But how does he know what he knows? And what is the source of this relative freedom?

An answer to this question was given in Part I of this book: the individual orders his daily life in the light of a conscious relationship with one or more species-essential objectivations 'for itself' or integrations. The norms, the conceptual stock, the requirements of the species-essential objectivations 'for itself' (or conjoint 'in-' and 'for itself'), of integrations, and those everyday needs that point towards species-essentiality – these are the factors which go to form his assessment of the requirement structure of everyday life; and he can discard this requirement structure whenever it fails to match up to the generic requirement structure, or whenever it conflicts with the generic values which he has internalized from higher-rank species-essential objectivations or with needs which have affinities with these values.

This is not to say that man lives his everyday life 'philosophically' – that he can conjure up some sort of homogeneous medium therefrom. But it does mean that, in a certain sense, he does homogenize his life in so far as he consciously 'hierarchizes' it, orders it in a hierarchy. What is the meaning of this conscious 'hierarchical ordering'?

Our everyday activities have their own built-in hierarchical ordering, one created by the exigencies of socio-economic life. If one has to work twelve hours a day, it is clear that work is going to take the lion's share in one's everyday agenda. Where participation in communal affairs is incumbent on members of a community, such communal activity will score high in the hierarchy of daily activities. But the hierarchy which the individual creates for himself in conscious relationship with species-essentiality differs from this in character: what it centres on and around is the distinction of the essential from the inessential. The individual establishes, in conscious relationship with species-essentiality, what the highest values are and how he can observe them on the basis of his personal gifts and needs, so as to ensure complete assertion of his own personality. Such an individual hierarchy may even run counter to the hierarchy inscribed in the species-essential objectivations 'in itself'. For example, in a society centred on and around private interest, the individual may choose and order his life around communal activity – a life 'for others'. Or vice versa.

The personality who has consciously ordered his life in the light of his own chosen hierarchy of values will evaluate the traditional ready-made hierarchy in that same light. From it, he will take in his own time and in his own way, whatever fits in with his own chosen hierarchy. As a result, he often lives and moves on the periphery of a given society, but this is not always the case. It is not unusual for the individual who has consciously formed his life from a species-essential objectivation 'for itself' to become a model to emulate; and in such cases the individual hierarchy, the individual life-style becomes – or at least tends to become – the hierarchy and life-style of that community.

I said that it is the species-essential values 'for itself' and the individual relationship thereto that go to form the individual hierarchy inscribed in an individual conduct of life. By this, I do not mean that species-essential activities are invariably and simultaneously brought into play in direct (non-mediated) fashion. If this were so, then anyone who wanted to lead an individual life would have to be an artist, a philosopher or a scientist – perhaps even a statesman: which is manifestly not true. As a rule, individual choice of life-informing order ensues indirectly, through the mediation of a world-view (*Weltanschauung*). A world-view is neither a scientific nor a philosophical synthesis, it is not a political ideology: it is rather the manifested form taken by an amalgam, a fusion of the resultants of these factors (or of some of them), and it is their internalization for service in the everyday life of the individual. So, my assertion that it is a conscious relationship with generic values that goes to formulate individuality and an individual hierarchy of priorities, requires a rider: namely, that this always happens through the mediation of a world-view. The world-view transposes the species-essential values to the personal level; and it is through the world-view that these values become the guiding forces in the individual's activity.

What this amounts to is a reunification of the object of action with the motivation of action. Let us recall what I said earlier: action as specifically human activity emerges in the process in which the objectivation 'in itself' is appropriated; it is action precisely because the object of, and the motivation for, action have been separated. The two factors have now been reunited – but consciously, not spontaneously, not from the point of view of satisfying the basic needs of life, but as a way of satisfying the need for a *human life*.

Thus, the life of the individual does not fall apart into either a simple succession or a simple simultaneity of heterogeneous activities. The activities remain heterogeneous, but each action has its place, its consciously ordered place in human life. Thus, whatever the extent to which heterogeneous 'ready-made' action must be duly performed on a basis of repetitive praxis, the life of the individual becomes unified.

The personality objectifies itself into a definite type of *subiectum*. As I said, the particularistic personality is the *subiectum* 'in itself' while the individual personality is the *subiectum* which has been objectivized into the 'for itself'.

(b) Individuality as 'being-for-itself' of the personality

In what sense can the individual (in our sense of the word) be said to embody 'being-for itself'? What does this mean?

Let us first recall the criteria we used to distinguish 'being-for-itself' as a type. The first criterion was that it does not necessarily belong to society (in contrast to 'being-in-itself'). We know that societies can and do exist, whose members are purely particularistic.

Our second criterion was that 'being-for-itself' cannot exist otherwise than in the 'intention-towards' it. Now, we know that every individual makes himself consciously the object of his own action and reflection.

Our third criterion of the species-essential was that it is not primary but secondary. And in fact individuality is built on the particularistic personality and its needs: this is the soil it grows out of. It cannot change its inborn set of gifts and potentialities; it can only seek to shape these in accordance with generic values. Like any other objectivation 'for itself', the individual life is an answer, as it were, to the questions put to it by the species-essential 'for itself' – an answer to not just any question, but to the question 'How should I live?' itself.

It has been said of 'being-for-itself' that it is the sphere in which freedom expresses itself – namely, the degree of freedom attained by human beings at a given time. From the standpoint of personality, the degree of development attained by individuality is the yardstick of personal freedom at that time.

I said of the species-essential objectivations 'in itself' that while they provide material for the objectivations 'for itself', they do not determine the inner structure of the latter. To what extent this is so in relation to the particularistic personality on the one hand, and to the individual on the other, is something that is particularly illuminated by the problem of value-hierarchy. The value-hierarchy which is taken over ready-made from the species-essential objectivations 'in itself' does indeed provide material for the hierarchy which the individual builds into his life; but the latter is constructed relatively freely.

As the 'being-for itself' of the personality, being an individual has an intrinsic value, even though there are morally ambiguous individuals (in the same way, there are fetishized objectivations 'for itself'). We are instinctively aware of this intrinsic value. A kind of 'aura' radiates from personalities: and the more pregnant the personality, the stronger the aura. Of course, it is not only individuals who may radiate this kind of aura. There are certain personal properties as well as certain moral virtues which have attractive force even when they are not specifically associated with developed individuals (beauty, courage, etc.). In general, however, this type of attractive force is transitory, fortuitous, and likely to have effect only on particularistic persons. Only the aura of the personality can be said to exercise a durable effect. The lineaments of beauty are devalued where they do not express a personality. Indeed, we can say that personality confers beauty, in that it illuminates the face with its value-content. We are less impressed by an act of courage when we realize that it was, in fact, fortuitous, or perhaps simply motivated by insensitivity to fear. In contrast, the attractive power of the courage vested in the individual increases in step with the development of the given individuality or with our exposure to it. There is nothing mystical about the demonic power of attraction so eloquently described by Kierkegaard; it is simply ascribable to that obdurate and homogeneous individuality which enables a Don Juan or a Mephistopheles to turn his back on the accepted system of norms, although in this case, personality is constructed *via* moral indifference or on outright evil principles.

The aura of individuality has always been *felt*, even though personality has not always been given the credit. Even in communities where (developed) individuality was suspect as being 'stubborn' and threatening to public order, the outstanding personality could attract admiration with an admixture of respect and/or fear. It was from the age of the Renaissance onwards that personality became an incontestable value: and no one has ever put this better than Goethe did in his unforgettable lines in the *Westöstlicher Divan*:

> Volk und Knecht und Überwinder,
> Sie gestehn zu jeder Zeit:
> Höchstes Glück der Erdenkinder
> Sei nur die Persönlichkeit.
> Jedes Leben sei zu führen,
> Wenn man nicht sich selbst vermisst:
> Alles könne man verlieren,
> Wenn man bliebe, was man ist.

(High and low, ruler and ruled, victor and vanquished – people of every degree have at all times avowed that mankind's chief blessing is *individuality*. Each life is to be lived, and can be, provided we do not mistake our true measure; we can lose everything else as long as we remain what we are.)

Let us recall that in any given historical period, science presents generic knowledge at its maximum potentiality, art represents generic self-consciousness, and philosophy presents the unity of knowledge and self-consciousness at their maximum potentiality.

What is embodied, represented by the personality 'for itself'?

The answer is that it embodies these possibilities which are available for the free assertion and development of human capabilities within a person's lifetime. It follows that the force-field of the personality 'for itself' (i.e. individuality) is by no means limited to everyday life, but covers life in general, which is, as we have seen, based on and partially at least reflected in, everyday life. Since individuality constructs the world-view which guides its everyday life, in conscious relationship with species-being, it is clear that no individual can be guided by species-essential objectivations 'in itself' alone. But he/she can introduce certain values which have been engendered by higher objectivations into his/her relationship with the objectivation 'in itself'. The extent to which this correlation incorporates values 'for itself' varies, and there is no need to repeat our analysis of the part played in this variation by the degree of alienation attached to the individuality itself. The reader should also bear in mind our analysis of the way in which the content of the chosen values forms or deforms the individuality itself. In what follows, I shall confine myself to a brief discussion of one type – the most valuable type – of individuality: moral individuality.

I said that his world-view is the medium *via* which the person unifies and hierarchically orders his everyday experience; we have now to ask – into what is the personality objectified? We can say straight away that world-views of identical conceptual content and identical value-content can be found in association with markedly different personalities: which is tantamount to saying that their ways of hierarchically ordering their everyday lives will also tend, at least, to be similar. This is why we can speak of types of individual. But the individuality of an individual is not simply reducible to its type affiliation. The uniqueness and singularity characteristic of every man are here raised to a higher level. In its creative and hierarchical ordering of its life, 'individuality' fuses the complex of uniquely conferred inborn gifts into a unified whole *via* the intermediary stage of a world-view: or, to put it another way, it so orders these properties that unity of the personality can ensue. This is why I say that man 'individualizes' the world-view, unites it with his personality. Morals provide the driving force for this individualization: moral praxis acts as an indicator for the conduct of life. The more developed the moral individuality, the less does this mean the subordination of the 'person' to the ruling (or at least accepted) moral code: and the more it signifies that the individual in question is transforming the internalized moral order into his own essence, his own substance. That is, he humanizes his own inborn qualities and inclinations, and creates from within himself a normative exemplar. Here lies the role of the great moral personality: he is able to humanize his own fortuitous and ready-made repertory of qualities, singular and unique as this repertory is, and turn them into paradigms for others, thus raising them (while still preserving inert particularistic properties and motivations) to the generic level, the level of species-essential representation.

What does it mean when we claim to live our life in such a way that it becomes the active terrain for a humanized personality, a terrain in which this personality can realize itself? It means that everyday life has become 'being-for-us'. 'Being-in-itself' becomes 'being-for-us' because we relate to it in the measure afforded by our personality.

Let me repeat what has been said more than once in previous pages: the extent to which our life can become 'being-for-us' does not depend totally or even primarily on the *subiectum*. The more alienated everyday life is in general, the more difficult it is to create a life that is 'being-for-us'; and the greater the achievement if we succeed – though this is given to very few. Communism, as Marx conceived it, might be defined as that society in which the social conditions requisite if every *subiectum* is to make his everyday life 'being-for-him', are met.

(c) The 'being-for-us' of everyday life

There are two types of 'being-for-us' as manifested in everyday life: one is happiness, the other is the meaningful life.

Happiness is a 'being-for-us' in everyday life, in the sense of 'limited fulfilment'. That is to say, it is a 'being-for-us' which is limited and complete: it is principially incapable of development or of extension: it is its own *terminus ad quem* and limitation.

For these reasons, happiness was central to the ethos of the ancient world. The world of the Greeks and the Romans was a world of limited fulfilment (brought to the highest degree of perfection mankind has every known); its boundaries were not obstacles to be overcome but termini. For these reasons, and since the Classical personality is a limited personality, the greatest good in this world was held to be happiness. That is, life is 'being-for-us' as it is imagined and is attainable in this world of limited fulfilment.

Given that it was Plato who experienced most deeply the crisis of the ancient polis, it is hardly surprising to find a second concept of happiness in his works, alongside the consensual one. This second concept is the happiness 'of the moment' – of moments of fulfilment which occur, according to Plato, in love and in the contemplation of the beautiful (of the ideas).

In antiquity, limited fulfilment (happiness) was an exclusively positive category: a different kind of fulfilment was not possible. Since the Renaissance, however, the social foundations of this limited form of fulfilment have been steadily eroded. From the Renaissance onwards, happiness has had to be achieved in a world of continuous change and conflict: and man has sought for a 'being-for-us' while continually surpassing all previous stages of achievement. But this would seem possible only if the person could bracket himself off from life's conflicts, if he could enclose his life. To the process whereby reality becomes 'being-for-us' for modern man belong confrontation with the world's conflicts, continual transcendence of the present, the continual taking-up of new challenges, along with all the losses and casualties which the person suffers in that process – in a word, it includes unhappiness as well.

This is the new problem which Goethe was the first to tackle (in *Faust*). As soon as Faust reached a state of 'happiness' his pact with the devil was to be fulfilled: his soul would be forfeit, and he would go to hell. Goethe's solution is to let Faust find his way, not to a state of 'happiness' but to a vision of the meaningful life, and thus he escapes perdition.

But if happiness as the 'being-for-us' of everyday life appears in a negative light, it has not yet lost all meaning for the individual in his everyday life, where it retains the function which Plato assigned to it – the 'being-for-us' in the fulfilment of a given moment. Since by definition this happiness is 'of the moment' there is no need to see it as a state of life, in terms of finality. Union in love, the contemplation of the beautiful, artistic creation, moral resolve – these and similar experiences awake in us powerful unmistakable feelings of 'being-for-us': and though they are 'of the moment' it is a moment that recurs over and over again. Life is not dissolved in these moments; it does not end with them. These are the great moments of everyday life, but they do not exhaust nor are they a substitute for its continuous 'being-for-us'.

The reciprocal of happiness is contentment. As we have seen, contentment derives not from 'being-for-us' in general, but from the satisfying of two needs – pleasure and usefulness. Hence, the feeling of contentment ranks lower than happiness even when it is contentment attendant upon being useful to others. It is true that like moments of happiness, contentment remains part of high-rank 'being-for-us'. But only in a tendential sense: moments of contentment engender dissatisfaction, since satisfaction does not have a fulfilment boundary, especially not where the contentment is attendant upon being useful to others.

The meaningful life is the 'being-for-us' of everyday life in an open world which is characterized by prospects of development through a succession of new challenges and conflicts. If we can make our world into 'being-for-us' so that both it and we ourselves are continually being renewed – we are living a meaningful life. The individual who is living a meaningful life is not a closed substance but a developing one who shrinks from no new challenge and who, in meeting it, unfolds his own individuality. It is a process to which death alone sets a term. This individual does not constrict his personality and impose limitations upon it but 'measures himself against the universe'. Within the possibilities open to him, he chooses his own values and his own world – the universe against which he measures himself.

Aristotle says of happiness that if we are to be happy we need not only virtues but also 'gifts of fortune' such as wealth, beauty, wisdom, etc. The same is true of the meaningful life. Above all, the world in which the meaningful life is to be lived must be one which permits this. The more alienated the social relations the greater the need for some 'gift of fortune'. The man doing brute labour will have little chance of leading a meaningful life. Acumen and endowment are indispensable 'gifts of fortune', though it is difficult to distinguish these from morals. A man can be morally endowed; and 'brains' are simply raw material.

If contentment is the reciprocal of happiness, we can say that 'aesthetic life' is the reciprocal of the meaningful life. 'Aesthetic life' is also a way of handling everyday life, so that it becomes 'being-for-us': the 'artist of life' – the person living an aesthetic life – unfolds his abilities on a personal plane. Is there then no difference between this way of life and the way of the meaningful life? The difference is that the man who leads an 'aesthetic life' has only one intention – to transform his own everyday existence into 'being-for-him'; and if a conflict threatens to impede him in this, he simply takes avoiding action. What is missing from his make-up is the 'useful to others' bit: he lacks the aptitude to feel for others in their need. The 'artist of life' wants to lead a meaningful life without raising the question whether the same is possible for others or for him alone. Thus, the 'aesthetic life' is aristocratic, while the meaningful life is democratic in principle. The guiding norm in the meaningful life is always generalizability, extensibility of the meaningful life to others: in the long run, to the whole of humanity.

Conduct of life is not absent from the state which we have defined as that of limited fulfilment, for here too, the individual consciously orders and arranges his life hierarchically. The role of conscious conduct is, however, less in this case than it is in the meaningful life, since the state of limited fulfilment rests on rigid and detailed value systems, and it is on this basis that the person must order his everyday life – once and for all, unless chance takes a hand. In the meaningful life, on the other hand, the role of conscious conduct of life is continually expanding, leading the individual on in confrontation with new challenges, in perpetual re-creation of life and personality, coupled with safe-keeping of the unity of that personality and of the chosen value-hierarchy. It is *via* the conduct of life that self-renewal for an everyday life of 'being-for-us' takes place.

The consciously chosen and accepted task of those individuals who today lead meaningful lives is to create a society in which alienation is a thing of the past: a society in which every man has access to the social 'gifts of fortune' which can enable him to lead a meaningful life. Not a 'happy' life – for there can be no return to the world of limited fulfilment. True 'history' is pregnant with conflict and continually transcending its own given state. It is history – consciously chosen by men and moulded to their design – that can enable all men to make their everyday lives 'being-for-them' and that will make the earth a true home for all men.

NOTES

4 The heterogeneity of everyday life

1 Some explanation of the distinction I make between *intentio recta* and *intentio obliqua* may be in order here. By the former I mean all knowledge arising from the fixing, ordering and collating of everyday experience or from the studied incubation of such experience into a homogeneous system. By *intentio obliqua* I mean all thought which is not incubated from everyday experience, but which arises only from the premised conceptual structure of generic objectivations. However, one type of theory engendered by *intentio obliqua* can be related to everyday experience, even if a second type cannot be so related, except in its consequences.

2 For an examination of the anthropomorphism of everyday thinking, see G. Lukács, *Die Eigenart des Aesthetischen*, ch. 1. At this point, we shall no go further into the pragmatism of everyday life and thinking, though it is closely related to the material under discussion as it comes up in Part 3 of the present work, in connection with our analysis of the structure of everyday thinking.

5 From the everyday to the generic

1 It will be clear to the reader that the distinction made here between 'work' and 'labour' is not the same as that made by H. Arendt (*The Human Condition*, Chicago University Press, 1958).

2 There is, of course, far more to Marx's pioneer analysis of work than this. But Marx's conception of humankind creating itself through its work, or of the work process as in the last resort the model for all human activity, or of work as metabolism with nature which pushes back continuously the 'natural frontiers' – all of this belongs to the philosophical concept of work. Here, however, we limit ourselves to what is immediately germane to our present theme.

3 In the third part of the present work we shall consider the concrete functions of language and custom in everyday life.

4 For an analysis of modern assembly-line methods, see G. Friedmann, *Problèmes humains du machinisme industriel*, Gallimard, 1946.

5 Max Weber, *Economy and Society*; ed. G. Roth and C. Wittich, New York, 1968, p. 580; my emphasis.

270

6 I do not agree with Durkheim when he asserts that all the properties of religion can be derived from the practices of 'primitive' religion: Durkheim was drawing general conclusions, ostensibly applicable to all religions, from the totemistic beliefs of Australian aboriginal tribes. I derive my ideas of religion primarily from the most developed forms of religion, mainly from Christianity.

7 In general this does not apply to the 'persons' in bourgeois society for reasons which we cannot go into here.

8 L. Kardos has carried out a very interesting study in the Bakonycserje area where the villagers are mainly Lutheran, with a Catholic minority and several sects. The study shows that only in the case of these sects is religiosity a formative factor in everyday life; by and large, adherents of the two major churches have a purely conventional, i.e. formal relationship with their religions. See L. Kardos, *Egyház és vallásos élet egy mai faluban*, Kossuth, Budapest, 1969.

9 The basic concept is Nicolai Hartmann's, but the use I make of it – with the reduplication introduced by *intentio recta* and *intentio obliqua* – is my own.

10 Scientific thought (and here I disagree with Lévi-Strauss) does not arise primarily from the ordering and systemization of everyday experience and observation, but is a specific development of religious thinking, in which we already find *intentio recta* of the second type, albeit in mythopoetic and fetishized format.

11 The concept of art which I outline here is, in general, based on the aesthetics of George Lukács (see: *Az esztétikum sajátossága*).

12 Needless to say, the concept of beauty presents many unsolved philosophical and aesthetic problems which we have no space to take up here.

7 Species-essential activity 'in itself'

1 C.K. Ogden, I.A. Richards, *The Meaning of Meaning*, Appendix I. Malinowski, *The Problem of Meaning in Primitive Languages*, Routledge & Kegan Paul, 1956.

2 Wittgenstein, *Philosophical Investigations*, Blackwell, 1963. p. 81.

3 A.N. Leontiev, *A pszichikum fejlődésének problémái*, Kossuth, Budapest, 1964, p. 285, my emphasis.

4 H. Lefèbvre, *Critique de la vie quotidienne*, II.

5 Here, I do no more than touch superficially on a very complicated subject.

8 The common properties of species-essential objectivations 'in itself'

1 Ferenc Jánossy, *A gazdasági fejlettség mérhetősége és új mérési módszere.* Közgazdasági és Jogi Könyvkiadó, Budapest, 1963.

2 W.V.O. Quine, *Word and Object*, Technology Press and John Wiley & Sons, New York and London, 1960.

3 A. Shaff expresses a similar opinion; see his *Bevezetés a szemantikába*, Akadémiai Kiadó, Budapest, 1967.

4 O. Jespersen, *Language, its Nature, Development and Origin*, Allen and Unwin, London, 1949. Whether this is to be regarded as development (Jespersen's thesis), or simply as change, is another matter.

5 See Quine, *Word and Object, op. cit.*

6 In the case of customs, this factor varies according to the type of custom. We shall return to this point later.

9 The special properties of species-essential objectivations 'in itself'

1 Rhees, 'Can there be a private language?', *Philosophy and Ordinary Language*, University of Illinois Press, Urbana, 1963.

2 L. Wittgenstein, *Philosophical Investigations*, p. 146.

3 N. Chomsky, *Cartesian Linguistics*, Harper & Row, New York and London, 1966, p. 35.

4 Audible range is less than visual range, but sound, unlike light, does not only travel in straight lines.

10 The general schemes of conduct and knowledge in everyday life

1 This problem is analysed in detail by Lukács in *Az esztétikum sajátossága*, I.

2 *Jacobsen, Essays,* quoted in Lefèbvre, *Le Langage et la société.*

3 *Spinoza,* Letter 56.

4 On evocative imitation, see Lukács, *Az esztétikum sajátossága* (the chapters on mimesis).

5 Subsumption and analogy – sharply separated in scientific thinking – usually coalesce in everyday thinking. Most subsumptions are mediated by analogy.

6 For a detailed treatment of this, see my *Társadalmi szerep es előítélet (Social Role and Prejudice)*.

7 Wittgenstein, *Philosophical Investigations*, p. 222.

11 Everyday knowledge

1 M. Bloch, *Das Prinzip Hoffnung*, I, Suhrkamp, Frankfurt am Main, 1967.

2 In this connection we may distinguish two extreme poles: on the positive side, putting someone to a test, on his mettle: on the negative side, 'using' people.

12 Everyday contact

1 I am well aware that the basis I take here for my classifications is not uniform; as I said above some degree of arbitrariness is unavoidable.

2 Question, command, request, summons, etc. are speech acts related to direct action and need not be considered here.

3 A.N. Leontiev: *A pszichikum fejlődésének problémái*, p. 500 (emphasis added by A.H.).

4 G. Simmel, *Soziologie*, Dennkerr Humblot, Leipzig, 1908.

5 Adapted from Lefèbvre: see *Critique de la vie quotidienne*, II.

6 E. Fischer, *A fiatal nemzedek problémái*, Gondolat, Budapest, 1964.

7 For a detailed analysis of Machiavelli's ideas, see my *Renaissance Man.*

8 See Albee, *Who's Afraid of Virginia Woolf?*

13 The personality in everyday life

1 M. Heidegger, *Sein und Zeit*, I.

2 In his study *Gelassenheit* Heidegger gives a similar analysis (though in different terminology) of the relationship between the 'person' and everyday life.

INDEX

273

Descartes, R., 208
Direct action, in everyday contact, 220–2
Disclosure, 225, 227
Discussion, 223–4
Don Giovanni, 26
Dostoievsky, F., 93, 231
Doxa, 203–5, 214

Economy, in 'in itself' objectivation, 143–5, 256
Egoism, 14, 22, 25
Epistémé, 203–5, 206
Everyday and non-everyday compared, 47–59
Everyday contact, 216 ff
Everyday knowledge: content of, 185–95; anthropological properties of, 195–203
Everyday life, as objectification, 47–8
Everyday thinking, 49–53; *see also under* Thinking

Familiarity, 239
Fantasy, 228–31
Feelings, in everyday contact, 231–6
Feud, 250
Fischer, E., 108, 112, 242
'For itself' objectivations, 117, 119–20, 194, 262–6
Fourier, F.M.C., 55, 61, 230
Friedmann, G., 67n
Fulfilment value, 149–52

Galileo, 50
Games, 227–31
Gattungsmässigkeit, 25
Gehlen, 129, 157, 158, 228
Goethe, J.W. von, 24, 39, 207, 264, 267
Goncharov, I.A., 199
Greece, Ancient, 90, 92, 94, 214, 266; *see also Polis*
Group, role of, 30–2

Habit, *see* Custom
Happiness, 266–7
Hate, 231–6
Hegel, G. W. F., 29
Heidegger, M., 256–7

Helvétius, C.-A., 50
Hierarchical ordering in everyday life, 260–1
Historical change, 241–2, 244
Hobbes, T., 50
Home, 239
Husserl, E. G. A., 202

Ibsen, H.: *A Doll's House*, 249; *Peer Gynt*, 26
Ideal community, 90–1
Ideology, 97–8, 105–6
Idyll, 250–1
Imitation, 170–2; of action, 170–1; of behaviour, 171–2; evocative, 172
'In and for itself' objectivation, 120
'In-itself' objectivation, 117–19, 121, 123 ff
Indifference, 231–2
Individuality, concept of, 15–27, 258 ff
Information, transmission of, 222–3
Intentio obliqua, 49–50, 100–1, 203
Intentio recta, 100, 101–2, 188
Internal speech, 145–6, 160–2
Intuitive thinking, 131–3, 147, 168, 174–5, 176, 181
Inventive praxis and inventive thinking, 128–30, 132–3, 143–4, 147, 150, 181
Ionesco, E., 226
Ipseity, 179
Islam, 94

Jacobsen, R., 167
Jánossy, F., 137
Jespersen, O., 144, 145n
Jesus Christ, 92–3; *see also* Christianity
Joy, 251–2
Judaism, 90, 94, 96

Kant, I., 50, 76, 77
Kierkegaard, S., 96, 243, 263
Knowledge, everyday, 185 ff; anthropological properties of, 195–203
Knowledge, particularistic, 193–4
Knowledge, religious, 188–9
Knowledge, scientific, 189–91, 203–5